THE PSALMS
THEIR STRUCTURE AND MEANING

THE PSALMS

THEIR STRUCTURE AND MEANING

by

PIUS DRIJVERS, O.C.S.O.

HERDER AND HERDER

HERDER AND HERDER NEW YORK

232 Madison Avenue, New York, N. Y. 10016

This book is a translation from the 5th revised edition of
"Over de Psalmen", published by Uitgeverij Het Spectrum,
Utrecht, 1964

The Scripture quotations in this publication are from the Revised
Standard Version of the Bible,
Copyrighted 1946 and 1952 by the Division of Christian Education,
National Council of Churches, and used by permission.

1st Edition 1964

2nd Impression 1964

3rd Impression 1967

Cum permissu Superiorum Ordinis

Nihil Obstat: Joannes M. T. Barton S.T.D., L.S.S.

Censor deputatus

Imprimatur: Patritius Casey, Vic. Gen.

Westmonasterii, die 31. Maii, 1965

Library of Congress Catalog Card Number: 65-19629

First published in West Germany © 1965 Herder KG

Printed in West Germany by Herder

Contents

AUTHOR'S PREFACE vii

FOREWORD ix

BIBLIOGRAPHY xiii

CHAPTER 1
THE PSALMS AS CHRISTIAN PRAYER . . 1

CHAPTER 2
THE ORIGIN OF THE BOOK OF PSALMS . . 16

CHAPTER 3
HEBREW POETRY 23

CHAPTER 4
THE VARIOUS TYPES OF PSALMS . . . 33

CHAPTER 5
THE PSALMS OF PRAISE, OR HYMNS . . 49

CHAPTER 6
THE PSALMS OF THANKSGIVING . . . 81

CHAPTER 7
THE PSALMS OF PETITION 104

CHAPTER 8
THE PILGRIM PSALMS 146

CONTENTS

CHAPTER 9
THE PROCESSIONAL AND ENTHRONEMENT
PSALMS 164

CHAPTER 10
THE ROYAL PSALMS 181

CHAPTER 11
THE OLD AND NEW COVENANTS . . . 204

AUTHOR'S NOTES 215

APPENDIXES
  I. THE GROUPING OF THE PSALMS . . 230
  II. THE PSALMS OF PRAISE 232
  III. THE PSALMS OF THANKSGIVING . . 235
  IV. THE PSALMS OF PETITION . . . 240
  V. THE PILGRIM PSALMS 254
  VI. THE PROCESSIONAL AND
      ENTHRONEMENT PSALMS 257
  VII. THE ROYAL PSALMS, OR PSALMS
      OF THE KING 259
  VIII. THE PSALMS IN THE NEW TESTAMENT 261

INDEX OF BIBLICAL QUOTATIONS . . 263

Author's Preface

It is with much pleasure that I take the opportunity of introducing the English edition of my book in this short preface, for it is a real joy to me that an English version is to be published very soon after several translations have appeared in other languages. I wish to thank the publishers, who have permitted me to revise the manuscript, so that I have been able to make numerous alterations in the light of the latest Dutch edition, which is now being printed, and into which I have tried to incorporate the latest evidence regarding the study of the Psalter. Since the first edition dates back to 1956, it was necessary for me to make a thorough revision, and I am gratified by the thought that this English version will be the first of the various translations to reflect the new perspectives envisaged by the latest Dutch edition.

I am especially indebted to the Rt. Rev. Mgr. John Mt. T. Barton, D. D., L. S. S., F. S. A., the well-known English exegete and English Consultor to the Pontifical Biblical Commission, who has kindly checked and amended the English version. For a young Scripture scholar it is an honour to be assisted by one who has already won a reputation in this field of studies.

I acknowledge with many thanks my debt to the unpublished lectures on the psalms by Professor Ernest Vogt, SJ., which were given in 1951–2 at the Pontifical Biblical Institute in Rome, of which he was for many years the Rector. Other literature which I have frequently consulted is listed at the end of the book.

With all my heart I would like to dedicate this Anglo-American edition to all my African friends, and especially to my brethren of the Trappist Monastery of Our Lady of Victory, Lumbwa, Kenya.

Abbey of Koningshoven   *Pius Drijvers, O.C.S.O.*
Tilburg, Netherlands

Foreword

In his epoch-making introduction to the Psalms, Hermann Gunkel compared the Psalter to a *Glockenspiel,* the old bells that one can still hear pealing out their message from the baroque German churches. The individual tones come through powerfully and majestically, each with its own modality and beauty. But only a knowledgable person can catch the melody that the artist intended. Writing in the tradition of Gunkel, Father Drijvers has enabled us to catch the melody and message of the Psalter more clearly and surely. It is simple truth to say that his book is the best introduction to the psalms available in English by a Catholic author. There are more learned commentaries, such as *The Book of Psalms* by the late Canon Kissane of Maynooth, and more sparkling treatments, such as Thomas Merton's *Bread in the Wilderness.* But Father Drijvers alone presents an approach which captures the essentials, yet remains appealing to the general reader.

This approach is less new than it seems. Basically the ancients tried to reach the "life-setting" *(Sitz im Leben)* of these poems, as is evident from the titles which have been prefixed to several psalms. (For example Psalm 34,

"A Psalm of David when he feigned madness before
Abimelech, so that he drove him out, and he went away.")
Thanks to modern research into ancient literary style, we
are able to correct and refine these early efforts. We know
now that the poems of the Psalter were composed according to particular literary types current not only in
Israel, but throughout the Fertile Crescent. Gunkel
demonstrated this characteristic in the Psalms fifty years
ago in his studies on Old Testament literary forms. It is
enough to glance at the table of contents in Father
Drijvers' book to see that he is faithful to these literary
criteria: The Psalms of Praise, The Psalms of Thanksgiving, The Psalms of Petition, etc. The literary type
determines the peculiar genius of a poem — its motifs,
its spirit — and the explanation of these types is clearly and
attractively presented in the present study. This approach
is both the most fruitful and most honest manner of
reading and understanding the Psalms.

It was primarily, but not exclusively, within the liturgy
of Israel that the literary types of the Psalms evolved.
This undeniable fact has occasioned not a few far-
reaching interpretations lacking both nuance and proof.
There is some truth in all extreme positions: the liturgical
origins (which Sigmund Mowinckel extends to all the
psalms); the existence of a Covenant-Renewal Feast
(which for Arthur Weiser is the pivot of the Psalter).
Father Drijvers has struck a sound balance in the face
of these rigid positions, as can be seen in his judgment
on the so-called Psalms of Yahweh's Enthronement.
While we may not be able to pinpoint a particular feast
as the life-setting of these psalms, no one can deny their
liturgical roots or their relevance to the covenant.

Another valuable feature of this book is its thorough

treatment of doctrinal themes. The prayers of the Psalter were composed over a period of seven centuries in Israel's history; they reflect a rich variety of mood, belief, and aspiration. One must remember that God *gradually* revealed Himself to Israel; the Psalms are to be read in the light of the other Old Testament ideas and beliefs, of which they represent a cross-section. The author has given a proper emphasis to the central ideas of messianism, covenant, kingship, suffering, creation, and salvation-history. These themes have to be studied in and for themselves before their culmination in the person of Jesus Christ can be properly understood. A Christological interpretation of the Psalter is not to be achieved by using the Psalms as a spring-board for pious thoughts. The hopes and beliefs of the Old Testament have to be correctly evaluated, with all their limitations and potentialities, before we can appreciate the fullness of the revelation in Jesus Christ.

The Psalms, as perhaps no other book of the Old Testament, directly portray the encounter of God and man in various situations: in despair and trust, in public cult and in private, in thanksgiving over victory, in lament over sickness and death, etc. The major points of human life are reflected in the biblical account of the contact between God and man. And we may expect that this Introduction to the Psalter will succeed in deepening the encounter between God and Christian. Unlike many books "about" things, it will entice the reader to test what it says — by reading and thinking upon the Psalms. Books such as these, which generate the personal study and application of the reader, contribute greatly to the current biblical movement which has taken hold in the English-speaking world.

When the present writer conversed with Father Drijvers at Louvain in 1958, during the International Catholic Biblical Congress, his work was in its third edition. Since then translations have appeared in German and French. In 1964 the original edition was completely revised, and now it is a pleasure to extend a welcome to it in English dress.

Roland E. Murphy, O. Carm.

Bibliography

G. Castellino, *Libro dei Salmi,* Rome – Turin (1955)

C. Charlier, OSB, *The Christian Approach to the Bible,* E.T., London (1958)

C. H. Dodd, *According to the Scriptures,* London (1953)

W. Eichrodt, *Theology of the Old Testament,* Vol. I, E. T. by J. Baker, London (1961)

A. Gelin, *The Religion of Israel,* E.T., London (1959)

A. George, *Prier les Psaumes,* Paris (1962)

H. Gunkel - J. Begrich, *Einleitung in die Psalmen,* Göttingen (1933)

P. Grelot, *Sens chrétien de l'Ancien Testament,* Tournai (1962)

H. J. Kraus, *Psalmen,* Neukirchen (1961)

E. Osty, *Les Psaumes,* Paris (1960)

H. Renckens, *Israel's Concept of the Beginning,* New York (1964)

J. Steinmann, *Les Psaumes,* Paris (1951)

T. Vriezen, *An Outline of Old Testament Theology,* E.T., Oxford (1962)

A. Weiser, *The Psalms: A Commentary,* E.T., London (1962)

CHAPTER 1

The Psalms as Christian Prayer

The 150 psalms we find in the holy Scriptures are not the only ones that have been handed down from antiquity. The religions of other Semitic and non-Semitic peoples of the Near East had likewise their psalters. Long before Israel, Babylon had its own psalms, hymns, and chants of lamentation. We know of a quantity of religious songs from Egypt, that were chiselled into the walls of great Egyptian edifices. The library that came to light during the excavations at Ras Shamra (Ugarit) in Northern Phoenicia contained a number of examples of psalms. In the language of the Hittites, too, psalms have been preserved with other ritual texts. Moreover, in Israel itself there have been many other psalms apart from those known to us from the Bible: this is apparent from the apocryphal literature; for example the psalms of Solomon, which date from about 60 B.C. Among the recent discoveries at Wadi Qumran on the shores of the Dead Sea there are numerous manuscripts that appear to be those of hitherto unknown Jewish psalms.

Those psalms that have their place in the holy Scriptures are, however, far superior to any in this varied

treasury of literature. The basis for this assertion is that
they are the only ones of which we are sure that they
originated as an integral part of the history of redemption. They are phenomena, concurrent with the mystery
of redemption. In this mystery God seeks communion
with mankind. And because this mystery continues in
the Christian Church as the New Israel, God still works
through and in his people and the psalms still form part
of their life. We believe that the psalms are the word that
God speaks to us. They are not merely historical
documents, but they remain alive for us, they are still
able to build a bridge between God and ourselves. They
did not need to be excavated; they are neither objects of
interest only to learned men in their studies nor ex-
hibition pieces in a museum. They are just as much alive
today as they were in past centuries. They are still used
in the prayer of the Church; they still express God's
majesty and love, man's sin and ingratitude, as well as
his search for God, his restless longing, his penitence and
thankfulness. Because they are the word of God the
psalms echo through the community of the Church which
is, so to speak, their sounding-board. They are communal
songs, the songs of God's chosen people. They came into
existence in the community of God's people in Old
Testament times, and had their place in the Old
Testament worship. Today they live in the fellowship
of the Israel of the New Testament; and they strike
a new note when sung in Christian worship, that is to
say in fellowship with Christ in his Church. We shall
have to learn to understand the psalms from the standpoint of the liturgy because in it God's sacred dealings
with his people are made real once more; because it is
only in the liturgy that the Church is *ecclesia,* a body

called together by God for himself. It is in that community with God which we find in the liturgy, that the psalms, attain their richest and deepest significance. Here we touch the power of the psalms by which Christ is formed in us.

We encounter the psalms especially in the liturgy. St Benedict instructed his monks to sing the psalms in such a way that their minds should be in consonance with their song.[1] So, in the same way, it is our aim to know what we sing and pray.

Liturgical prayer is not primarily to be an absorption with ourselves but an entrance into the objective truth of God's redeeming work that is revealed to us in Christ, through the Church, and more especially through the sacraments. The liturgy has something to offer us: we must open ourselves to it and absorb it. Perhaps it would be better to say that it is not the liturgy itself that offers us something but that God offers himself there to us in order to mould us, by this gift of himself, into the people of God. Man must accept this gift: he must consent and take up God's saving work in Christ positively, in faith and love. Acceptance means redemption; God's action in our souls is accepted by us, and so is enabled to display its efficacy. Thus it is of the first importance that we for our part should try to understand the liturgy in both word and action. The Christian liturgy has its climax in the great *Actio,* the offering of Christ. But round this central act of holy Mass the Church sets the daily prayer in choir with its ceaseless psalmody. We should not load the psalms with our own thoughts and feelings, we must always keep in mind that these psalms are the word of God, that through them God's spirit must nourish, enrich, and strengthen us, so forming our spirits and our hearts to a yet more worthy and full participation in the mysteries of our redemption. Certain dispositions are required of us; we must *will* to pray in Christ and the spirit of the Church. But in order to do this more perfectly we must also know the psalms and understand their language.

What have the psalms to offer us? Have they a content not only for our lips, but also for our minds? Indeed, what have they to offer for our whole personality? It is the purpose of this book to try to answer this question.

We must always remember in this connexion that the Old Testament is the original homeland of the psalms. There they came into existence and developed; there they became active. They are not a marginal gloss on the Old Testament text, but on the contrary its culminating point. All the riches to be found in the other books of the Old Testament such as revelation, instructions, admonitions, promises and threats are, in a quite unique way, assumed into the psalms which express the personal contact between Yahweh and Israel at prayer. The whole life of Israel, the gradual development of revelation, the delight of knowing itself to be God's chosen nation, the trials of persecution, the desperation resulting from man's sin and ingratitude — all this is frankly experienced and candidly expressed in song in the psalms. In short, the whole of the Old Testament is reflected in the psalms. There is no single experience of the soul of Israel that is not put into words there. The psalms are the fullest expression of God's revelation in the Old Testament.

It may well be asked how the Christian Church, indeed more particularly we Christians of the twentieth century, can make use of these treasures. Is not the Old Testament a thing of the past? Here we come up

against the whole problem of the relationship between
the Old and the New Testament. Origen says concerning
this: "Before Jesus Christ the Old Testament was as
water, now it has become wine."[2] It is of the highest
importance to have an insight into the relationship
between the Old and the New Testament if we wish
to understand the place of the psalms under the new
covenant. Therefore we must look further into this
question.

God's plan for the world becomes reality in what is
called the history of redemption. This shows several
different stages of development in spite of its inner unity
and harmony. The inherent unity and comprehensiveness
are necessarily present because throughout this history
it is God who is at work. God is working solely for one
end, namely to draw all men unto himself in total
surrender. God works, moreover, in his own characteristic
manner; the ways of God are essentially quite different
from those of his creatures. In spite of the wilfulness of
his creatures God's plan always succeeds.

Thus this history of redemption forms one great whole.
We may describe it as the "adventure" of God with
mankind, it is God's competing for man's approval
through the agency of his eternal love. But yet, as we
have already stated, in this one great adventure several
phases are recognizable. As we contemplate the inscrutable plans of God we can trace a continuous line running
right through history from eternity, through the creation,
through Calvary to the end of the world and a "new
eternity" in which the whole company of the redeemed
has been finally and definitively taken up into the love
of God. Two great divisions can be seen in this line:
before Christ and after Christ. The first stage is the

period of time from the creation to the coming of Christ; this is the period we know as that of the Old Testament.[3] It is the period of preparation for the intervention of God in the person of Jesus. Even in this period we see God in personal and direct dealings with man. This is to be seen especially in the events of the Exodus from Egypt, the education of the chosen people, the giving of the Law on Mount Sinai, and so on. But in spite of their positive significance all these wonderful acts of God are only shadows of the real and final intervention that is to come in the person of Jesus Christ. The central point in this history is the life of Jesus and, more particularly, his death and resurrection. In him God has created a new people, namely, the long-desired "community of saints", Christ's Mystical Body, the Church. Mankind has again been given direct contact with God, and this definitively. Everything that follows in what we may call the period of the Church, up to and including our Lord's second coming, is only a consequence, a development of the Passion and Glorification of Christ in Jerusalem in the year 30 of our era. The period of the Church has its beginning after the ascension of Jesus. It is pre-eminently the period of faith, of symbols, and of the liturgy. Only at the end of time will the veil fall away completely and faith be crowned by full revelation. Then will come the end, when Christ appears riding upon the clouds. Then he will deliver his kingdom into the hands of the Father. God will be All in All. The visions of the book of the Revelation will be fulfilled.

We are living in the period after Christ, in the time of fulfilment. We are living after the sacred events of Jesus' death and resurrection, yet before the second coming of our Lord. This is the time of living "in Christ", in St Paul's phrase, of faith, of waiting and fidelity. We live entirely in the strength of the salvation that Jesus has brought about; we celebrate it among ourselves in the signs and symbols of the sacraments, above all in the sacrament of the Eucharist. It is through this festival of our faith that God realizes his plan of salvation in us. In the liturgy the history of salvation is developed and God's kingdom is formed and expanded. Yet, at the same time, man is seen to be looking forward to the end, the glorious end, when everything will be fulfilled and when the saving work of Jesus has come to full fruition in a humanity which is completely united to God and worships him face to face.

This threefold aspect and threefold dimension is admirably summarized in one of the antiphons that the Church sings on the feast of Corpus Christi: "O Sacred banquet in which Christ is received; the memorial of his Passion is renewal (an active celebration of an act in the past); the mind is filled with grace (the work of salvation in the present) and a pledge is given to us of the glory that is to come" (the longing that looks forward to the end).

Let us now return to our consideration of the psalms, of which the Old Testament was the primary setting. There they originated and were developed. However, their present-day context is the Christian liturgy. The psalms have been carried over into the new Christian "economy of salvation". If we Christians wish to understand the psalms we must bear in mind that the roots of their thought lie in the past, in the Old Testament, while their blossoming reaches out into the far future, to the end of the world, to heaven itself. As we study the psalms we find ourselves on several organically connected planes, namely the Old Testament, the new covenant in Christ and his Church, and heaven. The Old Testament, in which the psalms originated, and the Church in which they now live find their point of contact in Christ. He is the link binding them closely to each other. In the New Testament Christ has fulfilled the Old. The full wealth of the Old Testament is revealed to us only in the light of Christ; it is no longer just plain water, it is turned to wine. God's word has such power that it can be used on several planes at the same time. In the mouth of Christ and his Church the old words are clothed with a new meaning. This should not surprise us. We find the essence of the Old Testament in the mystery of salvation, God's dealing with mankind. This communion of God and man is realized only gradually. It started in a tentative way in the period of the patriarchs, took the features of a nomadic people, was incarnated in a state and a nation with a king and a temple, was destroyed in all its material framework, and went on as a spiritual flame until the coming of the Lord Jesus. Not only is the whole of the Old Testament period a preparation for the mystery of Christ, but in an incipient and vague realization people were already living the mystery of Christ. Abraham had already made an act of faith that had a specifically New Testamental character by the fact that he surrendered himself to the God who can restore life to the dead.[4] The faithful of the Old Testament found a bridge leading to God in God's revealing word, and in the institutions and the historical facts of the Old Testament. And in this way they touched the mystery of the Christian life. Everything indeed was made for and compressed towards this mystery of Christ. Surely the people of Israel did not know anything about the mystery of Christ's death and resurrection by way of ideas clearly and explicitly formulated, but in an authentic experience of faith they attained a personal surrender to the living God, who revealed himself gradually and who would manifest himself explicitly only in the historical appearance of Christ. The experience of real faith that they had was implicitly an experience already of Christ. The texts in which we find an echo of these earlier experiences speak to us in an implicit and obscure way about the mystery of Christ, because they speak about the living God, who consistently acts in the same way. The words and situations of the Old Testament, which tell us about God and his people, were deepened again and again in the Old Testament by a *rélecture* (A. Gélin) or a *Motivtransposition* (H. Gross), till they reached their real fulfilment in the New Testament, through the light of the mystery of Christ. For this reason we are justified in making the statement that the world of the Old Testament which, as we have already seen, we find in the psalms is incomplete: from beginning to end it is a progress towards the fullness of the Christian revelation. The basic ideas and expressions of the Old Testament are very simple, but at the same time very profound. In the course of revelation God himself shows us the hidden depths of these themes. That which first blossomed in the psalms has come to its full flowering in the New Testament. Through Jesus the themes of the psalms reach, in the Church, their full splendour. Or it might be better to say, a fuller splendour, for it is only in the light of Christ's coming in glory that they will obtain their most radiant lustre. When we see God as he is, then this medium of writings and psalms will be surpassed.

From the above we have learnt that the psalms are not merely things of the past nor are they the residue of an out-of-date system in the economy of salvation. Because they are God's word they could be enhanced and therefore they are still meaningful in the Christian scheme of salvation. This process is made possible and indeed even advanced by the unity we recognize in the history of our redemption.[5] This unity enables us to survey several planes at the same time. The truths of the Old Testament obtain a new and clearer perspective through the fullness of the revelation in Christ, in the same way as the thin sound of a twanged string is made fuller and deeper by the presence of a sounding-board. At this moment the sounding-board that deepens the melody of the Old Testament is the Christian revelation experienced through faith. At the last it will be the contemplation of God face to face. We shall thus understand the psalms in proportion to our growth in the understanding of the whole of the Christian mystery. This mystery covers the whole epoch of human history. The early Church always recognized a close connexion between the mystery of Christ and the psalms. The monks of old learned the Gospel and the psalms by heart. In this way they could feed their souls on the teaching and prayer of Jesus. St Augustine saw the Book of Psalms as a gospel of Jesus Christ translated into songs of praise, thanksgiving, prayers of supplication and propitiation. This insight into the mystery of Christ must grow and develop in the Christian through faith.

Fundamentally this is a question of our purity of heart (*puritas cordis*), our single-mindedness. In the instructions of the Biblical Commission concerning the teaching of the holy Scriptures it is emphasized that the teacher must lay stress on the deeper significance of the writings and that he will be able to do so "only in proportion to his own greater purity of heart"[6]. For those that are "pure in heart" possess the affinity of life and nature that enables them to understand the "things of God". Along with this personal growth in holiness it is important to have a vital insight into the whole of the Scriptures. Therefore we must read and re-read the Bible and become thoroughly familiar with it. A living and true insight into the whole of the Scriptures and a vital realization of the great themes of biblical revelation are of more importance than new and improved editions of the Bible, more faithful translations, or introductions and word-by-word commentaries. To obtain this true insight into the whole of the Scriptures a review of the historic development, the evolution of revelation is important. Dom Charlier says in answer to complaints about the monotonous, dry praying of the psalms: "A new version, even a vernacular one, will not help them to pray in the right liturgical spirit until they have acquired a deep familiarity with the whole of Scripture."[7]

Finally, a close and prolonged study of the writings of the Fathers of the Church, for instance St Augustine's explanations of the psalms, together with a more conscientiously and carefully prepared celebration of the liturgy will contribute much to the discovery of the Christian significance of the psalms. And it is this Christian meaning of the psalms that we Christians who live twenty centuries after the Old Testament, and thirty centuries since the appearance of some of the psalms, need above all.

Signposts pointing the way in which we must travel

lie close to our hand. In the first place, it is not a good method to puzzle out with zealous erudition all the literal details concerning the meaning of the psalms and then to think that we have reached our goal, while at the same time we leave the way open for what is called "accommodation" to make the text fit into the liturgy. In this way we fail badly in appreciation of the development that has taken place from the Old Testament to the New and we undervalue the connexion that exists between the original historical sense of the psalms and the deeper significance that they have gained, and must still gain, through the Christian revelation in the light of the person of Jesus Christ. By so doing, the mystery of God's word becomes contracted down to the limits of mere human erudition. In order to step from the Old Testament up to the level of our Christian liturgy it is not necessary to bridge, by hook or by crook, a wide chasm. On the contrary, we must show that no chasm exists but that we are dealing with an organic whole, one part of which flows into the other. In any system of "accommodation" there is absolutely no guarantee that what one actually wishes to read into the text is also, in very truth, God's word. Have we not already said above that in the liturgy God's word must fill us, and that this process cannot be reversed? God offers us himself in our liturgy. When we, in accord with labours of modern exegesis and the leadership of the Pope — especially in the encyclical *Divino Afflante Spiritu* of 1943 — delve deeper into what lies behind the literal sense of the words, we bring to light a new spiritual meaning which is the full depth of what, in germ, lies buried under the surface-meaning of the text. This deeper, holier meaning can only be discovered in the

period after Christ because in his light the text takes
on an altogether new perspective. This is the extension,
the organic completion of the historical, literal meaning:
it is the new dimension which has been added to the
development of the history of redemption by the coming
of Christ. Therefore it is the interpretation intended
by God who is the fulfiller of the whole vast plan
of man's salvation. When we explain the psalms in this
way we come at once into immediate living contact
with revelation. This is of incalculable value and is the
purpose of the liturgical texts. On the one hand, we
must not be bound by the purely historical, exclusively
Old Testament meaning of the text of the psalms, but on
the other hand we must not ignore this immediate and
literal sense by taking flight into the sphere of mere
"accommodation" and spiritual exegesis. If this is done
one simply falls back on one's own fantasy and in
place of grasping the essential meaning of a text and
viewing it with Christian insight, one remains bogged
down in all manner of unessential details or in the
various interpretations of a single unimportant word.

Between a stiff, superficial erudition and a false spirituality lies the golden mean of a scientifically grounded,
theological exegesis — that is to say an exegesis that
desires to bring to the fore the inner teachings of the
book in question. Therefore we shall start out in this
study with a conscientious exegesis of the text of the
psalms. That is, and will continue to be, the basis of
our labours. The crux of the matter is that we should
try and find out the intellectual content and spirit of the
psalms in order to absorb more fully the revelation that
lies hidden in them. Therefore our exegesis will not enter
into the details of particular psalms, but will try to

divide the psalms into definite coherent groups and to study the characteristics of these groups. This division has been based on the study, so strongly recommended in *Divino Afflante Spiritu,* of the so-called literary forms. Each member of a group so discovered will be seen to express a specific, intellectual outlook and to lend itself specially for expressing definite doctrinal themes. The discovery of these themes is very important. We can list them as: creation, deliverance, covenant with God, Jerusalem, kingship, messianism, sin, suffering, the Law, eschatology, and so on. They are avowedly Old Testament in expression, but the New Testament teaching is already proclaimed in them. We who live after Christ can, by virtue of our insight into God's purposes, carry the line through from the Old to the New Testament and so see the Christian fulfilment of the various themes. The creation is now a new creation, the redemption has a new dimension in Christ, the covenant has become a new covenant, Jerusalem is a spiritual city, the king is not of this world, the Messiah appears as a suffering Servant, sins are taken away by the Cross, suffering has become glorified through Christ, the Law is no longer an external rule, but an inner force, the end of time has begun, and so on.

At the same time, as a result of the understanding of God's plan brought to us by Jesus, we can indicate the line that extends still further to the end of time when everything will be completely fulfilled. When we have interpreted the psalms in this way we have laid the foundation for really praying and experiencing them. We have discovered that the subject-matter of the psalms, namely the themes of the Old Testament, are also our themes and are the realities which to an even greater

degree constitute the Christian life. Personal prayer in
purity of heart, detailed study of each separate psalm,
the consideration of the facts of Christian tradition, the
theology of the liturgy and its development — all these
can help us towards replenishing and deepening our
lives as Christians. However, the foundation of all this
lies in our understanding the great themes of the Bible
and seeing how these have been taken up into the psalms.
This we shall attempt to demonstrate in this book.
Summarized briefly, our system will be as follows: by
methods of exegesis to arrive at the division of the
psalms into various groups; to elucidate the themes of
these groups; and to transpose these themes onto the
Christian and liturgical plane. In this way the Christian
character of the psalms is brought out in clear relief,
and we obtain a background and a firm foundation for
a further detailed study of the psalms that fall outside
the scope of this work.

The first stage of our approach to the psalms is to
sort out the various types into groups and work out
their theological themes. Much of this has been done for
us in the outstanding commentaries on the psalms
published within the last few years. However, the next
step, the transposition to the present-day Christian plane,
has been attempted in only a few cases and then only
for some individual psalms.[8] Yet to consider the whole
book of psalms in this way seems the best approach to
the range of ideas of these inspired songs.

In the course of this book we hope to make clear, and
to apply in concrete form, what we have so far only
discussed in abstract theory.

CHAPTER 2

The Origin of the Book of Psalms

As is the case with almost all the books of the Old
Testament, the origin of the Book of Psalms is very
complicated. The collection of 150 psalms as we know
them did not appear all at once in the form of a book,
nor can they be ascribed to one particular author, nor
are they all derived from any one period of Jewish
history. Psalms had been composed from the earliest
days of Israel right down to the time of Christ. In the
fifth chapter of Judges we find the Song of Deborah,
which establishes the existence of sacred poetry in Israel
at a very early date; and the psalms of Solomon, those
of Qumran, Mary's *Magnificat* and Zechariah's *Benedictus*
are a proof for us that the composition of psalm-poems
continued throughout Israel's history well into the
Christian era. Many of the older psalms must certainly
have been lost; many of the newer ones only emerged
after the completion of our canonical Book of Psalms
and thus appeared later in apocryphal collections. Before
the great compilation that forms our psalter came into
being there were already smaller collections in existence
that were used in the making of our psalter. Later in this

book we shall see what was the living background, apart from authorship and date, from which particular psalms originated. It is not yet possible to order the psalms according to the customary trends of Israel's religious thought, such as deuteronomic, prophetic, or sacerdotal. It is sufficient to point out here how, in the course of time, small collections of psalms were made, sometimes specially for liturgical use, at other times for use as private books of prayer, and were finally assembled together to make up our present psalter of 150 psalms. It is understandable that a number of psalms were not absorbed into such collections and yet have been preserved for us in holy Scripture. We know, for example, songs of lamentation from the prophet Jeremiah (Jer 15:15–21, the third and fifth of the so-called lamentations), and from Job (ch. 10, for example), the hymns of Deutero-Isaiah (especially Is 44:23), the songs of praise of the three youths in the fiery furnace (Dan 3:26–90), the thanksgiving hymns of King Hezekiah (Is 38), the song of Hannah, mother of Samuel (1 Sam 2), the songs of Daniel (Dan 2:20–23), Jonah (Jon 2) and Tobiah (Tob 13). The Book of the Wisdom of Jesus the Son of Sirach (Ecclesiasticus) also contains many pieces of psalmody. However most of the psalms are found in the collection known to us as the Psalter. We find in this book clear traces of earlier, smaller collections. One of these which strikes us first is the so-called "Elohistic group" consisting of psalms 42–83. This collection can be recognized as such because in all the psalms found therein the specific name for Israel's God, Yahweh, is replaced by the more generic name Elohim (God).[1] Hence the nomenclature of "Elohistic" collection. These psalms have undergone an Elohistic editing and thus belong together.

In this collection of some forty psalms we can observe
again three smaller collections. First that of Korah
(psalms 42–49), then that of Asaph (50 and 73–83), and
the small Davidic collection, Psalms 51–72. In the
second book of Chronicles, chapter 20 verse 19, we
read: "And the Levites of the Kohathites and the
Korahites stood up to praise the Lord, the God of Israel,
with a very loud voice." The Korahites formed, thus,
a sort of levitical choir and used their own collection
of songs during liturgical celebrations. The psalms that
were in their repertory are lyrical in nature; they liked
to sing about Jerusalem and the temple of Yahweh. The
collection of Asaph has quite another character; it is
more didactic and historical with a strongly prophetic
flavour. Israel is here depicted as Yahweh's vine. The
image of the flock and the shepherd also appears quite
often. Asaph was a cantor in the time of David (1 Chron
16:4–7; 25:1–2), and his descendants took over the
function again after the return from the Babylonian
captivity. In the book of Nehemiah, in the list of names
of those who returned from the captivity we find "The
singers: the sons of Asaph, a hundred and forty-eight"
(Neh 7:44; and further Neh 11:17, 22). The psalms in
this collection of the family of Asaph may not indeed
be derived from Asaph himself but "they appear to
come from the beginning of the Babylonian captivity."[2]
The small Davidic group of psalms was apparently
crowded into the Asaph collection. Almost all the psalms
in this collection are attributed by their titles to David.

Along with the Elohistic group just described we find
still another large Davidic collection in our psalter,
namely psalms 3 to 41. According to the inscription
all the psalms in this collection, except psalm 33, are

connected with David. That is to say it is assumed that David was the collector, although it is not necessary to consider him as the author of these psalms. The titles indicating with which person or with what family the psalm is connected are certainly not inspired. They show sometimes what the historical background of a psalm is, or — in a way rather obscure for us — how it was to be performed musically; and they may be indeed, of a very ancient date, but they are not part of the original psalm and thus need not be regarded as binding us. They represent, however, Jewish traditions and so have for us a certain amount of value.

One often speaks of the "psalms of David", or "the Davidic psalter". By this we do not mean that David was the poet who wrote all the psalms; even less that all the psalms ascribed to him in their titles actually originate from him. Who would venture, for example, to ascribe psalm 51 to David? But it is quite true that "David is none the less the initiator of psalmody as a literary form, and the organizer of Israel's liturgy. We must also consider him as the principal author of the Psalter in the sense of being the most notable and remarkable among the psalmists. It is unfortunately quite impossible to know even approximately how many psalms have the royal poet as their author."[3]

Among the remaining group of psalms (84–150) we find a small collection, the "psalms of ascent" (120–34), which were presumably used as pilgrim songs for those who went on pilgrimage to Jerusalem. In the same group we find the "Hallel" psalms, which begin and (or) end with the cry of jubilation "Hallelujah". Perhaps the whole of this last group (84–150) was added to the total when the Davidic and Elohistic collections were put together. It was generally accepted that the Psalter of 150 psalms was divided artificially into five sections by the doxologies.[4] Each doxology closes a so-called book. The five books so obtained form an excellent pendant to the venerable five books of Moses, that is the Pentateuch. Recent studies give another solution to the question why the 150 psalms have been gathered together in this special order in the Book of Psalms. In the synagogues it was customary to read every sabbath a part of the Pentateuch. This gave 150 reading-parts in a three-year cycle. Each time (150 times) a special psalm was chosen that could be the response of the community to the reading.[5]

From what periods do the different collections come? We find in the time of King Hezekiah (721–693 B.C.) traces of the beginning of a collection of sacred songs. "And Hezekiah the king and the princes commanded the Levites to sing praises to the Lord with the words of David and Asaph the seer . . ." (2 Chron 29:30). And in the Book of Proverbs we read the following: "These also are parables of Solomon which the men of Hezekiah, King of Judah, copied" (Prov 25:1). These collections were made fully a hundred years before the people were led into captivity. After the return from the exile it is said of Nehemiah (445–33 B.C.), "that he founded a library, and collected the books about the kings and the prophets, and the writings of David, and letters of the kings about votive offerings" (2 Macc 2:13). It is not certain that the Psalter of that time had the same contents and form as our familiar Book of Psalms. In any case the collection in its present-day form was finished by the third century B.C., when it was translated into Greek, the so-called Septuagint translation.

The word *psalterium* came into use at this period, derived from the Greek word ψαλτήριον, a translation of the Hebrew *sefer tehillim*, meaning prayer-book, as also the word ψαλμός was used as a translation of the Hebrew *mizmor*, meaning a song for string-accompaniment, or harp-song.

The influence of the Septuagint has been very great indeed. It was in this Greek translation that the early Church used the Book of Psalms. In fact, it was in this form that Christians took over the whole Old Testament. The Hebrew text had not indeed been lost, but it had, in reality, less influence than the Septuagint. Most Latin translations of the Psalter have been made not from the original Hebrew, but from the Septuagint. The Vulgate translation of St Jerome, which was in general use in the Western Church, was also made (as regards the Psalter) from the Greek, and not from the Hebrew. Thus the Vulgate edition of the psalms is so to speak second-hand, and it has, as well as its own translators' faults, those of its original translation, the Septuagint. On the other hand the theological enrichments and profundities of the Septuagint were carried over into the Vulgate.

Hence it is understandable that men long for a purer and more reliable version of the text of the psalms, especially because they are used so much in the liturgy and must so often be recited by priests in their prayers. Therefore Pope Pius XII ordered the professors of the pontifical Biblical Institute to make a new translation of the psalms from the original text. This "new Latin interpretation of the original text" appeared for the first time in 1945. Thus along with the trusted and traditionally honoured Vulgate text, which was often not very clear, we possess a new Latin translation, which is more classical in language and clearer in expression, although less poetical. This translation is far more intelligible and comes closer to the original Hebrew text. Precisely because of its greater clarity it is of considerable help in the study of the Psalter, especially when we are trying to differentiate the form and structure of the various groups of psalms. In order to safeguard better the Vulgate text which had a profound influence on the Christian way of thinking and formulating, Dom R. Weber tried a new revision of the Vulgate text: *Psalterii nova recensio* (Clervaux, 1961).

Unfortunately the Septuagint version considered the Hebrew psalms 9 and 10 as one psalm, as also 114 and 115, whereas, conversely, it divided each of the psalms 116 and 147 into two parts. The result is that there is still some confusion in the numbering of the psalms. For instance, the Psalter in the Westminster Version (1944) prints above each psalm two numbers. The first figure gives the numbering according to the Hebrew text, the figure between brackets being that of the Greek and Latin translations. It comes down, in practice, to the number of the Hebrew text being in most cases one figure higher than that of the Septuagint and the Vulgate. The numbering followed in this book is that of the Hebrew text. This numbering is also followed in the Revised Standard Version which has been used for the quotations from the Bible.

CHAPTER 3

Hebrew Poetry

We must never forget when studying and systematizing the psalms that we are dealing with poetry. A psalm is a poem and from this fact arise a number of important considerations. First, one must absorb the psalms calmly and naturally. A psalm, which conveys an inner and emotional experience from one person to another, must be allowed to speak for itself. If it is a good poem it has an inner unity whose background of human experience is conveyed to us by its rhythm. A certain atmosphere emanates from a true poem that must not be disturbed by analysis and critical considerations, although these can help to a certain extent towards a better realization of the poem. But such an analysis must never obtrude so much as to damage the spontaneous and clear impression of the poem itself. The second thing which follows from the fact that a psalm is a poem is that it can easily be experienced on two levels, the concrete and the spiritual, at the same time. The inner experience of a man which he desires to express in something concrete, something tangible, is sometimes presented through pictures. Images and symbols are poetic mediums of expression; behind the everyday tangible reality often lies an inner and hidden experience. Poetry lends itself to a sort of double perspective. For lack of anything better the poetic vision projects itself on to the limited earthly plane; but behind, and above this, lies the spiritual plane that is the chief concern of the poem. This is more than ever the case with the psalms in which we are trying to give expression to sublime and eternal realities. Here one has, of necessity, to take refuge in imagery. Just in this way can Israel's history be made to reveal more easily a distant future.

The psalms are not, however, poems and nothing more. They belong to Hebrew poesy and are the fruits of the Hebrew spirit. They are permeated with the national spirit and character. The Hebrew by nature is poetic, contemplative, and introverted. He seeks earnestly for wisdom, for a philosophy of life that is not so mindful of organization and construction as is the technical spirit of the West. His nature is mature and thoughtful, he seeks the realities of life, he contemplates life. We see the expression of this character, first of all, in his readiness to express to the full his deepest feelings and experiences. His desire is not only to communicate to another the more ordinary and superficial experiences, as we Westerners do, but to quicken in another the same inward, spiritual, and emotional experience as he has had himself. He wishes to convey everything that he himself has undergone; and to this end the Israelite does not analyse his thoughts, he does not trouble himself about their logical order, but he utters it all spontaneously and then elucidates the whole over and over again from various angles. Thus we get what is called the concentric style. What he says is a piling up

of suggestions that touch upon the whole in its totality
but do not exhaust it. Over and over again something
new is made clear, another aspect is brought to the fore.
The experience that we learned about initially, complete
but vague, becomes in the end clearly and sharply defined
before our minds and is thus deeply implanted in our
hearts. There is thus a kind of circular movement, the
mode of thought is concentric. In the midst of repeated
statements, which seem to be more or less alike, there is a
central point. This is never fully touched upon and, in
a sense, is never quite exhausted. Examples of this
concentric mode of thought can most certainly be found
in St John's gospel. For example, in the sixth chapter
where he writes about the bread of life, and in the
fifteenth chapter in the parable of the vine. The expression of thought is musical in form, it is rhythmical. It
is like a piece of music in which the same theme is
repeated over and over again each time with slight
variations of mood and key, each time expressed differently. This repetition and expansion makes it possible
to appreciate the central theme more fully. It becomes
our personal possession, it is assimilated.

Having established these facts about the Hebrew
spirit we can say that even the prose of Israel is more
or less poetic. It has something rhythmical, at least in the
development of thought. A steady movement as of ebb
and flow can be observed; one notices a constant
parallelism. When the author of Genesis tells how the
sons of Jacob throw their young brother Joseph into
the well it is not sufficient for him to say that the well
was empty but he says: "The pit was empty, there was
no water in it" (Gen 37:24). A woman who comes to lay
her complaint before David says: "Alas, I am a widow;

my husband is dead" (2 Sam 14:5). An excellent example is
to be found in the prayer of Hannah, the mother of
Samuel: "If thou wilt indeed look on the affliction of
thy maidservant, and remember me, and not forget thy
maidservant, but wilt give to thy maidservant a son, then
I will give him to the Lord all the days of his life, and
no razor shall touch his head [a sign of the dedicated
state]" (1 Sam 1:11).

In this last example there is a fourfold parallelism
in the first part of the sentence and a twofold one in the
second. This parallelism is still more noticeably present
in Hebrew poetry. Already in the ancient Song of the
Sword of Lamech one is struck by the thought-rhythm:

> Adah and Zillah, hear my voice;
> you wives of Lamech, hearken to what I say:
> I have slain a man for wounding me,
> a young man for striking me.
> If Cain is avenged sevenfold,
> truly Lamech seventy-sevenfold. (Gen 4:23–24)

Parallelism is most striking in the verse technique of the
Hebrew writers. There is no thought of end rhymes in
this poetry although there are often splendid sound
assonances. Even less do we always find a strict metre,
although rhythm plays an important part. The verse
technique consists specially in the rhyming of thoughts,
or parallelism. Every line of verse has two sections or
half-verses which agree in content and in form. Only
taken together do they express the thought fully. They
complement each other like the two arms of a pair of
scales. Together they offer a fully balanced expression of
thought. As a rule one line of verse has two parts, so

we speak of a distich; sometimes three parts occur and then we have a tristich.

Before considering this parallelism further, we must mention that in Hebrew verse-technique strophes and rhythm also appear. In order to be able to judge the merits and flavour of these we should really be acquainted with the Hebrew tongue. In many translations the strophes are reproduced and give us the advantages of being able to separate the various ideas more easily from one another. Division into strophes helps thus to clarify the ideas. On the other hand it is very difficult to reproduce rhythm in a translation. Yet in the original verse the rhythm is extremely important. Artistic emotion is caught up by a personal life-rhythm which expresses itself in poetry first of all as a thought-rhythm and then in a rhythmic arrangement of words, which is sometimes accompanied by strict metre and rigid verse schemes. The rhythmic wording is very pronounced in Hebrew verse. By reason of regular accentuation there is a controlled excitement, a restful symmetry, and a deeper resonance of important ideas.[1]

There is no precise metre that can be scanned, but there are accentuations that are pronounced and give the rhythm. The number of these accents sometimes changes from line to line in the verses, and between the accents the number of syllables varies. Sometimes a whole psalm, or division of a psalm, has the same accentuation scheme, for instance in the so-called *qina* rhythm which originally appeared in songs of lamentation. This has three accents in the first half-verse but two in the second half-verse, as if to symbolize the rising complaint and the assurance that follows.[2] Parallelism is the thought-rhyme of the verse conveyed by the rhythm of poetical inspiration.

In this parallelism we discern several sorts, or types; the synonymous, the antithetic, and lastly the synthetic or progressive. In *synonymous* parallelism the ideas of the first part of the verse are repeated in the second; the type of syntactical construction is in both parts the same:

> Fret not yourself because of the wicked,
> be not envious of wrongdoers! (37:1)

> Hear my cry, O God,
> listen to my prayer. (61:2)

> Now therefore, O kings, be wise;
> be warned, O rulers of the earth. (2:10)

> The kings of the earth set themselves,
> and the rulers take counsel together. (2:2)

In the last two examples we notice also the chiasmus, that is to say, the verb and the subject of the sentence stand in directly opposite order in the two lines.

Antithetic parallelism develops and illuminates the theme presented in the first part by a directly opposite statement in the second, as a sort of clash of ideas. By reason of the strong contrast one gets a kind of shock, with the result that the idea which the poet desires to express comes more strongly to our minds.

> Some boast of chariots, and some of horses;
> but we boast of the name of the Lord our God.
> They will collapse and fall;
> but we shall rise and stand upright. (20:7–8)

> Many are the pangs of the wicked;
> but steadfast love surrounds him who trusts in the
> Lord. (32:10)

The third type of thought-rhyme, *synthetic* parallelism, has no repetition of the same thought, but there is a sort of connexion between the two parts of the verse. There is no real thought-rhyme, for the train of thought goes straight on, while the thought itself is worked out or defined further, in so far as it is worked out at all.

> O sing to the Lord a new song;
> sing to the Lord, all the earth!
> Sing to the Lord, bless his name! (96:1)

> They have mouths, but they speak not,
> they have eyes, but they see not. (135:16)

The thought behind the first half of the verse is here developed in the second. Other types turn the idea quite about and proceed further: in the second line a new thought appears and consequently one can scarcely speak of parallelism at all.

> I cry aloud to the Lord,
> and he answers me from his holy hill. (3:4)

According to the way in which the thoughts proceed in this last type of parallelism one can subdivide the synthetic, or progressive, parallelism still further. A short survey of the different possibilities shows us the variety of Hebrew thought-rhymes. First of all, both the parts of the verse can be co-ordinated with each other as in the example last given above. Here the relationship between them is that of cause and effect. This relationship can be of different kinds, for example, question and answer:

> How can a young man keep his way pure?
> By guarding it according to thy word. (119:9)

or by comparison:

> It is better to take refuge in the Lord
> than to put confidence in man. (118:8)

or by a contrast:

> The Lord has chastened me sorely,
> but he has not given me over to death. (118:18)

This last verse is antithetic and at the same time progressive.

As well as co-ordination we often meet subordination, that is, for example, in the second line the purpose of the first line is given.

> The face of the Lord is against evildoers,
> to cut off the remembrance of them from the earth.
>   (34:16)

In another case we have a change-over to a conditional sentence:

> Unless the Lord builds the house,
> those who build it labour in vain.
> Unless the Lord watches over the city,
> the watchman stays awake in vain. (127:1)

Finally one could include in progressive parallelism the rarely seen and less poetic form in which one simple sentence is split into two parts. This is something which we could call an expedient, and it betrays a lack either of skill, or of talent, or of inspiration:

> With my lips I declare
> all the ordinances of thy mouth. (119:13)

The stone which the builders rejected [subject]
has become the head of the corner. [predicate]
     (118:22)

A particular type with special poetic force and attrac-
tiveness is the so-called "stepped" rhythm or stair like
parallelism. A member of the first line is repeated in the
second, often quite literally, but the other piece is
dropped so that there is a gap that must be filled in.
To fill this the poet replaces the words dropped from the
first line by a broader synonym or very often adds an
altogether new element:

> What ails you, O sea, that you flee?
> O Jordan, that you turn back? [broader synonym
> for "flee"] (114:5)

> And gave their land as a heritage,
> a heritage to Israel his servant. (136:21–22)

Driver calls this type of parallelism *parallelismus cli-
maticus*. Herkenne names it *Stufenrhythmus*. In this type
of thought-development one goes step by step further.
This works very suggestively, as we can see clearly in
psalm 29:

> Ascribe to the Lord, O heavenly beings,
> ascribe to the Lord glory and strength.
> Ascribe to the Lord the glory of his name;
> worship the Lord in holy array.
> The voice of the Lord is upon the waters...
> The voice of the Lord is powerful...
> The voice of the Lord breaks the cedars,
> the Lord breaks the cedars of Lebanon...

The voice of the Lord shakes the wilderness,
the Lord shakes the wilderness of Kadesh.

This psalm shows some resemblance to the literature of
Ugarit (Ras Shamra) in the use of this particular thought-
rhyme. In the poetry found in Ugarit this stepped rhythm
is used in a really masterly way to express the strong
life-rhythm.

A knowledge of Hebrew parallelism is important for
us because it can almost always remain apparent in
translation. The fuller our insight into the nature and
structure of parallelism, the fuller our appreciation of
the beauty of the poetry of the psalms. We shall understand and enjoy the psalms more if we appreciate the
beautiful form that is an intrinsic part of them. Of this
beauty there remains for us, unfortunately, practically
only the thought-rhyme when we read the psalms in
translation. More specially, the parallelism helps the
expert to understand the more difficult passages in the
psalms or to perceive the meaning of the more obscure
Hebrew expressions.

And also in our prayer this thought-rhyme can help
us. When we pray in the words of psalm 148:2, "Praise
him, all his angels, praise him, all his host", it is clear
from parallelism that by the host of God the armies of
angels are meant. Finally this thought-rhyme helps to fix
our attention on the main ideas which are repeatedly
placed before our minds, in changing form but with the
same content, during the course of the meditative rhythm.

CHAPTER 4

The Various Types of Psalms

In the previous chapters we have confined ourselves principally to more or less introductory matters. Now we are going to approach the psalms themselves. The first question concerns the how and why of the different types of psalms.

Bible study, especially that of the Old Testament, has developed enormously during the past decades. The new element arose out of the study of literary forms and the research into the different types to be found in the Old Testament *(Gattungsforschung)*, together with the consideration of the growth and development of literary forms in the four gospels *(Formgeschichte)*. The literary criticism that is connected with the name of Julius Wellhausen has established the fact that there are several documents in the five books of Moses, namely: the Yahwist, Elohist, Deuteronomist, and the Priestly Code. From the study of these documents we find there existed also an earlier source, not concerned with written authorship but with tradition passed down by word of mouth. The spiritual trends in Israel and the literary forms corresponding to them did not develop in sequence, but several

schools of thought or tendencies grew up together side
by side, each predominating in turn according to the
conditions then obtaining. The question of the authorship
of a book of the Bible, which was considered so
important during the period of literary criticism, has thus
lost some of its meaning. On the other hand, the issue
about the concrete situation at any particular time in
the life and worships of Israel, out of which the
particular literary work under discussion had originated,
received greater emphasis. This was because, when this
problem had been answered, the relationship between the
writings under considerations and the religious life of
Israel became clearer, and so the text could be more
easily and realistically understood. Rowley wrote in
1950: "Of no single book in the Old Testament, in the
form in which we have it today, do we know the
author."[1] Even if we do not know the author of any
particular book of the Bible, today we have more and
more insight into the material that this unknown author
used. We see now how this material grew naturally out
of the daily life of the people of Israel, and out of
Yahwism, which was so full of life. The Bible is set back
again in its social, psychological, and historical context.
We study the texts carefully to discover in different
passages of Scripture certain general features and related
patterns, which can then be connected up with institutions, customs, and modes of life in ancient Israel. Thus
we examine a particular group of texts of one special
literary genre for what Gunkel calls *Sitz im Leben,*
that is the concrete situation out of which the literary
form has developed. We look for the living background
against which it can be placed and thus understood and
fully appreciated. Behind the externals of a text we seek

the spiritual trends, the usages, the tradition of which the text is an expression. Thus a psalm, for example, after a philological and critical examination and an inquiry into its authenticity, remains just a dead thing. It represents just another lifeless detail so long as we do not know how to place it against its living background, in its right place in the nation's literary and doctrinal development. As long as we cannot penetrate into the author's psychology and into the soul of the Jewish people, in whose midst the psalm was first written and experienced, just so long does this psalm remain quite inanimate for us.

This modern method of Bible study was begun and brought to full flower by Hermann Gunkel (1862–1932). He and the school of thought which followed him assuredly went too far with the application of their method. They wished to deduce and explain the development of Israel's religion entirely from social, psychological, and historical factors. In this way Gunkel studied the Book of Genesis and above all the Book of Psalms. The results of his study of the psalms were decidedly fruitful, so that one can truthfully say that several conclusions that Gunkel arrives at about the form of the psalms almost command general agreement.[2]

From the Catholic side, round about 1900 Lagrange O.P., de Hummelauer S.J., and Prat S.J., began to direct their attention to literary styles. But their standpoint was too strongly apologetical and the background of their knowledge on this subject was too limited. It was only in 1943 that the encyclical *Divino Afflante Spiritu* gave a stimulus to Catholic biblical research into literary genres. The Pope wrote in this encyclical: "It is absolutely necessary for the interpretation to go back in spirit to these remote centuries of the East, and make proper use of the aids afforded by history, archaeology, ethnology, and other sciences, in order to discover what literary forms the writers of that early age intended to use, and did in fact employ. For to express what they had in mind the ancients of the East did not always use the same forms and expressions as we use today; they used those that were current among people of their own time and place; and what these were the exegete cannot determine *a priori,* but only from a careful study of ancient oriental literature ... Consequently, if the Catholic exegete is to meet fully the requirements of modern biblical study, he must, in expounding sacred Scripture, and vindicating its immunity from all error, make prudent use also of this further aid; he must, that is, ask himself how far the form of expression or literary idiom employed by the sacred writer may contribute to the true and genuine interpretation; and he may be sure that this part of his task cannot be neglected without great detriment to Catholic exegesis." And at the end of the passage that treats of this subject we read: "Thus a knowledge and careful appreciation of ancient modes of expression and literary forms and styles will provide a solution to many of the objections made against the truth and historical accuracy of Holy Writ; and the same study will contribute with equal profit to a fuller and clearer perception of the mind of the sacred Author." [3]

The consideration of their literary forms means a great step forward in our study of the psalms. All the commentators on the psalms try to bring them together into groups, because by elucidating a whole group each separate psalm in that group becomes clearer. All the experts mention songs of praise, songs of thanksgiving, and songs of lamentation. These three types of psalm strike a student of the psalter at once. But the homely proverb, "Too many cooks spoil the broth", can be said to apply here. Bäthgen speaks of psalms of gay mood, psalms of sad mood, and psalms of restful mood; Kautsch, following the Greek nomenclature, writes of Odes, Hymns, and Elegies. So many divisions of the psalms can be made on the grounds of their contents. Thus, for instance, there are psalms with historical motifs, psalms about Jerusalem, and about the Messiah. The new Latin translation divides the Psalter in this way. Steuernagel distributes the psalms according to the different phases of Israel's religion; thus we have psalms from the milieu of the prophets, from deuteronomic reform circles, from the priestly class, from the schools of the "wise men", and so on. Robert worked, in combination with Gunkel's system, also in this direction and not without some justification. Thus each commentary tends to use a different system of division.

Gunkel argues as follows: we are looking for a system of division for the psalms. Well, the psalms are a literary product. A good grouping must be first, if perhaps not principally, a literary one. We must seek a literary agreement between a number of psalms. We find then a number of psalm types. In order to understand each type properly we must see how it came into being, from what events and circumstances it grew. We must consider how it is that this particular form of poetry, and not any other, was used. At first sight the psalms are often not clear to us because they originated in a milieu and a civilization having little in common with our very different world of the twentieth century and our Western culture. Therefore we must try to discover for each type of psalm the concrete situation out of which it developed, and the function it had in life. When all the psalms of a certain type are put back in the situation which, as it were, forms their original background, they become clear and intelligible and do not require an elaborate interpretation. This method seems to be very fruitful indeed. Instead of taking the text of the psalm as the point of departure for raising a theological edifice, which had already been mostly designed beforehand, Gunkel considered such a text as first of all a point of arrival, as the goal of a long process of evolution. By tracing back the course of this evolution we should, according to Gunkel, finally arrive at the original situation in which the psalm again becomes meaningful.

Here we must call to mind that Israel's poetry is not, in general, individual; it is not an outpouring from the heart of a personal experience like much of our modern verse-making. Israel's poetry was born out of the life of the whole people. It has a collective character. It is a product of the people as a whole. The poet is above all an interpreter of the soul of his people. *He* says what *they* think and feel. He himself may feel more strongly and more personally than do the masses, but he expresses that feeling within the limits of a fixed framework and almost entirely according to the possible range allowed by the traditional forms. Hence this poetry is a pure reflection of the time and the culture wherein it was written. These poems are products of life as a whole. Now it is a song chanted by the women as the victorious armies return; on another occasion it is the lament over the bier of some dear, departed friend that is sung. In still another instance it is a prophet's oracle spoken to the people assembled in the temple. All these songs are different in form and style according to the varying situations from daily life into which they fit. We can find in the Bible a song of a well:

Spring up, O well! — Sing to it! —
the well which the princes dug,
which the nobles of the people delved,
with the sceptre and with their staves. (Num 21:17)

again a song of the sword:

Adah and Zillah, hear my voice;
you wives of Lamech, hearken to what I say:
I have slain a man for wounding me,
a young man for striking me. (Gen 4:23)

We can recognize love-songs, harvest-songs, songs of victory, etc.

Religion was, however, Israel's principal source of inspiration. Repeatedly we find stories in the Bible of holy deeds coupled with a song or some other fixed formula. The Book of Numbers (10:35) relates: "When the ark was lifted up, Moses said: 'Arise, O Lord, and let thy enemies be scattered; and let them that hate thee flee before thee.' And when it was set down he said: 'Return, O Lord, to the ten thousand thousands of Israel.'" (Compare psalm 68). After Judith's victory her people unanimously extolled her and said: "You are the exaltation of Jerusalem, you are the great glory of Jerusalem, you are the great glory of Israel, you are the great pride of our nation! You have done all this singlehanded; you have done great good to Israel, and God is well pleased with it. May the Almighty Lord

bless you for ever. And all the people said: so be it!"
(Jud 15:9—11). Think of Exodus ch. 15 in connexion
with this. Here it is related how Miriam, the prophetess,
the sister of Moses and Aaron, had a tambour in her
hand, while all the womenfolk followed her with
tambours and dances and took up from her the refrain:

> Sing to the Lord, for he has triumphed gloriously;
> the horse and his rider he has thrown into the sea.

These songs came into being because of God's spectacular
intervention in the life of the generation then living.
Yet not every religious experience in Israel was founded
upon an actual, visible intervention of God's power.
"For the Israelites, as for us also, the liturgy forms a
normal framework within which the people lived their
religion."[4] The public worship, in which the Israelites
experienced above all the fact that they knew themselves
to be God's chosen nation, formed the most important
source of inspiration for the growth of the ancient
Israelite psalmody: "The Psalter was not only the prayer-
book and hymn-book of the second temple and the
synagogue; it reflected in many cases the pre-exilic
cultus; many a psalm came into being in and through
the public worship of primitive Israel."[5] The actual
situation in which the psalms were composed was
especially the liturgy of Israel.

The public worship of the people of Israel, which
took shape in the great yearly festivals, in the daily
sacrifices, in ceremonies of thanksgiving, days of prayer,
the formal reading aloud of the Law, the renewal of
the covenant, and so on, meant the celebration of
Yahweh's holy action, the acknowledgment of Yahweh

as their God. Liturgy was for them, just as it is now for us, not just a mere memorial of happenings in a remote past. The actions of sacred history, especially the Exodus from Egypt and all that was connected with that event, were not only remembered but were in some sense re-presented as veritable sacred acts and words of God, so that the faithful could re-live them. The holy acts of Yahweh were proclaimed to the community — the congregation was as it were the sounding-board for God's word. This authentic proclamation of the word of God had a definite result; it offered salvation. This active recollection (*anamnesis*) of the past which was itself the fruit of belief, would awaken an even fuller belief — ultimately a belief in Christ. It was enacted by telling and celebrating in song all the sacred acts of God in the midst of the whole community of Israel. Thus these sacred events of the past were actively at work in the present, although not by means of a sacramental presence such as we know in the Christian Eucharist.

It is more helpful to compare the presence that existed there in Israel with the presence of the saving events in Christian history that are celebrated in the Church's calendar throughout the year, when the events are not historically re-enacted, but there is no mere act of remembrance: "The mysteries of Christ's life ... live on in their effects in us, since each ... in its own way is the cause of our salvation."[6] During the proclamation referred to above, the reading of historical passages from the sacred books took a prominent place. The reading was done within the circle of the whole community, *in medio ecclesiae*. In whatever way this repetition of events of the past took place something actual and up-to-date was experienced so that each man linked himself

with it and became, by faith, part of it. That this is
so can be seen, for example, from the repeated use of
words such as "this day", "us", "we"; "Not with our
fathers did the Lord make this covenant, but with us,
who are all of us here alive this day",[7] and in the story
of the renewal of the covenant at Shechem after the
death of Joshua (Jos 24). The sense of the present
actuality of the sacred facts would be increased still
further by a symbolic, sober performance or representation of what was in process of being told. Such, for
example, according to Weiser, was true of the commemoration of the covenant made on Mt. Sinai. Incense,
a flourish of trumpets, the voice of the reader etc., all
combined to symbolize the great events on Sinai. The
supreme fact that formed the basis of every liturgical
celebration in Israel was the unchangeable faithfulness
of Yahweh; his will to redeem and save endured for ever.
Yahweh never regrets his benefactions, his faithfulness
does not depend in any way on any reciprocal faithfulness on our part. His word, his revelation stands fast to
eternity. Whenever Israel appears assembled before the
face of God these eternal facts apply as much today
as ever they did in the past.

It is from these liturgical celebrations that the psalms
took their origin. Unfortunately we know practically
nothing of the rubrics and instructions that were
followed during the ceremonies. No ritual directions
concerning the actions that were performed have come
down to us with the psalms. Yet we repeatedly come
up against indications in the psalm itself of particular
actions that accompanied its recitation:

Bring an offering, and come into his courts. (96:8)

Enter his gates with thanksgiving,
and his courts with praise. (100:4)

Open to me the gates of righteousness. (118:19)

I go about thy altar, O Lord,
singing aloud a song of thanksgiving,
and telling all thy wondrous deeds. (26:6–7)

The processions of my God, my King, into the
    sanctuary —
the singers in front, the minstrels last,
between them maidens playing timbrels.
    (68:24–25)

I will come into thy house with burnt offerings . . .
I will offer to thee burnt offerings of fatlings,
with the smoke of the sacrifice of rams;
I will make an offering of bulls and goats.
    (66:13–15)

These indications are valuable; by very careful study
of the psalms and by the combination of such details
we can often arrive at the precise method of celebration,
the celebrant, and other particulars about the ceremony
from which the psalms originated. In the same way we
can imagine someone quite unacquainted with Christen-
dom being able through careful study of the prayers
used during the sacrament of baptism to puzzle out
in some degree the ceremonies used and the teaching
contained therein.

From what has been said above we may take it that
the worship and the liturgical feasts of Israel form the
stage with its scenery on which the psalms originated.

The psalm, as it was required for any particular feast, came spontaneously from the hand of a writer, who was king, priest, or prophet. These psalms, however, were repeated on every occasion that followed and so became traditional; and in Israel, where tradition and the sense of community were so very strong, a ceremonial once established remained, although the circumstances changed. A certain fixed form of composition grew out of this spontaneous psalm-writing to which every author felt he must adhere. A hymn should be composed thus and in no other way. A psalm of thanksgiving followed in this way a certain standardized pattern that was demanded by the rules of literary style. Thus when we know, for example, that the psalms of thanksgiving originated from a particular liturgical thanksgiving ceremony and that the genre of these psalms shows also the features of that particular ritual, then we are entitled to explain each individual psalm of thanksgiving with reference to that ceremony. This does not mean to say that each and every psalm of thanksgiving had a liturgical origin. Perhaps it was written far away from Jerusalem in some out-of-the-way place. But even in that event we must turn to the liturgical thanksgiving ceremony for our explanation, because it set its stamp upon the genre of this type of psalm, from which even an isolated extra-liturgical psalm cannot escape. What Guardini says about liturgical style can also be adapted to the literary genres in Israel: "Where previously the movement seemed to be bound to precisely defined circumstances, to a certain fixed assessment, it can now be adopted to a certain degree by everybody."[8] It is just in the personal and individual use he makes of old forms and fixed expressions that the poet shows his artistry.

He knows how to put new life into the ancient tradition that has grown somewhat stale.

As not all psalms originated in the cult of Israel so we must assert also that not all psalm genres are liturgical in their origin. This is true in particular of the personal psalms of petition; these probably did not develop from liturgical celebrations but from the desperate situation in which the psalmist found himself. Still these psalms also, in spite of their non-liturgical origin, were used later in the cult. This was especially so after the captivity. Such psalms serve a quite different purpose from that for which they were originally written. This is verified in practically all psalms. A psalm written as a personal prayer is taken over and used as a form of intercession for the whole people. We can see this if we examine, for example, psalms 51 and 69. A psalm of thanksgiving such as psalm 30 is, as appears from the Hebrew title, used for the feast of the dedication of the temple. Moreover we can perceive later blendings of the various genres; they overflow into each other as can be seen from psalms 9, 10, 34, and 119. Added to this, we have the influence of the prophetic style and the occurrence of prophetic oracles (see Pss 50, 81). We see the stronger emphasis on a more spiritual life of a personal stamp brought to the fore in such psalms as 51 and 63; and the imitation of the moralizing style of the Wisdom literature that emphasizes intellectual reflection in psalms such as 37, 49 and 73.

In this later period Hebrew poetry suffers from affected and artificial forms. This was the time of the alphabetic psalms in which every verse, or half-verse, begins with successive letters of the alphabet.[9] These various developments of the styles of psalmwritings that

have left their traces in the psalter do not make research
into the various genres any easier, and they force us to
employ in reality still more subdivisions. In this book,
for practical reasons and in order to increase our
appreciation of the underlying principles, we shall try
to the best of our ability to demonstrate the various
genres in their original and purest forms.

When are we justified in classifying a psalm under a
particular genre? The fact that several psalms show
agreement among themselves does not yet bind them
to any single psalm-type. With Gunkel we can state
three criteria that will indicate that we are dealing
with a particular literary genre. First, the songs that
belong to the same type grew originally out of the
same situation in life and thus proceed very often from
the worship of Israel. Secondly, they have a common
treasure of thought and mood. Thirdly, they show a
similar literary style and a resemblance in structural
form. All three of these criteria must be satisfied before
we can say quite definitely that a particular psalm
belongs to any determined psalm type. To satisfy one
of them is not by any means sufficient to establish
a literary genre. It is especially important to see that
the psalms under discussion agree as to their contents.
Psalms with historical motifs, for example, do not make
a separate group simply because they are historical; such
motifs can occur in all types of psalms whether they
are psalms of praise, thanksgiving, petition, processional,
or for use on royal occasions. Yet in each of these groups
of psalms the historical motif has its own special
function. Thus, when dividing the psalms into types
we must observe, along with this question of contents,
the actual concrete situation out of which the psalm

originated. Thus we must try to find out what part
the psalm played in Israel's life. After that, attention
must be given to its literary form. The psalm will only
ultimately become quite clear to us through our knowledge of the circumstances behind its writing, coupled
with an understanding of its literary construction.

We do not need to enter further into the subject of
the importance of a knowledge of literary genres in our
study of the psalms. In order to explain each psalm in
its immediate and literal sense one must keep in mind
its literary genre first of all. It is precisely the putting
back of the psalm into its own individual setting that
makes it clear and brings it to life. But the division into
groups and into types signifies a great gain for the
understanding of the teaching, contents, and theology
of the psalms, both from the Old Testament standpoint
and when considering them in the light of the Christian
revelation. Each group is distinguished by its own
setting, its own mentality and its own range of thought.
Each group has its own central idea and expresses the
corresponding attitude of mind. It is for us now to try
to discover just what that underlying idea and attitude
may be. Our examination of the literary genres will
prove of great help in doing this. We can thus "introduce
some sort of order into the rather heterogenous mass of
150 psalms",[10] and bring to the fore groups and special
themes. When we examine each psalm separately we see
more clearly the principle, the fundamental attitude of
soul that lies behind the group to which that particular
psalm belongs. When we gradually learn to place that
central idea, that theme, that attitude of mind in a
Christian perspective, we find a really fruitful way of
using the psalms as prayers.

In Appendix I the division of the psalms into particular types, according to the method followed in this
book, can be found. Undoubtedly this division is
somewhat formal and rigid and the gradual evolution
of Israel's religious life, which runs right across our
system of grouping, has not been sufficiently emphasized.
The evolution of Israel's religion in general and in so
far as it is represented in the different types of psalms
has not yet been studied sufficiently to give us data from
which we can establish facts about them more or less
definitely. Knowledge of the chronological development
of the religious doctrine and the literary forms of ancient
Israel are very important in order to understand better
the religious message of the psalms and their real place
in the life of the people of Israel. But it is still very
difficult to tie down literary styles, choice of words and
thematic development to fixed dates. Time and again
it becomes clear that we start from inevitable *a priori's*.
When is a text deuteronomic? When really post-exilic?
Why is the style of Deutero-Isaiah really tied to a
certain period? [11]

CHAPTER 5

The Psalms of Praise, or Hymns

Some few short songs having the character of hymns have
been preserved for us from the earliest period of Israel's
history. These may be regarded as models or patterns
for the hymns of a later date. The song of Miriam, the
sister of Moses, is one of the best known of these:

> Sing to the Lord, for he has triumphed gloriously;
> the horse and his rider he has thrown into the sea.
>   (Ex 15:21)

This short hymn, which is expanded still further in the
so-called song of Moses (Ex 15:1–18), grew spontaneously out of the experience of God's mighty intervention
in the affairs of his people at the time when they passed
through the Red Sea. The Israelites celebrated this divine
benefaction with song and dance. A song of praise
developed naturally, and they called out to one another,
"Sing to the Lord". The Strong One of Israel is the
central figure of this song. "For he has triumphed
gloriously, the horse and his rider he has thrown into
the sea." God's holy action, his powerful intervention,

is the stimulus to the praise of God. The introduction to the ancient song of Deborah is, in the same way, a little hymn:

> Hear, O kings; give ear, O princes;
> to the Lord I will sing,
> I will make melody to the Lord, the God of Israel.
> 　(Judg 5:3)

Now when God brought deliverance by the hand of Jael, the wife of Hebr, the Kenite, who drove a tent-peg through Sisera's temples, the joy of victory welled up. Deborah and Barak sang a song of thanksgiving to the honour of God: "Hear, O kings; give ear, O princes . . ."

In the vision that Isaiah saw at the time of his call we hear the song of praise sung by the seraphim:

> Holy, holy, holy is the Lord of hosts;
> the whole earth is full of his glory. (Is 6:3)

After the revelation of the holy God follows the trembling and awe-inspired song of praise of his creation repeating that he alone is holy. He is holy in the essence of his being, he is holy also in the revelation of his goodness and mercy, experienced repeatedly by the people of Israel. The best-known cry of praise and joy, very much in the form of a hymn, that the people uttered, is echoed repeatedly in psalms and countless other places in the Bible and runs as follows:

> O give thanks to the Lord, for he is good;
> for his steadfast love endures for ever.

We shall see later how often and how spontaneously the people make use of this hymn to sing their praise to God. Whenever God reveals himself, a song of praise is always heard. Sometimes the theophany is so direct that it awakens deep feelings of fear and awe; on other occasions it takes the form of a divine intervention in their history. In later times we also find this reaction, this spontaneous hymn of praise. When the heroic acts of Judith, a later version of the deeds of Jael, demonstrated 800 years later God's wonderful care for his people, a song of praise known as the song of Judith was sung:

> Begin a song to my God with tambourines,
> sing to my Lord with cymbals.
> Raise to him a new psalm;
> exalt him, and call upon his name.
> For God is the Lord who crushes wars. (Jud 16:2 f.)

and yet further:

> I will sing to my God a new song:
> O Lord, thou art great and glorious,
> wonderful in strength, invincible. (v. 13)

These songs of praise, born spontaneously, derive from a direct experience of God's intervention on behalf of his people and are brought to life again, given as it were a sacramental form, in the meeting of Yahweh and his people that took place in the liturgy of Israel, as we saw in the last chapter. In this liturgy the people (in Hebrew *qahal*, in Latin *ecclesia*) lived anew the holy acts of God once shown to a former generation and still working as a living force in the religious worship of Israel. There, in community, were celebrated the ancient traditions regarding the Exodus and Sinai, and the fact that they were the people of the covenant was experienced in a very real way. Again and again the songs of praise resounded: "Lord, great art thou, and glorious in thy power, and no one can overcome thee", "Holy, holy, holy" and ". . . his steadfast love endure for ever".

Because the great feasts were the normal framework into which the psalms of praise were fitted and sung, we must examine these Israelite ceremonies further. They were all of a religious nature, because the whole life of these people of Yahweh was coloured by their religion. Even when they had set up the golden calf in the wilderness, while Moses was on the mountain with God, songs of praise were sung and the people shouted together: "These are your gods, O Israel, who brought you up out of the land of Egypt" (Ex 32:4). Elkanah, the husband of Hannah, went once a year to Shiloh, not only to offer sacrifice but also, as it is written, "to worship the Lord of hosts at Shiloh" (1 Sam 1:3). The prophet Amos when speaking about false worship satirized the worshippers' gifts and offerings of fatlings and the "noise of your songs", and "the melody of your harps" (Amos 5:23). Songs were sung without ceasing throughout the feasts of Israel. They were sung during the entry into the temple-porches which were a structure quite apart from the main building. They were sung in the templehalls during the offering of the sacrifices, and during the various processions, and so on. Large crowds of Israelites, in happy mood and clad in festive garments, showed their joy and jubilation in numberless songs of praise. Priests or trained choirs, such as those of Asaph and Korah already known to us, led the singing, while the people joined in or repeated

the refrain over and over again. Psalm 136 has such a
refrain. Throughout the whole length of the psalm the
second half-verse is continually: "For his steadfast love
endures for ever." Psalm 118 begins with the call:

> O give thanks to the Lord, for he ist good;
> his steadfast love endures for ever!
> Let Israel say, "His steadfast love endures for ever."
> Let the house of Aaron say, "His steadfast love . . ."
> Let those who fear the Lord say, "His steadfast
>   love . . ."

Sometimes choirs sing alternately:

> O house of Israel, bless the Lord!
> O house of Aaron, bless the Lord!
> O house of Levi, bless the Lord!
> You that fear the Lord, bless the Lord! (135:19–20)

Along with the voices of the people raised in song and
jubilation there sounded the richly varied tones of
musical instruments. One should not think too meanly
of the technical possibilities of musical instruments
3,000 years ago. There were string-instruments such as
the lyre and harp (a psalm was originally a song intended
to be sung with harp accompaniment), and there were
wind-instruments such as trumpets, horns, and flutes,
while the percussion instruments consisting of tambou-
rines, drums, and cymbals accentuated the rhythm. With
the help of all these instruments the musicians could
introduce a good measure of variety and produce an
impression of grandeur. At the end of the book of psalms
we see as it were a great conductor indicating to each
instrument in turn where it must join in:

> Praise him with trumpet sound;
> praise him with lute and harp!
> Praise him with timbrel and dance;
> praise him with strings and pipe!
> Praise him with sounding cymbals;
> praise him with loud clashing cymbals!

And the final chord:

> Let everything that breathes praise the Lord!
> Praise the Lord! (150:3–6)

The congregation took their own active part by uttering loud shouts of jubilation, and repeated exclamations accompanied by rhythmical hand-clapping.[1] Many places in the Bible make it clear how we must picture to ourselves the people's enthusiasm. When the priest Zadok had anointed Solomon as king we read: "Then they blew the trumpet; and all the people said: Long live King Solomon. And all the people went after him, playing on pipes, and rejoicing with great joy, so that the earth was split by their noise" (1 Kings 1:39–40). We read something similar when, at the coronation of the little seven-year old Joash, all the people called out, "Long live the king" to the accompaniment of fanfares of trumpets (2 Chron 23:11–13). It was often the king himself who, at the great religious gatherings, called the people to bear witness to their joy. "Then David said to all the assembly: Bless the Lord your God. And all the assembly blessed the Lord, the God of their fathers" (1 Chron 29:20). How did they praise God? What exclamation did they use? The principal cry of joy was undoubtedly their name for God "Yahweh" often shortened to Yah, or Yahu. This cry has remained in the word "Hallelu-jah". "Hallelu" means "Praise ye!", and is thus an invitation to utter sounds of praise. Yah is the shortened form of Yahweh, thus "Hallelujah" means "Praise ye Yahweh". Sometimes a priest or elder invites the people to join in the praise by the call "Hallelu" whereupon they all answered enthusiastically "Yah, Yah, Yah". Or in place of "Hallelu", another word was used such as "shout", "rejoice", "be glad". The answer was always "Yah, Yah, Yah". Another cry of joy was "Amen". "And all the people said, 'Amen' and praised the Lord" (1 Chron 16:36), just as at the eulogy of Judith, "And all the people said, 'So be it!'" (Jud 15:10).

We have spoken already of the cry "For his steadfast love endures for ever" with which we are familiar in many psalms.[2] When we compare the story of the transference of God's ark to Solomon's temple (2 Chron 5:13) and that of the dedication of the temple (2 Chron 7:3, 6) we see that when the cloud filled the temple, and the House of God was filled with his glory (kabod) the people bowed down in worship and raised the song of praise: "For he is good, for his steadfast love endures for ever." King Jehoshaphat had a band of consecrated singers and group of musicians clad in festive garments to march before the troops on the occasion of a warlike expedition. These had to sing: "Give thanks to the Lord, for his steadfast love endures for ever" (2 Chron 20:21). And Jeremiah prophesied in days of stress: "Thus says the Lord, the voice of mirth and the voice of gladness shall be heard again, and the voices of those who sing: Give thanks to the Lord of hosts, for the Lord is good, for his steadfast love endures for ever" (Jer 33:10–11).

The people took an active part in the celebrations by

joining in certain ceremonial actions, as well as by songs and shouts of rejoicing. These actions often evolved during the solemnities themselves quite spontaneously. We find the best description of these solemnities in later writings from the time after the captivity such as the books of Ezra and Maccabees and the books of Chronicles, probably written by a cantor, as appears from many liturgical notes. It is precisely in this period that the psalms of praise, which are the concern of this chapter, attained great popularity[3] and were sung, in some sense dramatized, in the liturgy. Although the details given by these late books were somewhat embellished to fit in with the ideas of the times when the books were written, yet the fundamental parts of the liturgical celebration there described originated from the earlier era of the kings. We read in many places in these books that the people stretched out their hands, bowed down, knelt, placed their foreheads to the ground, prostrated themselves, and so on during the temple services.[4] A few examples must suffice. At the solemn dedication of the temple King Solomon's prayer was introduced in this way: "Then Solomon stood before the altar of the Lord in the presence of all the assembly of Israel, and spread forth his hands. Then he knelt upon his knees with his hands spread forth towards heaven and said . . ." After his prayer was over fire came down out of heaven and the glory of the Lord filled the new temple building. When all the Israelites saw how the fire descended and how the temple was filled with God's glory they bowed down with their faces to the ground in worship and sang the hymn of praise: "For he is good, for his steadfast love endures for ever" (2 Chron 6:12 to 7:3). Two centuries later, in 721 B.C., King Hezekiah dedicated the purified temple again. The description tells that on this occasion similar ceremonies took place. "The whole assembly worshipped, and the singers sang, and the trumpeters sounded; all this continued until the burnt offering was finished. When the offering was finished, the king and all who were present with him bowed themselves and worshipped" (2 Chron 29:28–29). After the foundation of the new temple had been laid under Zerubbabel — it had been destroyed in 587 B.C. at the time of the captivity — the song "Give thanks to the Lord, for he is good and his steadfast love endures for ever" echoed once again, "and all the people shouted with a great shout, when they praised the Lord, because the foundation of the house of the Lord was laid" (Ezra 3:11). Finally we read that on the occasion of the feast of rededication under Judas Maccabeus in 160 B.C. after the violation of God's House by Antiochus Epiphanes, the temple "was dedicated with songs and harps and lutes and cymbals. All the people fell on their faces and worshipped and blessed Heaven,[5] who had prospered them. So they celebrated the dedication of the altar for eight days..." (1 Macc 4:54–56).

We must set Israel's psalms of praise against this background. The unrestrained rejoicing and active participation of the people resound through these psalms.

After this general sketch of the situation, before going on to consider the teaching and religious contents of the psalms of praise, we must make some remarks concerning the wording characteristic of this group of psalms. For it is by their wording that we can recognize the groupings of the psalms; this is true also when we are praying them.

At the beginning of this chapter we quoted various fragments of ancient hymns in which we could establish

some arrangements of words that later became characteristic elements of psalms of praise. A psalm of praise begins
usually with an introduction in which the psalmist invites
the people to sing their praise to God. Then follows the
main body of the hymn stating the precise reasons for
this particular act of praise. Generally the psalm ends
with a concluding formula.

First of all then comes *the invitation*. It is the call to
praise as this existed originally in the rites of Israel's
feasts. Such words as: praise, bless, bear witness, sing,
play upon the harp, rejoice, and shout, are often used.
We see the priest or the king or, perhaps, the precentor
or leader of the orchestra standing behind these formulas,
inviting the people to be glad, to sing, to shout, to play
certain musical instruments, to enter, to fall down and
worship, to clap their hands or to stretch them out to
Yahweh who dwells in the holy of holies. Above all, the
incentive to be glad, to give thanks and seek God's
presence in this rejoicing, and to ask for favours and
mercy, can be heard in this invocation:

> Seek the Lord and his strength,
> seek his presence continually. (105:4)

The call is directed in the first place to those present:
Praise and bless, O ye sons of Israel, servants of Yahweh,
ye men of piety, ye who stand in Yahweh's House
(meaning those present, or perhaps also the temple choirs),
you, O house of Israel, Jerusalem, Zion (meaning the
believers assembled on Mount Zion, or in the temple
area), you priests, you levites, the whole nation. But
Yahweh's chosen people are not the only ones to whom
this call to utter songs of praise has gone out. The writer
of the psalm, whether he be a choir-leader at some

earlier date or a later poet working according to the traditional pattern, sends out the call to praise God to all the earth, all peoples, all kingdoms, countless islands and lands, kings of the earth to the uttermost confines of the world. He calls also on all beings above the earth, all angels and spirits, to join in this hymn of praise. All creation must join together as one great choir to praise God and his ineffable majesty. There are instances in which the entire psalm is nothing other than a great call on all created things to join in song with man, who alone of them all knows his own utter helplessness and lack of power. The end of the Psalter gives us two such psalms, 148 and 150. The "Benedicite", the song of praise of the three youths in the fiery furnace, is another of this type that has come down to us (Dan 3:57–88).

In this call, or invitation to praise, all the persons who are to be celebrated are mentioned, and at the same time the reason for the eulogy is very briefly stated. The name that appears over and over again here is Yahweh:[6] sing before Yahweh, rejoice before Yahweh, shout before Yahweh and so on. We find also such expressions as: call upon the God of Jacob, play before our King, thank his holy name, bless his name, etc. We find summarized in this introduction, as a motive of the eulogy, the theme of the psalm itself. Yahweh is to be praised because of certain of his acts or qualities. The following expressions tell us this fact: proclaim his glory, proclaim his wonderful works, tell of the deligths of his kingdom, praise him in all his majesty, and so on. After this invitation the psalm of praise can take its course.

It is necessary to lay emphasis on the importance of thoroughly understanding the structure of this first invitatory section of the psalm. The formulas are not always those we have given above. There are others such as: let us exalt his name, let us worship, let us shout, be glad, kneel, etc. In some psalms the writer speaks to himself: bless Yahwe, O my soul; let me play before you, O Lord. By way of conclusion, less vivid and declamatory modes of address appear such as: may Yahweh be blessed, Yahweh's name be praised. However, in most cases the form follows the pattern of "Praise Yahweh, O house of Israel." Whenever we recognize this formula, in whatever dress it may appear, then we have an indication that we are dealing with a hymn, with a particular state of mind and with a particular religious theme. By grasping this fact we help ourselves to a better understanding of the psalm. Hymn motifs and portions of hymns are not only to be found in the seventeen psalms that are classified as psalms of praise. The pilgrims' psalms and the enthronement psalms are also very much in the nature of hymns. In these also we can find a somewhat similar state of mind expressed by way of the same literary formulas. We find also much that reminds us, both as regards form and content, of hymns in the psalms of thanksgiving, especially those that are intended to accompany folk-dances. Not all psalms of praise, however, begin with an invitation; in many cases the psalm opens with words of praise and an indication how Yahweh is to be praised. For instance, we find such formulas as: the heavens proclaim the glory of God; exalt Yahweh, O my soul; my heart rejoices. These lead directly into the main part of the psalm.

This main section, or *body* of the psalm, which is the real song of praise, announces the motives that have prompted and underlie the song of joy.

The invitation section runs: "O give thanks to the Lord, for he is good and his steadfast love endures for ever."[7] The *body* of the psalm elaborates the particular acts of goodness and mercy; in this section God is proclaimed in all his glory and in his mighty deeds. This proclamation is both the highest possible form of praise and, as we shall show later, a means of working out our salvation. This particular section of the psalm has also its own special formulas. It begins in most cases with a conjunction such as "because" or "for".

> Declare his glory among the nations,
> his marvellous works among all the peoples!
> *For* great is the Lord, and greatly to be praised;
> he is to be feared above all gods.
> *For* all the gods of the peoples are idols;
> but the Lord made the heavens. (96:3–5)

> Sing unto him a new song,
> play skilfully on the strings, with loud shouts.
> *For* the word of the Lord is upright;
> and all his work is done in faithfulness ...
> *For* he spoke, and it came to be;
> he commanded, and it stood forth. (33:3–9)[8]

Very often a relative clause is the form characteristically used, as we can see clearly from psalm 136.

> O give thanks to the Lord, for he is good ...
> Who alone does great wonders ...
> Who by understanding made heavens ...
> Who spread out the earth upon the waters ...
> Who made the great lights ...
> Who smote the first-born of Egypt ...

> Who divided the Red Sea in sunder ...
> Who led his people through the wilderness ...
> Who smote great kings ...
> Who gives food to all flesh ... (v. 4–7, 10, 13, 16,
> 17, and 25) [9]

Naturally God himself is the chief object of praise. The people sing about what he does, and has always done, in the work of providence. The people rejoice over his intervention in their own national history and in the history of the whole world. More especially they rejoice that he created the world and all mankind, and that he delivered the people of Israel from slavery in Egypt. Sometimes they give praise to God for a deliverance they foresee in the future and in the coming establishment of the kingdom of God: "The Lord sits enthroned as king for ever" (Pss 29:10, 96:13), "For God will save Zion and rebuild the cities of Judah" (Ps 69:35). Clearly Yahweh is the object of their praise whenever his name occurs, as it does repeatedly (see footnote 6):

> The Lord sets the prisoners free;
> the Lord opens the eyes of the blind.
> The Lord lifts up those who are bowed down;
> the Lord loves the righteous.
> The Lord watches over the sojourners,
> the Lord upholds the widow and the fatherless.
>   (146:7–9)

In a suggestive way the word "thou" and the possessive pronoun "thine" make God the immediate object of praise. The psalmist then speaks personally to God and bears witness to him of his great joy in God's glory. So, for example in this meaningful text:

O Lord God of hosts,
who is mighty as *thou* art, O Lord?
Thou dost rule the raging of the sea;
when its waves rise, *thou* stillest them.
Thou didst crush Rahab like a carcass,
thou didst scatter thy enemies with thy mighty arm.
The heavens are *thine*, the earth also is *thine;*
the world and all that is in it, *thou* hast founded
them.
The north and the south, *thou* hast created them;
Tabor and Hermon joyously praise thy name.
(89:8–12)

Also in the following psalm which fulfils ancient folk rules:

Thou didst divide the sea by thy might;
thou didst break the heads of the dragons on the
waters.
Thou didst crush the heads of Leviathan,
thou didst give him as food for the creatures of
the wilderness.
Thou didst cleave open springs and brooks;
thou didst dry up ever-flowing streams.
Thine is the day, *thine* also the night;
thou hast established the luminaries and the sun.
Thou hast fixed all the bounds of the earth;
thou hast made summer and winter. (74:13–17)

Just as in the invitatory section, so also here all sorts of other literary forms are possible. We find exclamations of wonder such as "O Lord, our Lord, how majestic is thy name!", or the rhetorical question "Who is like unto thee, O Lord?" Word-pictures are drawn illustrating

God's might by contrasting it with the helplessness of idols:

> Their idols are silver and gold,
> the work of men's hands.
> They have mouths, but do not speak;
> eyes, but do not see.
> They have ears, but do not hear;
> noses but do not smell. (115:4–6)

However, the body of these hymns is mostly in the form of a story or a statement of fact: such is Yahweh; thus does he work.

There is not always a formal *ending* to a psalm of praise and where one exists it has not invariably the same form. Sometimes the psalm ends simply because the rejoicing comes to an end; at another time the introductory verses are repeated at the end, either word for word (in the manner of an antiphon), as we find it in psalm 8, or in accordance with the general meaning, so that the invitation occurring at the beginning of the psalm appears again in a somewhat varied form. So in psalm 103 ("Bless the Lord, O my soul; and all that is within me, bless his holy name!") we find, after a description of God's mercy and goodness, the following verses by way of conclusion:

> The Lord has established his throne in the heavens,
> and his kingdom rules over all.
> Bless the Lord, O you his angels,
> you mighty ones who do his word . . .
> Bless the Lord, all his hosts,
> his ministers that do his will!
> Bless the Lord, all his works,

in all places of his dominion.
Bless the Lord, O my soul! (103:19–20) [10]

Now and then a short prayer provides the ending for
a hymn: "May my meditation be pleasing to him"
(104:34), or: "Let the words of my mouth and the
meditation of my heart be acceptable in thy sight,
O Lord, my rock and my redeemer" (19:14). [11]

A certain fixed group has been detached from the
whole collection of 150 psalms by means of our study
of the literary structure and our sketch of the situation
from which these psalms arose. This group is known
as the psalms of praise, or the hymns. These psalms lay
stress quite clearly on the note of joy. This is what we
should expect when we consider the conditions out of
which these psalms developed, that is the joyful festivals
of Israel. The great enthusiasm, the boundless joy expressed during these gladsome festivities can be heard
in these psalms. We are made aware of a joy that is
centred entirely on God. The songs that are sung issue
from a fresh and youthful religious experience, from the
sense of wonder, the *admiratio*, that forms the undertone
of all authentic spiritual life. There is no sign here of
"being in a rut", of being enslaved to a routine of boredom
(*taedium, acedia*); there is no trace of formalism, no cult
of the letter of the law. On the contrary, we see the sur-
prised and joyful discovery of God, of his glory, his power,
goodness, and love. We can feel in these verses how pure
and spontaneous is this enthusiasm for God. It is something really experienced and comes straight from the
heart. Enthusiasm does not argue, does not analyse God's
truths piecemeal. In fact it does not treat of truths at
all but of Yahweh himself and his deeds. Yahweh and

his works are considered as an entity. God stands in the
full lustre of his majesty and love, and demands the
whole of the psalmist's attention so strongly, indeed, that
man and all that concerns him falls quite into the
background. Here we find that a comparison with, for
example, the hymns of Babylon is very instructive. The
insertion of petitions in these Babylonian hymns is the
rule; in those of Israel it is the exception.[12]

In the case of the chosen people the hymn is almost
entirely taken up with pure worship, with joy in God
and the qualities that have been revealed in his holy
actions. "The hymn is a reflex, an echo; it is the Amen
of the congregation following the divine self-revela-
tion."[13] This reflex is at the same time a proclamation,
a *kerygma*. When this proclamation occurs in its correct
setting, that is in the congregation *(qahal)* of Israel, it
provides a means to the attainment of holiness. It is then
that God's loving and creative word echoes through it.
And this proclamation of God's word is not a mere
statement of a teaching or a system of human reflections
on the verities of God. The things that are proclaimed
are historical events and facts. The psalm handles facts
in the same way as we celebrate primarily historical
events in our own liturgy. The psalms of praise present
the facts, and the reactions to the events of history that
are shown to us in the hymn are those of the chosen
people. They sing of an experience of God.

An analysis of the main section of the hymn, in which
the reasons for the act of praise are set out, shows us
clearly that the experience of God is founded on two
main facts, creation and deliverance, but in the very first
place upon deliverance, that is, salvation. Both subjects
come before us repeatedly and often they are linked

together and strengthen each other. Only two psalms are thematic, that is devote themselves entirely to a single theme and work this out fully, namely psalm 103, which has creation as its theme, and psalm 104, which treats of deliverance. The remaining psalms treat of both subjects with varying degrees of emphasis.[14]

When we ask ourselves how the Israelites developed their thought about creation and deliverance we must remember that their religious experience was first of all an experience of deliverance, and thus their whole conception of God was built on experience of him in the events of sacred history, on the fact, in short, that God was close to his people. It was only much later after further reflection that the conviction of the Creator's relationship to his creatures grew out of this. The Bible does not approach theology by way of philosophy but by way of religious experience, that of being God's chosen people. Only later after long meditation on this experience were conclusions arrived at about their own being, about the world and creation. It is always so in the Bible. It was the reconciling light from Calvary that first revealed in full clarity the meaning of the past since Adam.

Professor T. Vriezen of Utrecht formulates this priority of salvation over creation thus: "Israel's belief in God itself did not, however, originate in these reflections, but it preceded them; for it was born from the spiritual experience of God's activity directed towards the people and the individual; *Israel met its God as a Living God,* who revealed himself in the history of the people and in the life of the individual; Israel came to know God as *the Saviour and the Leader, the Redeeming God.* Israel did not derive its knowledge of God first and foremost from nature, as the ancient oriental peoples did, but from the acts of God in the history of the people as they appeared in the light of his revelation to Moses and the prophets."[15] Father Renckens says: "Israel could have known God from observation of the created world, but in fact learned to know the God of Israel much sooner and much more intimately from his intervention in its own national life and history. Yahweh was known to the Israelites through the things he did on their behalf. Yahweh revealed himself to Israel by making Israel consciously experience him."[16]

It was this God whom men knew and had experienced personally who first of all was honoured in song in the hymns. God is represented there as "He who acts".[17] The beliefs about creation that were already latent came into the foreground only during the times of the later kings. They became then, especially through the medium of priestly thought during and after the captivity, a counterpoise to the possibly too exclusive connexion of Yahweh with the chosen people alone. The danger of the idea of God being weakened and made less pure by the presumptious concept of Yahweh as one who was merely an instrument in the hands of the people of Israel, or as one who was only interested in those who belonged to the seed of Abraham, was very much reduced. The danger that the people should think themselves safe simply as a result of their election as the holy and chosen people of God, because they were by carnal descent of Abraham, was thus counterbalanced by the idea of God as creator and ruler of the whole world and of all nations.[18]

The *salvation* about which the psalms speak is principally the act of welding the nation into the chosen people

of the Old Testament by means of such events as the
Exodus and the experience in the Sinai desert. Yahweh's
marvellous acts *(mirabilia* and *prodigia Dei)* referred to
most specially are the coming out of Egypt, the rescue
at the shores of the Red Sea, the wanderings in the
desert, the giving of the Law on Mount Sinai, and the
occupation of the promised land. In these events Yahweh
revealed himself as the deliverer, the *go'ēl* (redeemer)
of Israel who set free his people from slavery. He was
someone who had paid ransom for them, like a member
of a family who takes upon himself the commitments
of his poor relations. Yet this family-tie between Yahweh
and Israel is not considered as a bloodrelationship but
as one depending upon choice. The ransom itself did
not consist of so many pieces of silver or gold but was
a completely free gift. He to whom all nations, including
the Israelites, belong delivered his chosen people from
slavery.

This is *the deliverance* that appears time and again in
the Old Testament:

> It is he who remembered us in our low estate,
> and rescued us from foes. (136:23–24)
> He has not dealt thus with any other nation;
> they do not know his ordinances. (147:20)

And the reason for this experience of God is one we
hear echoing through the song of Moses (Ex 15:1–21).
It is God's mercy, God's free election, "For you are a
people holy to the Lord your God; the Lord your God
has chosen you to be a people for his own possession, out
of all the peoples that are on the face of the earth.
It was not because you were more in number that any

other people that the Lord set his love upon you and chose you, for you were the fewest of all peoples; but it is because the Lord loves you, and is keeping the oath which he swore to your fathers, that the Lord has brought you out with a mighty hand, and redeemed you from the house of bondage, from the hand of Pharaoh, King of Egypt" (Deut 7:6–8). The author of the book of Judith lets the Ammonite captain, Achior, tell Holofernes who the Israelites are (Judith 5). He does not picture him as describing race, country, capital, language, or manners but makes him tell the story of the Exodus from Egypt. Those people are the Jews, "a people delivered by God".

Those events of the Exodus left their mark on Israel's national life for thousands of years. Then indeed men had experience of God, that was the ideal time. Through the mouth of his prophet Jeremiah God speaks to Israel about "the devotion of your youth, your love as a bride, how you followed me in the wilderness, in a land not sown" (Jer 2:2).

The time of the Exodus was greatly idealized. Yet, at the same time, we find numerous prophetic texts in which Israel's proverbial ingratitude and presumption are referred back to those earliest days: "I am the Lord your God from the land of Egypt . . . It was I who knew you in the wilderness, in the land of drought; but when they had fed to the full, they were filled, and their heart was lifted up; therefore they forgot me" (Hos 13:4–6).[19] This theme of their deliverance at the time of the Exodus occurs repeatedly in the Psalter. Over and beyond the numerous more or less clear allusions to the events of the Exodus, it forms the chief theme of fifteen psalms.[20]

To begin with, God's wonderful intervention during the Exodus is a reason for expressions of joy and gratitude above all in the psalms of praise. But in other psalms, chiefly the pilgrim hymns written under prophetic and Deuteronomic influence, the infidelity of the Israelites, shown even during the journey through the wilderness, is regarded as a warning for the generation then living (see psalms 81 and 95). When the people of God's mercy, as a result of their repeated infidelities, found themselves in great need and realized that the deliverance of the Exodus had not a lasting and definitive character — then a longing for a new intervention of God in their history was born. Looking back to that ancient deliverance, they besought Yahweh for a new and better Exodus that should deliver them for ever out of the bonds of slavery. They prayed that he would entice his people again into the wilderness and make with them there a new and everlasting covenant.[21]

> Turn again, O God of hosts!
> Look down from heaven, and see;
> have regard for this vine,
> the stock which thy right hand planted. (80:14–15)

> O God, why dost thou cast us off for ever?
> Why does thy anger smoke against the sheep of thy
>   pasture?
> Remember thy congregation, which thou hast
>   gotten of old,
> which thou hast redeemed to be the tribe of thy
>   heritage! (74:1–2)

The psalms look forward to the new deliverance that Jesus will bring in the future. In the new Israel the proclamation of the facts of their deliverance in their hymns no longer concerns only the passage over the Red Sea and the rescue out of the hands of the Egyptians. During the celebration of the Eucharist the Church prays in her psalms about the exodus under the new covenant, which was consummated by the redemptive work of Jesus. "Jesus knew that his hour had come to depart out of this world to the Father" (Jn 13:1). He discussed this departure with Moses and Elijah on the Mount of the Transfiguration (Lk 9:31), while, at the beginning of his public life, during the forty days in the desert he gloriously underwent the trial that Yahweh had inflicted for forty years upon Israel in the wilderness (Mt 4:1–11).

For this reason Christians offer the true Paschal Lamb, who is Jesus (Jn 19:36; 1 Cor 5:7). The crossing of the Red Sea meant for the Israelites the development into the chosen people bound together under Moses, who typifies Christ. What this event signified for the Israelites, baptism signifies for the Christian (1 Cor 10:4). Believers under the new covenant eat of the manna of the Eucharist (Jn 6:48–52). For them the water gushes out of the rock (Jn 7:38; 1 Cor 10:4) and the brazen serpent set up in the desert typifies Jesus lifted up on the cross (Jn 3:14). The plagues referred to in the book of Revelation are pictured according to the model of those in Egypt.[22] The seal of the Living God, the naming of the twelve tribes of Israel, the clothes washed in the Blood of the Lamb, the leading of the people to the living fountains referred to in the seventh chapter of that same book — all these set the Christian life in the context of the Exodus.

The Old Testament deliverance was as it were the first actualization of God's plan for man's salvation.

It was a picture of, a preparation for, and an implicit, veiled participation in the real and final deliverance in Jesus. When we bear all this in mind it cannot be difficult for us to return over and over again to the psalms of praise in order to worship God for the great gift and benefaction of *our* personal salvation and redemption, which forms a part of the whole Christian exodus. St Paul writes a hymn as a tribute to the salvation that is ours in Christ, "To the praise of his glorious grace" (Eph 1:3–14). He encourages the Christians, "Give thanks to the Father, who has qualified us to share in the inheritance of the saints in light. He has delivered us from the dominion of darkness and has transferred us to the kingdom of his beloved Son, in whom we have redemption, the forgiveness of sins" (Col 1:12–14).[23] We are delivered, but not yet completely. Only at the end of time when Jesus comes in glory will our salvation be perfect. God will be all in all, and along with the Exodus canticle of Moses will sound the great canticle of the Lamb: "Great and wonderful are thy deeds, O Lord God the Almighty! Just and true are thy ways, O King of the ages. Who shall not fear and glorify thy name O Lord? For thou alone art holy" (Rev 15:3–4). "Worthy art thou to take the scroll and to open its seals, for thou wast slain and by thy blood didst ransom men for God from every tribe and tongue and people and nation, and hast made them a kingdom and priests to our God" (Rev 5:9–10). In this fullness of the kingdom of God the cry "For his steadfast love endures for ever" acquires its deepest meaning and truest fulfilment.

As the central point of the psalms of praise, alongside the idea of salvation, stands the theme of *God as*

Creator. Already from the very beginning of Israel as nation there had been a conviction, although at times a somewhat vague one, that the God of history *(Geschichtsmächtige),* was at the same time the God of nature *(Naturmächtige).*[24] "Israel first of all learned to know God as a national God, Yahweh, as their *deliverer.* By experiencing God's acts of deliverance Israel learned to know him also as *creator.* On the basis of historical facts Israel's insight ripened; Yahweh was not only the God of Israel, their Elohim. The election of Israel as the chosen people lies just here, that God is absolutely Elohim."[25] When we speak about the idea of creation in the psalms of praise we use this word in its widest sense and mean: God should be recognized as Lord of nature, as Providence. When later this idea was more fully considered there came a purer conception of what we mean by Creator, creation, and creature. The starting-point of Israel's thinking was the meeting with the living God in the history of their own nation. When they considered God's revelation of himself in the history of his chosen people: "The gods and the constitution of Egypt's land, the heart and military might of Pharaoh, the peoples of Canaan and the land between the two great rivers (Mesopotamia), in short, all nature and all history, appear to be subject to Yahweh's authority. He rules them all, he has everything in his hands. From all this they learned that he is the maker of everything, including mankind itself."[26] Yahweh, Israel's God, is mighty in nature and among the nations, Yahweh looks down from heaven; the eyes of Yahweh regard all those who petition him. The psalms tell of his providence:

> Sing to the Lord with thanksgiving;
> make melody to our God upon the lyre!
> He covers the heavens with clouds,
> he prepares rain for the earth,
> he makes grass grow upon the hills.
> (And plants for man to cultivate.)
> He gives to the beasts their food,
> and to the young ravens which cry. (147:7–9)[27]

and elsewhere:

> The Lord is gracious and merciful,
> he provides food for those who fear him.
>   (111:4–5)[28]

Gradually they became conscious of the idea of creation in its strict sense as it is worked out in Genesis 1, as compared with the older chapter, Genesis 2, and expressed in Isaiah 54:5 "Your Maker is your husband . . . and the Holy One of Israel is your Redeemer."[29] The prophets see God's creative might as a guarantee of his fidelity:

> Thus says the Lord,
> who gives the sun for light by day
> and the fixed order of the moon and the stars for
>   light by night,
> who stirs up the sea so that its waves roar —
> the Lord of hosts is his name:
> If this fixed order departs
> from before me, says the Lord,
> then shall the descendants of Israel cease
> from being a nation before me for ever.
>   (Jer 31:35–37)

Also the psalmist of psalm 89 refers to this:

> For thy steadfast love was established for ever,
> thy faithfulness is firm as the heavens. (v. 2)

The belief in God as creator comes to the fore in the psalms, especially in order to emphasize the sublimity and power of God:

> By the word of the Lord the heavens were made,
> and all their host by the breath of his mouth.
> For he spoke, and it came to be;
> he commanded, and it stood forth. (32:6, 9)[30]

The point that is so momentous here is the discovery, if we may so name it, that Yahweh, who is their God and is so near to them, is he who has created everything by his word: "He makes each thing in its totality, yes, the very totality of being has its foundation in him."[31] And he creates in perfect freedom, instantaneously by his sovereign word. By his work of creation something quite new has been begun, the cosmic order has been set in motion. There is no threat to man from creation, for Yahweh is the centre both of the belief in creation and the belief in his saving power. The holy acts of Yahweh in creation do not only proclaim his splendour but reveal his wonder and majesty.

There is a unity and harmony in the life of the believing Israelite. He knows that Yahweh is great and glorious, is ruler of the whole earth because he is its creator. He knows, too, that man is as nothing compared with God and is completely dependent upon him, and can only approach God's awful majesty in the fear of the Lord.[32] This Yahweh, the Holy and Unassailable

One, is at the same time the God who has called Israel into existence and who loves his people. Israel has nothing to fear, Yahweh their God is the Creator-God. The description of Yahweh's revelation in a tremendous thunderstorm, in which Yahweh is pictured for us as the terrifying God of nature, ends with the words:

> The Lord sits enthroned over the flood;
> the Lord sits enthroned as king for ever.
> May the Lord give strength to his people!
> May the Lord bless his people with peace!
>   (29:10–11)

and psalm 95 says:

> Let us kneel before the Lord, our Maker!
> For he is our God,
> and we are the people of his pasture,
> and the sheep of his hand. (v. 6–7)

The full meaning of the creation is only revealed in the New Testament. The idea of creation is here presented in terms of Christ. It becomes clear how creation has its foundation and fulfilment in Christ. The Word of God was realized in creation: "All things were made through him, and without him was not anything made that was made" (Jn 1:3). St Paul says in one of his hymns about the Christ that: "He is the first-born of all creation, for in him all things were created in heaven and on earth." He says, too, that "all things, visible and invisible were created through him and for him" who died and rose again (Col 1:15–17). This is the mystery that God wills to reveal to us now in the fullness of time "according to his purpose which he set forth in Christ, to unite all things in him, things in heaven

and things on earth" (Eph 1:10). All creation culminates
in Jesus Christ, he is its highest point (as in psalm 8:
The Man is the crown of creation). It is made for him
and for us in him.

Yahweh's creative work consists not only in setting
the cosmic order in motion but also in the ordering of
the events of salvation. It is on a still higher plane;
it is a re-creation.[33] Yahweh's dealings with the Israelites
are a part of creation (Deut 4:32). God made a people
for himself, as Deutero-Isaiah likes to express it (the
formula occurs twenty times): "Bring my sons from
afar ... every one who is called by my name, whom I
created for my glory, whom I formed and made" (Is
43:6–7). But now God speaks to Jacob, his creature, to
the Israel he fashioned: "Fear not, for I have redeemed
you; I have called you by name, you are mine" (Is 43:1).
The psalmist prays that God will create a new heart
in him: "Create in me a clean heart, O God, and put a
new and right spirit within me" (51:10). God goes still
further; he creates a new race upon the earth (Jer 31:22).
Paradise returns, the clouds drop justice. "I the Lord
have created it" (Is 45:8). Yes, God creates a new earth:
"For behold, I create new heavens and a new earth; and
the former things shall not be remembered or come into
mind. But be glad and rejoice for ever in that which I
create; for behold, I create Jerusalem a rejoicing, and her
people a joy. I will rejoice in Jerusalem, and be glad in
my people" (Is 65:17–19).

This new creation is the salvation of mankind and
the world. Creation and re-creation merge into each
other. Jesus, as the Saviour is the centre of creation.
"He is the first-born of all creation ... He is the head
of the body, the Church ... the first-born from the dead,

that in everything he might be pre-eminent" (Col 1:15 to 18). In him the Christian is a new creation (2 Cor 5:17; Gal 6:15). Therefore the true believer must "put on the new nature, created after the likeness of God (= Christ) in true righteousness and holiness" (Eph 4:24).

The whole creation has a share in the re-creation of mankind, it yearns and reaches out to the revelation of the children of God. All nature hopes "to be set free from its bondage to decay and obtain the glorious liberty of the children of God. We know that the whole creation has been groaning in travail together until now" (Rom 8:21–22). It is the struggle, experienced daily, of our first and fallen creation with the new creation in Christ which sounds through this text. But from our wrestling here the Scriptures direct us to the vision of the new heaven and new earth which is to come. "But according to his promise we wait for new heavens and a new earth, in which righteousness dwells" (2 Pet 3:13). And in the Revelation the author speaks from Patmos: "I saw a new heaven and a new earth, for the first heaven and the first earth had passed away ... and he who sat upon the throne said: 'Behold, I make all things new'" (Rev 21:1, 5).

The psalms of creation sing about God's creative intervention, about the relationship of Creator to creature. In the light of Christ we obtain a better perspective. Christ himself is the centre of creation. The reason for the first creation was, in fact, the re-creation according to his spirit. Since the coming of Jesus we have looked forward to the foundation of a new heaven and a new earth. "Behold I make all things new!" When we sing the hymns of Israel, it is not only a question of

looking back into history. In those hymns we make
contact with the soul of Israel, with the people of Israel,
who have had experiences with God in creation and in
redemption, with Israel that answers in a personal
surrender to the Creator-God and the Redeemer-God,
who is Yahweh. To what extent he was Creator and
Redeemer was not yet known and could not be known.
But they were completely convinced of the fact that he
was Creator and Redeemer. In this manner God was able
gradually to reveal the fullness of his grace to the old
Israel and the Christian Church, the new Israel. The texts
that tell us about Israel's experience of faith are ready to
be given a new dimension. Through the Christian experience the new dimension has been given to the old text.
That is why we sing the hymns in a Christian manner,
from our own new knowledge of the mysteries of creation
and redemption, which God gave in his Son, Jesus
Christ.

CHAPTER 6

The Psalms of Thanksgiving

The psalms of thanksgiving can be divided into two groups. There are those in which thanks are offered to Yahweh for his goodness towards a particular person; these we may call *private* psalms of thanksgiving. Other psalms in which Yahweh is thanked for his gracious intervention on behalf of the whole people of Israel we may style *communal* psalms of thanksgiving. In contrast to the hymns in which God is praised for the qualities that the people discovered in him or for his mighty acts of former days in creation and deliverance, in both these groups of thanksgiving psalms God is praised for one particular act of goodness towards either an individual or the whole nation. This chapter will deal more specially with the private thanksgiving psalms, while at the end it will touch upon some especially noteworthy points about the communal thanksgiving psalms.

The setting into which we must fit the private thanksgiving psalms is the liturgical thanksgiving ceremony. This took place preferably during the great, year by year recurring feasts of Israel, and constituted a minor

part of the festivities as a whole. But they could be used
also during the normal course of the year.

We know the essentials of these rites from the psalms,
and can reconstruct their setting as follows: the Israelite
who had been delivered from some great emergency, in
most cases from some danger to his life, came full of
joy to the temple, surrounded by his family and friends
carrying the sacrificial animal, which may have been
promised beforehand, in order to make his offering to
God:

> I will come into thy house with burnt offerings,
> I will pay thee my vows,
> that which my lips uttered
> and my mouth promised when I was in trouble.
> I will offer to thee burnt offerings of fatlings,
> with the smoke of the sacrifice of rams;
> I will make an offering of bulls and goats.
>   (66:13–15)

Sometimes the celebrating priest together with the
congregation comes out to meet the happy man to
congratulate him and wish him good fortune:

> Blessed is he whose transgression is forgiven,
> whose sin is covered.
> Blessed is the man to whom the Lord imputes no
>   iniquity. (32:1–2)

The fact that God delivered him in his necessity was the
proof that the sins that had burdened him were now
forgiven. And, as was the custom of the ancient peoples
of the East, they spoke quite openly about it. Having
come into the temple the Israelite stood with uplifted
hands to give thanks to God:

> So I will bless thee as long as I live;
> I will lift up my hands and call on thy name.
>   (63:4)

He invited the people who were standing round to listen to his story:

> Come and hear, all you who fear God,
> and I will tell what he has done for me. (66:16)

> I will tell of thy name to my brethren;
> in the midst of the congregation I will praise thee:
> You who fear the Lord, praise him!
> all you sons of Jacob, glorify him! (22:23–24)[1]

Then he began to tell his story, how he was in great trouble and called upon Yahweh who intervened in a marvellous way. During the telling of this story he repeatedly urged the people present to give thanks to God and sometimes he called upon all creation to be joyful with him:

> Sing praises to the Lord, O you his saints,
> and give thanks to his holy name. (30:4)

> All the kings of the earth shall praise thee, O Lord,
> for they have heard the words of thy mouth;
> and they shall sing of the ways of the Lord. (138:4)

At the same time he interposed pieces of good advice: so good and faithful had God once more shown himself to be, that they must always put their trust in him.

> Gracious is the Lord, and righteous;
> our God is merciful.

> The Lord preserves the simple;
> when I was brought low, he saved me. (116:5–6)

When the actual words of thanksgiving had been uttered together with the story of God's deliverance, the sacrifice of thanksgiving often followed.

> My vows to thee I must perform, O God;
> I will render thank offerings to thee. (56:12)

> With a freewill offering I will sacrifice to thee;
> I will give thanks to thy name, O Lord, for it is
>   good. (54:6)

When the sacrificial offering was brought, a procession was sometimes made round the altar, while God's goodness was celebrated in song, as is told us in the following attestation of innocence:

> I wash my hands in innocence,
> and go about thy altar, O Lord,
> singing aloud a song of thanksgiving,
> and telling all thy wondrous deeds. (26:6–7)

The sacred meal, consisting of the remains of the sacrificial gifts, was held after this. It took place in the temple annex, and, according to the custom in Israel,[2] friends and the poor were invited to join in, especially when there was a large quantity of sacrificial meat. "The poor shall eat and be satisfied" (22:26; see also 34:8).

We probably find an echo of this festive meal as an essential part of the thanksgiving ceremony in psalm 23, where we are told of the preparation of the table,

about the anointing of the head with perfumed oil as
a token of joy, about the goblet overflowing, and all
this "under the eyes of my enemies" who may happen
to visit the temple at the time of the feast and see their
victim offering thanks to Yahweh for his rescue from
their hands.[3]

Such a ceremony of thanksgiving could take place
any and every day, but many Israelites were glad to
put off their thanksgiving till one of the great pilgrim
feasts, preferably till the feast of tabernacles that was
observed after the harvest. Because of the vast numbers
who wished to celebrate their thanksgiving at this time
the custom arose of dividing them into groups according
to the types of need out of which they had been
delivered by Yahweh. A typical example can be found in
psalm 107. It begins with a call to praise and a liturgical
command to all those who streamed into Jerusalem in
order to thank God:

> O give thanks to the Lord, for he is good;
> for his steadfast love endures for ever!
> Let the redeemed of the Lord say so,
> whom he has redeemed from trouble
> and gathered in from the lands,
> from the east and from the west,
> from the north and from the south. (107:2–3)

In the verses that follow come four different groups. A
priest, or some other leader of a group, speaks the words
of thanksgiving in the name of all who compose that
group, perhaps following definite instructions. He utters
the formula, "Praise the Lord, for he is good and his
steadfast love endures for ever"; one after another the

travellers (vv. 4–9), the released prisoners (vv. 10–16), the sick (vv. 17–22), and the seafarers (vv. 23–32), are called upon in turn.

Each formula of thanksgiving is built up in a precisely parallel pattern: first, they were in need; secondly, they cried to Yahweh in their anxiety; thirdly, he delivered them from their affliction, and, fourthly, they must thank Yahweh for his mercy and his wonderful works for the children of men. After these four divisions follows a more general summary of God's acts of goodness, perhaps added later (vv. 33–41). The whole of the psalm is brought to a conclusion by two verses in the form of a hymn (vv. 42–43). This psalm offers us a reliable picture of the course of one of the combined thanksgiving ceremonies. It is very noticeable that in other psalms, for example psalm 66 and psalm 118, we find singular and plural forms alternating, as between an individual and a group.

A splendid description of the thanksgiving liturgy is given us in psalm 118. After the call in hymn form in the first few verses, a prominent person, perhaps the king himself, took over and gave expression to his thanks in the form of a narrative:

> Out of my distress I called on the Lord;
> the Lord answered me and set me free . . .
> I was pushed hard, so that I was falling,
> but the Lord helped me . . .
> I shall not die, but I shall live,
> and recount the deeds of the Lord.
> The Lord has chastened me sorely,
> but he has not given me over to death.

Then the man in front entered the temple and the whole procession followed him. He first asked the priests:

> Open to me the gates of righteousness,
> that I may enter through them
> and give thanks to the Lord.

The priest at the gate answered:

> This is the gate of the Lord;
> the righteous shall enter through it.

The leader called:

> I thank thee that thou hast answered me
> and hast become my salvation.

While the procession comes in we hear the exclamations and the cries of joy of those who stand around watching:

> The stone which the builders rejected
> has become the head of the corner.
> This is the Lord's doing;
> it is marvellous in our eyes.
> This is the day which the Lord has made;
> let us rejoice and be glad in it.
> Save us, we beseech thee, O Lord!
> O Lord, we beseech thee, give us success!

The priests from within welcomed the procession which was now entering the temple:

> Blessed be he who enters in the name of the Lord!
> We bless you from the house of the Lord.

The people shouted with joy:

> The Lord is God, and he has given us light.

A priest then commanded:

> Bind the festal procession with branches,
> up to the horns of the altar!

Meanwhile the leader murmured softly:

> Thou art my God, and I will give thanks to thee;
> thou art my God, I will extol thee.

The psalm finishes with a final call from the priests which is at the same time, a repetition of the first verse:

> O give thanks to the Lord, for he is good;
> for his steadfast love endures for ever!

No other single psalm gives us such a vivid picture of the actual setting in which a psalm of thanksgiving was used as does this psalm 118.

The original milieu of the personal psalm of thanksgiving is evidently to be found in the liturgical thanksgiving ceremony. This, for the Israelite, was originally the normal means for the expression of his gratitude to God. Still, this is not to say that no psalm of this type existed outside the liturgy. In these psalms the accent is shifted more and more to the spiritual condition of gratitude that thankfulness brings with it, and falls with less and less emphasis on the external expression of it as the fulfilment of a ritual. Many psalm texts stress the relative values of the two types of sacrifice. God does not wish for sacrifices that are merely ritual gestures.

> Sacrifice and offering thou dost not desire;
> but thou hast given me an open ear.
> Burnt offering and sin offering thou hast not
>   required.
> Then I said: Lo, I come. (40:6–7)

I will praise the name of God with a song;
I will magnify him with thanksgiving.
This will please the Lord more than an ox
or a bull with horns and hoofs. (69:30–31)

For thou hast no delight in sacrifice;
were I to give a burnt offering, thou wouldst not
    be pleased. (51:18)

This all concerns the inner attitude of a man, his penitent
and broken heart. Thus we see that the song of gratitude
originally intended for the ceremony of thanksgiving
has become freer and more spiritual. Originally it was
indeed intended for use in the temple ceremonial, it was
sung "in God's presence" (41:12); "in the gates of the
daughter of Zion" (9:14); "near God's altar" (43:4);
"in the sanctuary" (63:2). But later all links with the
temple were severed. The song of praise and thanksgiving could be offered and sung anywhere, even in the
belly of a fish (Jonah 2:2–9). Still, however, the literary
form indicates that the original setting of this type of
psalm was the ceremonial thanksgiving liturgy.

   This group of psalms has also its characteristic
formulas. From the actual setting from which they
originated these psalms have gained their own individual
form, their own special structure. In most cases they
contain three elements: first, the introductory declaration;
secondly the account of the blessing received that has
led to this act of thanksgiving (and this is the essential
element), and thirdly, a section intended to stimulate
the congregation to do their part. Each of the three
parts is easily recognizable because of its structure, but
there is often no very emphatic dividing line between
the second and third parts; they merge into each other.

The form of the introduction is usually as follows: "Let me", "Let us", which is more freely translated as "I will", "I will tell of": "I will announce", "I will glorify thee, O Lord", "I will praise thee", " I will tell", "I will play on the harp", and so on. Sometimes we find the third person used here: "My soul praises thee", "My spirit rejoices", and so on. The declaration is thus usually something in the form of a hymn and indeed sometimes acts as the introductory hymn to the main recital of the story in the thanksgiving psalm. So in psalm 66:

> Make a joyful noise to God, all the earth;
> sing the glory of his name;
> give to him glorious praise!
> Say to God, "How terrible are thy deeds!
> So great is thy power that thy enemies cringe
>   before thee.
> All the earth worships thee;
> they sing praise to thee,
> sing praises to thy name."
> Come and see what God has done. (vv. 1–5)

The climax of the thanksgiving psalm occurs in the narrative section. The form that is characteristic of this summary of the facts is in Hebrew the third person of the perfect tense, "because he has heard me, has freed me, has turned his ear to my petition". Or we find the second person, spoken directly to Yahweh himself: "Because thou hast healed me, hast broken my bonds, hast forgiven me", and so on. In this way psalm 9 prays:

> Thou hast maintained my just cause;

> thou hast sat on the throne giving righteous
> judgment.
> Thou hast rebuked the nations, thou hast destroyed
> the wicked;
> thou hast blotted out their name for ever and ever.
> The enemy have vanished in everlasting ruins;
> their cities thou hast rooted out;
> the very memory of them has perished. (vv. 4–6)

Another psalm begins abruptly:

> I waited patiently for the Lord;
> he inclined to me and heard my cry.
> He drew me up from the desolate pit,
> out of the miry bog,
> and set my feet upon a rock,
> making my steps secure. (40:1–2)

The narrative is often built up of three parts. An example of this can be seen in psalm 107. It opens with a description of the trouble in which the psalmist found himself; he describes such things as illness, humiliation, treachery on the part of his friend, and craftiness on the part of those who brought charges against him, with other similar misfortunes. It is noticeable that this description is usually very vague and generalized. "The cause of this deficiency is to be found in the influence exerted by the use of formulas and in the cultic tradition's shaping of the personal saving experience on the lines of the representation of the salvation of the cult community as a whole."[4]

We are struck by the narrow margin between penitential and thanksgiving psalms. It is altogether in the atmosphere and the fashioning of the psalms of petition

that we find ourselves here. After the joy and jubilation
of the introductory declaration, which bears some relation
to the psalms of praise, this similarity of form to the
psalms of petition can be very confusing. We must,
however, bear in mind that the psalmist relives, as it
were, the troubled state he has passed through and for
the relief of which he is giving thanks. He describes
not only how he has fallen on difficult times, but he
dramatically recalls the situation; he lives again in his
time of need, he remembers the petitions he offered to
God in his trouble, and makes them again real by their
repetition. That is why the narrative is repeatedly
introduced by such words as: "I spoke", "I said", followed
by the prayer of petition that was offered at that moment
in the past.[5]

After describing the calamities that afflicted him the
psalmist speaks of his trust in God and how he has
prayed for deliverance, "Waiting, I waited for the Lord";
"Anxiety overcame me but I called on the name of the
Lord"; "Then they cried unto the Lord in their need."
Sometimes these prayers for help were expressed dramatically in the present tense: "Unto thee, O Lord, I call";
"God have mercy on me"; "Lord have pity upon me."
An important factor in the right understanding of these
psalms is, therefore, to know how to relate these petitions
and calls for help that occur throughout the psalm back
to the mood of thanksgiving; otherwise we shall be in
danger of seeing only disconnected sections instead of a
united whole.

Finally, the narration contains the story of God's
intervention, of the deliverance, the healing, or the
acquittal. After the great sorrow the later happiness
is described in vivid colours. The reversal of fortune is

a very striking event, and the contrast between sorrow
and joy is strongly accentuated. It is a passage from a
prison to the open spaces, from weeping to laughter,
from sorrowful complaint to gay dances, from sackcloth
to wedding garments, from the gates of death to the gates
of the daughter of Zion, and from the twilight realm
of the dead to the bright land of the living. The
accessories of the feast are described with enthusiasm;
the psalmist offers thanks in festive garments, anointed
with the purest oil; the festal board is laid and goblets
stand waiting, filled to overflowing with wine (Ps 23).

Woven into the narrative section are interruptions or
interpolations such as advice to those who are standing
around, or groups of words that the members of the
assembly themselves utter. This element of the psalms
of thanksgiving is not only rather varied in contents
but also in form, in contrast to the introductory an-·
nouncement and the narrative itself, which are more
stereotyped. The subject matter of all the variations is the
close bond between the psalmist and the people who
surround him. In some instances the psalmist invites them
to hear him and to praise God with him in such terms as:
"rejoice"; "come and see"; "hear"; "play upon the harp". In
other cases he moralizes and draws conclusions from the
happy event being celebrated that apply to everybody:
"How great are thy works, O Lord"; "The Lord is merciful and just"; "The righteous flourish like the palm tree."
Or the psalmist stammers to himself: "How wonderful
indeed"; "Many are thy wondrous deeds, O Lord my
God" (40:5); "Return, O my soul, to your rest, for the
Lord has dealt bountifully with you" (116:7); "Thou
art my God, and I will give thanks to thee" (118:28).
Sometimes it is the assembly round about him which

proclaims something, who wish the psalmist good fortune, as we saw in psalm 118. Then, sometimes, we find a description of the festive meal in which all people present share (116:14 ff.). In each and every one of these various interpolations the hymn-like element appears quite clearly, while we can notice a strong influence of the sapiential literature in the parts which moralize.

Thanksgiving psalms of this type, characterized by introductory announcement, narrative, and exhortations of various sorts to the people assembled are not only found in the nineteen psalms of personal thanksgiving that occur in our Psalter. The songs of King Hezekiah (Is 38:10–20), of Hannah the mother of Samuel (1 Sam 2:1–10), of Jonah in the belly of the whale (Jon 2:2–9), are clearly also songs of thanksgiving. The psalms that were discovered at Qumran show in their form the closest relationship to our canonical psalms of thanksgiving,[6] while the *Benedictus* of Zechariah and the *Magnificat* of the mother of God exhibit strong likenesses in their literary form to the thanksgiving psalms, and thus also to those of Qumran. Often in our Psalter itself we find an element of the psalms of thanksgiving at the end of the psalms of petition and lamention.[7] After the prayer for help comes suddenly an act of thanksgiving. Could the reason for this be that the psalmist is already quite sure that his prayer will be heard as a result of a prophetic pronouncement during the temple service?[8] Or are we indeed in quite another setting? Is it that, after the answer to prayer, the earlier petitionary psalm is repeated as a form of thanksgiving with an extra formula of thanks added? This is very difficult to ascertain and it seems best to make a separate judgment in each case as does Weiser.[9]

After having sketched out the general setting and indicated the literary characteristics of this group of psalms we can pass on to their teaching, contents and themes. The significance of these psalms for the people of Israel, as also for us as Christians of today, can best be appreciated by studying the central portion of the psalms, that part which we have called the narrative. This is considered of greater importance than the sacrifice of thanksgiving itself — it may never be omitted, God's praise must be sung aloud: "that my soul may praise thee and not be silent. O Lord my God, I will give thanks to thee for ever" (30:12). The Israelites are so convinced that God saves in order that the people shall proclaim him that we find this stated in the psalms of petition as a motive for an answer to their prayer; it is as if the psalmist said: "Save me from this mortal danger, for if thou dost not deliver me, I cannot proclaim thy praise."

> Dost thou work wonders for the dead?
> Do the shades rise up to praise thee?
> Is thy steadfast love declared in the grave,
> or thy faithfulness in Abaddon?
> Are thy wonders known in the darkness,
> or thy saving help in the land of forgetfulness?
> (88:10–12)

> For in death there is no remembrance of thee;
> in Sheol who can give thee praise? (6:5)

Therefore King Hezekiah said, when he had been cured of his illness:

> For Sheol cannot thank thee,
> death cannot praise thee;

> those who go down to the pit cannot hope
> for thy faithfulness.
> The living, the living, he thanks thee,
> as I do this day. (Is 38:18–19)

To praise God is the lifelong task of every Israelite. A man offers his praise by proclaiming to all God's people what Yahweh has done for him personally, how Yahweh has kept the promise of his covenant and listens to the godly, whenever they call upon him. This faithfulness of God towards every member of the people of his covenant is the main idea at the back of the psalms of thanksgiving. This idea "is easy to put into words and understand, but much more difficult to believe and hold firmly in all the emergencies of this life." [10] Yahweh's faithfulness has been demonstrated yet once more; the psalmist stands as a living example of one who has experienced Yahweh's love; the story that he now tells in public is the latest proof of this fact, and he bears witness to it in some such terms as: "Come, behold, and rejoice"; "All men shall see and rejoice, and so put their trust in God." Yahweh is he who stepped into the breach:

> How great are thy works, O Lord!
> Thy thoughts are very deep!
> The dull man cannot know,
> the stupid cannot understand this. (92:5–6)

Before all else must man know that Yahweh's hand, and none other, was at work:

> Posterity shall serve him;
> men shall tell of the Lord to the coming generation,

and proclaim his deliverance to a people yet
  unborn,
that he (Yahweh) has wrought it (22:30–31)

Let them know that this is thy hand;
thou, O Lord, hast done it! (109:27)

The narration is not only an expression of gratitude to
God, it is also an acknowledgment and confession of the
benefits conferred. It is a testimony before his fellow
nationals; a testimony which, of its very nature, has
the character of a recruitment. To praise Yahweh often
means to confess him in his relation to the closed group
of the people of Israel, to acknowledge him, to bear
witness to him.[11] During the song of thanksgiving Yahweh
reveals himself anew to his people.

In order to understand this we must place the thanksgiving ceremony in its correct setting which is the
festivals of Israel, where the blessings of the covenant,
both past and present, are celebrated. The private person
acts solely as a member of the whole people of the
covenant in his contact with Yahweh. The fact that he has
been blessed by Yahweh personally and has been privileged
to experience the deliverance of his God, is not considered
to have a purely personal significance. This private experience of salvation is absorbed into that of the nation
as a whole, and is but a very small part of it. On the
other hand, while the people celebrate Yahweh as their
national God, they do not remain indifferent to the more
limited acts of beneficence which God performs for private
people. On the contrary, they find in such personal proofs
of God's faithfulness to the covenant a reinforcement of
their faith in God's presence and his willingness to act
on behalf of his chosen nation. The purpose of the

narrative is then, as Weiser states, "to incorporate the witness borne to the saving experience of the individual worshipper in the representation of this corporate salvation of the cult community as a whole, to whom the account is mostly addressed".[12]

The special and particular expressions of God's love are quoted for the purpose of stimulating the faith of the whole company of God's people:

> Come, O sons, listen to me,
> I will teach you the fear of the Lord. (34:11)

> Be glad in the Lord, and rejoice, O righteous,
> and shout for joy, all you upright in heart! (32:11)

> Be strong, and let your heart take courage,
> all you who wait for the Lord! (31:24)

Israel's liturgy is always concerned with the revelation of God. This revelation is directed either towards the whole assembly or to some private person, yet, through him, to every single one of God's people and ultimately to the whole world:

> That thy way may be known upon earth,
> thy saving power among all nations. (67:2)[13]

The Revelation of St John calls Jesus "the true and faithful witness" (Rev 3:14), "Jesus Christ the faithful witness, the first-born of the dead" (Rev 1:5). By his Passion and death Jesus proved that he was the witness; as St Paul says, "Christ Jesus, who in his testimony before Pontius Pilate..." (1 Tim 6:13). The early Church considered him as the One who testified that the Father raised him from the dead, and who gives thanks to the Father for his death and resurrection. Was not psalm 118 interpreted by the earliest Christian writings, and even in the New Testament itself, as being the Easter song of Jesus? Did not they see in psalm 22 and 31 the description of Christ's Passion and Glorification?[14] Was it not he who spoke:

> I will tell of thy name to my brethren;
> in the midst of the congregation I will praise thee.
> (22:22)[15]

Later generations of Christians put into the mouth of Jesus numerous other texts from the psalm of thanksgiving: "Thou hast brought up my soul from Sheol" (30:3); "When my enemies turned back, they stumbled and perished before thee" (9:3); "The Lord who shows steadfast love to his anointed" (18:50); "The snares of death encompassed me " (116:3) and so forth. He is pre-eminently the thankful man. His thankful witness lives on, in and through the Church who testifies to her gratitude to God the Father in and through Jesus, the Lord.[16] This witness has above all, the power to attract men to faith, for the death and resurrection of Jesus are not just a part of God's plan, but are the very central point in the whole course of sacred history. Therefore publicly to give thanks to God is to reveal God, to bear witness that it is God who has done this great work, and through such witness to lead men to submission to the facts.

When therefore, during the blessing of bread and wine, Christians, in imitation of the Jews, not only thank God for the food itself but also for his benefits and for his

special guidance of his chosen people, they put in the
forefront the thought of the death and resurrection of
Jesus. L. Bouyer says quite rightly: "The simple thanksgiving, the central act of Jewish piety, finds its fuller
and higher fulfilment in the Christian Eucharist." [17]
Christian thanksgiving concentrates wholly on the historical events in the life of Christ. The earthly and
material blessings of the Old Testament covenant, in
gratitude for which this group of psalms was composed,
appear spiritualized and deepened in the New Testament
as the gifts of salvation brought by Jesus. These gifts
are the Holy Spirit, peace, and unity. The ritual of the
Eucharist, the "Thanksgiving", is the expression of
Christian gratitude for these gifts of the new covenant.
Justin, Origen, Irenaeus, and others, regarded the Mass
as not primarily a sacrifice. They placed a strong
emphasis on the idea that here we celebrate a memorial,
and therefore a thanksgiving. It is precisely the twenty-
third psalm that had so great an influence on early
Christian thought and expression. It served as a starting-
point of their teaching about baptism and the Eucharist;
it was their text of Christian initiation. [18]

All the distinguishing marks of the Jewish ceremony
of thanksgiving, and thus also of this group of thanksgiving psalms, we find once again in the holy Mass. We
have first the narration of certain definite facts. God's
benefits bestowed in Christ are again recalled: "On the
night when he was betrayed he took bread into his holy
and adorable hands." This narrative is both testimony
and proclamation. "As often as you eat this bread and
drink this cup, you proclaim the Lord's death" (1 Cor
11:26). "Therefore, O Lord, we thy servants, as also thy
holy people, calling to mind the blessed Passion of Christ

Jesus, our Lord, his resurrection from the grave, and his glorious ascension into heaven" (Canon of the Mass). This declaration is founded on an upwelling of belief that brings a renewed confession of faith in its train, a Credo. The summing-up of the saving events in the story of our redemption that we find in the Eucharistic prayer, in the ancient prefaces and elsewhere, is as it were a profession of faith. Also the Eucharistic sacrificial meal with the spread table (Ps 23) and the cup of salvation (Ps 116) and the overflowing cup (Ps 23)[19] is the continuation of the Jewish sacrificial meal and of the "cup of blessing" along with which the Jewish father uttered the formula of thanksgiving at home. At the Christian sacrificial meal the poor are invited and can be satisfied, and the echoes of this New Testament thanksgiving ceremony go, by way of the faithful, out to all nations, all men, and all times.

The thanksgiving of the Eucharistic meal is to last "until he comes" (1 Cor 11:26). When our Lord appears again in glory the thanksgiving will find its completion in the liturgy of heaven. The narrative and good tidings of salvation will be replaced by the contemplation of God himself. All redeemed mankind will take part in this great act of gratitude, thanks to the recruiting witness of the Eucharist. The psalms of thanksgiving indicate this universal and eschatological prospect:

> All the ends of the earth shall remember
> and turn to the Lord;
> and all the families of the nations
> shall worship before him. (22:27)[20]

Then all men will acknowledge God's hand in the wondrous acts of redemption that they have seen in the

death and resurrection of Jesus. As we read in Revelation: "We give thanks to thee, Lord God Almighty,
who art and who wast, that thou hast taken thy great
power and begun to reign" (Rev 11:17). "Worthy art
thou to take the scroll and to open its seals, for thou
wast slain and by thy blood didst ransom men for God
from every tribe and tongue and people and nation"
(Rev 5:9).

As a conclusion to this chapter let us consider briefly
the communal thanksgiving psalms. These did not develop
as part of the ceremonial described above, which was
performed by an individual Israelite. They had their
origin in the great festivals of joy which were held either
during the yearly recurring pilgrim feasts or on the
occasion of some special gathering for public thanksgiving, usually a celebration of Israel's deliverance as
a nation from the peril of war, or for a particularly rich
harvest. We can imagine such a ceremony as corresponding to the days of prayer and penance that will be
discussed in the following chapter. Three of these
communal thanksgiving psalms offer thanks for an event
of political significance, which for Israel had also importance as a religious event. These psalms are 46, 48,
and 76. There is good reason for believing that psalms
48 and 76 deal with the liberation of Jerusalem from the
siege by Sennacherib in the year 701 B.C. in the time
of King Hezekiah (2 Kings, chs. 18–19). Psalms 65 and
67 show us a thanksgiving liturgy for a good harvest.
The event celebrated in psalms 124 and 129 remains for
us very vaguely indicated.

These psalms are like hymns in their literary form
while they have also explicitly the distinguishing mark
of psalms of thanksgiving, the narrative.[21] In the psalms

46, 48, and 76, three elements clearly appear in regard to the central fact about which Israel gives thanks. These three are the story of the event being celebrated, the actual celebration itself, and, thirdly, the prophetic glance into the future, when God's kingdom will be fully established.

Narrative

> For lo, the kings assembled,
> they came on together. (48:4)

> The earth has yielded its increase;
> God, our God, has blessed us. (67:6)

Actual celebration

> We have thought on thy steadfast love, O God,
> in the midst of thy temple. (48:9)

> We shall be satisfied with the goodness of thy house,
> thy holy temple! (65:4)

Prophetic glance

> Those who dwell at earth's farthest bounds
> are afraid at thy signs;
> thou makest the outgoings of the morning and the
>   evening. (65:8)

> Make a joyful noise to God,
> all the earth. (66:1)

CHAPTER 7

The Psalms of Petition

More than one-third of the Psalter is made up of chants
of lamentation or psalms of petition. Most of these
psalms are ascribed to King David. They fall into two
groups, the private and the communal psalms of petition.

The first group grew out of the needs of a single private
person and developed into an intimate personal contact
with Yahweh, the helper and deliverer of the man who
trusted in him.

The psalms of the second group were sung in God's
house on the occasion of some national calamity or threat
of disaster to the nation, on special days of prayer and
petition. Further, there are rather more than twenty
psalms that show much affinity with the psalms of
petition, although they do not have all the characteristics
of this type of psalms. At the end of this chapter we
shall make a survey of these songs.

The private psalms of petition came into being extra-
liturgically. They had their origins in the troubles and
dangers to which a single Israelite found himself exposed.
The chief misfortune to cause an Israelite to lament and
to turn to God for help was the threat of death. Nothing

alarmed him more than the thought of an early, untimely demise. His ideal was always to live, to live long, to achieve the full number of his day. For him God is, in truth, the God of the living.

I say: "O my God, tak... in the midst of my days." (102:24)

King Hezekiah p... ing:

I said

I

... my life;
... m. (Is 38:10–12)[1]

...nd wrongdoing was a premature

...ood and treachery
...not live out half their days. (55:23)

This idea is in great part attributable to the fact that in Old Testament times people had no more than a vague, ill-defined idea of the hereafter. They knew little about a life after death passed in the underworld, sheol, a place under the earth to which all men must descend. Anything more than this about the after-life was for them a great mystery. They thought that those who live in sheol, the weak and helpless, the *repha'im*, led a life that is a mere shadow of their former earthly existence. Man lived on there as a complete person, but in a markedly feeble and wretched state. Everything there merges in forgetfulness; they called it "the land of forgetfulness"

(88:12). Everything there is weak and shadowy, without joy or light (49:19). Of speech there is hardly any above a whisper.[2] Nobody is aware of what may be happening in the land of the living. Even with Yahweh, there could be no companionship.

> Like one forsaken among the dead,
> like the slain that lie in the grave,
> like those whom thou dost remember no more,
> for they are cut off from thy hand. (88:5)

In that land of the dead, Yahweh and his wonderful works are no more remembered:

> Dost thou work wonders for the dead?
> Do the shades rise up to praise thee?
> Is thy steadfast love declared in the grave,
> or thy faithfulness in Abaddon?
> Are thy wonders known in the darkness,
> or thy saving help in the land of forgetfulness?
>   (88:10–12)

Thus in the land of shades, in sheol they cannot praise Yahweh.[3]

The underworld is often seen as an enclosed space like a prison with gates and bars, or like a deep hole or pit through which men fall into the kingdom of the dead, or as a well the bottom of which is slimy water:

> Rescue me from sinking in the mire;
> let me be delivered from my enemies
> and from the deep waters.
> Let not the flood sweep over me,
> or the deep swallow me up,
> or the pit close its mouth over me. (69:14–15)

In other places the kingdom of the dead is thought of
as a vast land a very dusty one, the dust being that of
the dead, through which rivers flow and where there
are deep waters. Psalm 141 verse 7 speaks of "the mouth
of Sheol" as if to picture death as a beast waiting to
receive us into its wide-open jaws.

There are also other personifications, or pictorial
expressions. One is that of the hunter with nets and cords:
"the snares of death" says psalm 116, verse 3; Psalm 18,
verse 5 speaks of "the cords of death"; another image
is the shepherd who leads people into sheol:

> Like sheep they are appointed for Sheol;
> Death shall be their shepherd;
> straight to the grave they descend,
> and their form shall waste away;
> Sheol shall be their home. (49:14)

When an Israelite was in great danger of death he
expressed himself very often in exaggerated terms; he
spoke as if he were already come to the gates; already
the waves of death were washing over him:

> Thou who liftest me up from the gates of death.
>   (9:13)

> Rescue me from the deep waters. (69:14)

> My life draws near to Sheol. (88:3)

Also, when offering thanks, the psalmist speaks as if
he has returned from the kingdom of the dead:

> Thou hast brought up my soul from Sheol. (30:3)
> He drew me up from the desolate pit, out of the
>   miry bog. (40:2)

> The Lord brings down to Sheol and raises up.
> (1 Sam 2:6)

The descent of the soul *(nephesh)* into Sheol means thus
not death, but chiefly the danger of death. Moreover,
the word "soul" does not mean what we understand by
that word, the spirit of a man as opposed to his body.
"Soul" meant for an Israelite life; it replaced the personal
pronoun. Thus "my soul" means "I", so "my soul sinks
into Sheol" means "I sink into Sheol".[4] For what lives
on after death is, for an Israelite, not a part of a man
such as the part we call his soul, but a shadow of the
whole man. Only in later hellenistic times, under the
influence of Greek philosophy, did men learn to think
of the dual character of man as body and soul. This
appears, for example, in the second book of Maccabees
and in the book of Wisdom. The knowledge regarding
the survival of a part of a man, the soul, gave a clearer
insight into the life hereafter.

The first cause of death and danger of death is illness.
The psalms give us a clear picture of how men regarded
illness in the Old Testament. Yahweh is he who sends
an illness and is also the one who cures it. The Israelite
tended to overlook the "secondary" causes of illness. He
took only notice of the primary cause, and saw God as
the only source of illness.

> For thy arrows have sunk into me. (38:2)
> For thou hast taken me up and thrown me away.
> (102:10)

> For they persecute him whom thou hast smitten,
> and him whom thou hast wounded, they afflict
> still more. (69:26)

For day and night thy hand was heavy upon me.
(32:4)

From day to night thou dost bring me to an end.
(Is 38:12)

When a man had called upon Yahweh and pleaded for
restoration to health he acknowledged, in his thanksgiving: "Thou hast healed me" (30:2)

Often the psalmists speak about the reasons why
God sends illness; it is because of sin and evil in a man.
In the eyes of an Israelite bodily suffering was a punish-
ment and was of a purifying character:

Some were fools through their sinful ways,
and because of their iniquities suffered affliction.
(107:17)

Heal me, for I have sinned against thee. (41:4)
There is no soundness in my flesh
because of thy indignation;
there is no health in my bones
because of my sin. (38:3)

When the psalmist pleads for recovery he paints his
illness and its symptoms in lurid colours. Especially
in psalms 38 and 102 we find such descriptions: "There
is no soundness in my flesh", "My wounds grow foul
and fester", "My loins are filled with burning", "My
heart throbs", "The light of my eyes has gone from
me", "My bones burn like a furnace", "My bones cleave
to my flesh", "I lie awake and sleepless"; and in Isaiah:
"Like a swallow or a crane I clamour, I moan like a
dove". (Is 38:14)

Along with illness there appears continually the words, "my enemies". Enemies are those who leave the psalmist in the lurch, even though he could say: "I stood by them in their sickness" (35:13–15). Enemies are those who said: "When will he die, and his name perish?" (41:5) They are those who gossip unkindly after a visit:

> All who hate me whisper against me:
> "A deadly thing has fastened upon him,
> he will not rise again from where he lies." (41:7–8)

Also in many psalms there are oft-repeated allusions to enemies, not the enemies of the nation, but personal enemies.

This frequent reference to numerous enemies makes a strange impression on us; therefore it is necessary to go further into this question. The Israelite knew three types of enemy. First of all, those who were, in truth, members of this circle of friends of the man who was sick or otherwise afflicted, yet who now in these unhappy circumstances imagined evil of him. "He must be guilty (they said) of a secret sin, if God punishes him so." In the New Testament the disciples of Jesus ask: "Rabbi, who sinned, this man or his parents, that he was born blind (Jn 9:2)?" The whole book of Job is full of this problem. The sick man naturally noticed the attitude of his friends, that they thought ill of him; the suspicions that they cherished added new and extra pain. Thus his friends had become his enemies.

The second group of enemies were those who scorned and failed to take seriously either God or religion. "Now you see", said they, "how all your piety has helped you!" They laughed and mocked at everything that religious and pious people did.

When I humbled my soul with fasting,
it became my reproach.
When I made sackcloth my clothing,
I became a byword to them.
I am the talk of those who sit in the gate,
and the drunkards make songs about me.
　　(69:10–12)

Here we see two types of people contrasted, two mental
attitudes. Formerly there was friendship, now there is
trouble and division, and the ungodly have appeared in
their true colours. The psalmists often show great
indignation about this type of enmity, because their
enemy was not only against them personally, but was
also against Yahweh and his commandments. They
called God's vengeance down upon such a man: "O
Yahweh, may the godless be brought to shame!"

The last category of enemies consisted of those who
had always been the psalmist's adversaries, those who
had persecuted him, those who had robbed him or
slandered him and who now took the opportunity of his
illness to crush him, preferably, by bringing an action
at law against him or by uttering maledictions against
the psalmist, which maledictions in a popular and magic
way were considered as causes of the illness and its
aggravation. They had a strong argument against him
before the law because Yahweh seemed to be on their
side, for he had stricken the accused down with illness,
and thus their allegations seemed certainly to be founded
upon truth:

For they persecute him whom thou hast smitten,
and him whom thou hast wounded, they afflict
　　still more. (69:26)[5]

After danger of death and illness, false accusation before a court of law was considered as the cause of deadly peril of the type we meet in the psalms. Actions at law are typical of ancient Israel. They had a real passion for ligitation; it was as if a man could not live without bringing an action before a court. These legal affairs were not always carried out fairly, for deceit, bribery, and blackmail were the order of the day. The great differences between rich and poor played a leading part here. Very often poor, pious men were oppressed by members of the rich ruling class. We know the stories of how David treated Uriah (2 Sam 12), of Ahab's, or rather Jezebel's appropriation of Naboth's vineyard (1 Kings 21), and of the elders' calumnies against Susanna (Dan 13). Isaiah says also: "Your princes are rebels and companions of thieves. Every one loves a bribe and runs after gifts. They do not defend the fatherless, and the widow's cause does not come to them" (Is 1:23). "And he (Yahweh) looked for justice, but behold, bloodshed; for righteousness, but behold, a cry" (Is 5:7). "Woe to those who acquit the guilty for a bribe, and deprive the innocent of his right" (Is 5:23). It is not for nothing that Isaiah says about the Messiah, on whom God's spirit will rest: "He shall not judge by what his eyes see, or decide by what his ears hear; but with righteousness he shall judge the poor, and decide with equity for the meek of the earth" (Is 11:3–4). Others among the prophets criticize unjust dealings of judges and the deceit of officials.[6] And it appears that the situation had not much improved by the time of Christ's coming. This can be seen, for example, from the following parable: "In a certain city there was a widow in that city who kept coming to him and saying, 'Vindicate me against my adversary'. For a while he refused; but afterward he said to himself: 'Though I neither fear God nor regard man, yet because this widow bothers me, I will vindicate her, or she will wear me out by her continual coming'." (Lk 18:2–5)

There had been rules in the codes of law against unrighteous judgment and the giving of false evidence since the earliest days of Israel's existence as a nation. Already in the ten commandments we find: "You shall not bear false witness against your neighbour" (Ex 20:16). In the twenty-third chapter of Exodus are a number of instructions for the administration of justice; we find among others: "You shall not pervert the justice due to your poor in his suit ... and you shall take no bribe" (Ex 23:6–8). To combat the evil of false witnesses as much as possible, the law of retribution, the *lex talionis*, was applied. This law is formulated in the book of Deuteronomy as follows: "If the witness is a false witness and has accused his brother falsely, then you shall do to him as he had meant to do to his brother; so you shall purge the evil from the midst of you. And the rest shall hear, and fear, and shall never again commit any such evil among you" (Deut 19:18–20). We hear repeatedly in the psalms an echo of this law of retribution.[7]

It is impossible to draw a precise picture of the administration of justice in Israel. The details given to us are too contradictory and originate from so many different periods of history. We mention here a few particulars that will give us a better understanding of the psalms. Justice was usually administered at the gate of the city, so that "in the gate" often means the same thing as "before the lawcourts" or "in a lawsuit".

Judgment was also sometimes given in the King's palace, where the royal princes of David's house were the judges.[8] And sometimes justice was administered in the local synagogue. The early morning was by preference the time for hearing law cases: Thus Absalom stood in the early morning to wait for those who came for lawsuits to the city gate (2 Sam 15:2). The psalms often speak of the early morning. Those persons especially, who had had to spend the night before the sessions in custody and had spent anxious hours in prison prayed urgently for deliverance:

> For to thee I pray, O Lord,
> in the morning thou dost hear my voice. (5:3)
> I will sing aloud of thy steadfast love in the
>   morning. (59:16)

> As for me, I shall behold thy face in righteousness,
> when I awake, I shall be satisfied with beholding
>   thy form. (17:15)

The law-session itself took place less quietly. No regular order of procedure was known. The accusations were shouted out all at the same time, one mingling with another.

> You love evil more than good,
> and lying more than speaking the truth.
> You love all words that devour,
> O deceitful tongue.
> But God will break you down for ever;
> he will snatch and tear you from your tent;
> he will uproot you from the land of the living.
>   (52:3–5)

In order to arrive at a judgment the hearing of witnesses both for the prosecution and for the defence was of the greatest importance. If a man wanted to be declared innocent he had to seek out the best possible witnesses. Psalm 127 speaks about this:

> Lo, sons are a heritage from the Lord,
> the fruit of the womb a reward.
> Happy is the man who has
> his quiver full of them!
> He shall not be put to shame
> when he speaks with his enemies in the gate.
>   (vv. 3, 5)

When God had delivered the righteous man and had shown himself to be the best witness on his behalf, the psalmist prayed:

> With my mouth I will give great thanks to the
>   Lord;
> I will praise him in the midst of the throng.
> For he stands at the right hand of the needy,
> to save him from those who condemn him to
>   death. (109:30–31)

Another way, apart from the evidence of witnesses, for a man to declare the justness of his cause was by swearing an oath: "O Lord my God, if I have done this, if there is wrong in my hands, if I have requited my friend with evil or plundered my enemy without cause, let the enemy pursue me and overtake me, and let him trample my life to the ground, and lay my soul in the dust" (7:3–5). Very often the accused asks Yahweh to "procure justice for me", that is to say, "see to it that I am judged rightly and fairly."

The false witnesses and the accusers, from whom the psalmist suffered so much, are often spoken of metaphorically. They are referred to as soldiers of an armed force: their throat is an open grave, their tongue a sharp razor or a sword, their teeth are arrows. They are pictured as hunters who wield their accusations as nets and cords or who dig snares; or they are robbers who lie ambushed in the dark. Again they are likened to lions, dogs or snakes that threaten to attack the psalmist and tear him apart.[9]

In order to arrive at the correct setting in which the psalms of petition evolved we must, after giving details of the danger of death in its various forms, also consider some points about the so-called anthropomorphism. The Bible is full from beginning to end of anthropomorphic ideas and they occur repeatedly in the psalms, especially in these psalms of petition. To appreciate this, we need only reflect that it is wholly impossible for us to represent God as he really is, and that nothing remains but to have recourse to figurative expressions and to adopt an anthropomorphic manner of speaking. We must bear in mind that to the Israelites Yahweh was known above all as a personal, living God. He was not, according to their manner of conceiving, an unmoved prime mover who had withdrawn himself from any interest in man and his world. Israel's belief in God is not upheld by philosophical reflections on the fact that God is a spirit, but on a living experience of his personality and mighty presence. Therefore it was easy for them to think of him in human terms and associate with him as man to man in a free and easy style that seems strange to us. In the Bible we read how freely and openly great men of God such as Moses, Joshua, Elijah, and Jeremiah associated with God.[10] Yet in spite of this very human sphere of concepts and representation, they did not lack in any degree the sense of God's transcendence. We need only think of the prohibition of graven images in the Old Testament. Vriezen says, quite rightly: "Wherever there is knowledge of God, communion with God, all reserves imposed by reason are abandoned, consciously or unconsciously, and human feelings and a human shape are attributed to God without any hesitation."[11] It is the anthropomorphism that reveals to us the special character of Israel's idea of God: "They guarantee the purity of the concept of God, because they continually bring to the fore the notion of how immediate, how real and personal is God's intervention, how near and living is Israel's Holy One."[12] Added to this is the fact that the Oriental's psychological approach to things is very different from the Westerner's. His is the way of concrete imagery rather than that of abstract thought, and he can only free himself with difficulty from the concrete. The psychically tense condition of the psalmist was particularly active in regard to the psalms of petition. He painted his condition as black as possible and called with all his might upon God for his gracious intervention; Yahweh *must* help and help as soon as possible. And this call goes out, not to a far away inaccessible and shadowy godhead, but to a living and personal God who is Yahweh. Therefore this call for help is so entirely human. It was just in their state of need that they saw God as the powerful and intimately near Person who could and would help them.

The climate in which the private psalms of petition developed is the result of the disturbance and uncertainty that life's trials — especially illness, death, persecution, and enmity — bring to us all. This corporate climate accounts for the fact that all these psalms of petition have the same build and structure. That is why they are so easily distinguishable. Four elements are present: the call to Yahweh, the lament, the petition itself, and the motivation.

Among the first words of the psalm of petition is, in most instances, the name of God, Yahweh. In Elohistic psalms this is replaced by the simple words "God", or "my God". "O Lord, how many are my foes" (3:1); "O Lord, rebuke me not in thy anger" (6:1); "O Lord my God, in thee do I take refuge" (7:2); "Have mercy on me, O God" (51:1); "Save me, O God, by thy name" (54:1), and so on. In this last example we see how the psalmist ascribes a saving force to the very name of God; the name alone represents a godlike power, that name performs wonders and is creative.

> Our help is in the name of the Lord. (124:8)
> Some boast of chariots, and some of horses;
> but we boast of the name of the Lord our God.
>   (20:7)
>
> We trust in his holy name. (33:21)

Therefore the psalmist always begins his petition by calling upon the name of Yahweh, God, and by the very uttering of the holy name he feels that he is in contact with God. From the very first word we are in the presence of a true prayer. Contact is made, God's power to help already flows out. This happens simply by the utterance of the name of Yahweh without any additional words or phrases, and without a whole litany of glorifying epithets such as are characteristic of the prayers of the heathen. It is clear that the psalmist and Yahweh are no strangers to each other and the atmosphere of trust that is a distinctive feature in the impetratory psalms of Israel surrounds us. The single word "Yahweh" is sufficient to place the psalmist in the very presence of God.

Having made his address the Israelite proceeds to make known his trouble in God's presence. He describes and illustrates his need in great detail, so as to make it perfectly clear, and he does this in so vital and direct a way that he cannot fail to awaken Yahweh's pity. He tells of all his torture of mind and body, all that Yahweh himself has done to him, all that he has suffered at the hands of friends and enemies. He describes his illness, noxious maledictions, as also the false accusations that have been brought against him and declares that now he has reached a climax:

> Many bulls encompass me,
> strong bulls of Bashan surround me. (22:12)

> Yea, I hear the whispering of many,
> terror on every side,
> as they scheme together against me,
> as they plot to take my life. (31:13)

He repeats the words and threats of his enemy, or enemies:

> He committed his cause to the Lord; let him
>   deliver him,
> let him rescue him, for he delights in him! (22:8)

> May his days be few;
> may another seize his goods! (109:8)

He paints the state of exhaustion that has overcome him:

> I am weary with my crying; my throat is parched.
> (69:3)

> I am cut off from thy sight. (31:22)

He makes his moan in order to awaken Yahweh's pity and reveals his trouble before the face of Yahweh, who is thus as it were compelled to help him. The expression of his grief itself is the first reason for his being heard, but it has at the same time an altogether different function. While grief brings about tension in the soul, the expression of it reduces the tension. Therefore the psalmist wishes to express to Yahweh everything that makes him unhappy. Whether Yahweh helps him directly or not, there is in any event this psychological effect: his heart is lightened and he acquires fresh courage.

> I pour out my complaint before him,
> I tell my trouble before him. (142:2)

The title above psalm 102 reads also: "A prayer of one afflicted, when he is faint and pours out his complaint before the Lord".

After the invocation and the psalmist's statement of his troubles comes the heart of the psalm of petition; the petition itself. It is in this section of the psalm that we can see how simple, spontaneous, and human is the psalmist's relation with Yahweh. The prayer comes from his very heart: "Hear me, help me, save me, preserve me, have mercy on me." Sometimes he prays: "Yahweh may I not be ashamed!" or "May Yahweh help me, may

Yahweh hear me!" and suchlike petitions. The lively style of speech is well illustrated in this section of the psalm, and especially so when God's help seems to be delayed and the psalmist tries harder than ever to attract attention to his pleading. To put it in the manner of speech of the heathen (1 Kings 18:27), he wakes Yahweh from sleep with such words as: "Wake up! Arise! Put aside thy other activities and listen to me! Turn thy face towards me! Give ear unto me! Behold me! Cast thine eyes down upon me!" And further we find such expressions as: "Answer me! Let me hear joyful tidings! Say to me 'I am thy salvation'." Or we have expressions such as: "Send in very deed your help. Come thyself Yahweh to my rescue! Rise up and lift me up. Come to meet me; make haste, stand not aside." The forceful character of these prayers comes out even more clearly in questions which certainly reach the limit of admissible familiarity: "How much longer art thou going to forget me? Why hast thou cast me off? Why dost thou remain so far distant? When wilt thou regard me?"

The Israelite knew how to pray. Faith in God's nearness was the controlling force in all his prayers and he believed Yahweh could not do otherwise than intervene on his behalf and deliver him from his trouble. In later days, under the influence of the prophets, the idea progressed still further. Yahweh had not only to deliver him from his troubles, but had to prevent evil and sin; he had to make his will known and make clear his commandments. Yahweh himself must teach Israel how to do his will; he must create a new heart:

> Create in me a clean heart, O God,
> and put a new and right spirit within me.

> Cast me not away from thy presence,
> and take not thy holy Spirit from me.
> Restore to me the joy of thy salvation,
> and uphold me with a willing spirit. (51:10–12)

The New Testament sounds clearly through these verses which are a prayer for re-creation in the spirit of the firstborn to whom the fullness of redemption has come.

Finally, there is a fourth element in the psalms of petition. It is a sort of summary of the reasons why the psalmist considers he has a right to be heard. He wishes to convince himself that he is sure to be heard, because there is so much to be said on his behalf and he wants to persuade Yahweh, so that he may move him to intervene. Yahweh's own qualities are the chief reasons for the psalmist's confidence: these are God's mercy, goodness, righteousness, and omniscience. This is usually expressed shortly by a word in apposition to the name Yahweh: my Lord, my helper, my deliverer, my salvation, my strength, rock of my salvation, my shield, my guardian. Or it is worked out briefly in a sentence such as: "Thou hearest those that call upon thee"; "Thou snatchest the poor from the hands of the violent man"; "Thou art kind to those who hope in thee", and so forth. Similar expressions appear in the hymns and the psalms of thanksgiving but there they have a quite different function and are intended to stimulate man to the praise of God. Here, in the psalms of petition they serve as statements of reason why the prayer should be heard.

Another important theme is the expression of the psalmist's trust: to thee I flee; in thee I put my trust; unto thee I lift up mine eyes; in thy hands I place my fate; I hope always in God; God cares for me; and other expressions of this type. This trust rests upon the covenant and Yahweh's election of Israel to be his people. The upright man, for this reason, cannot be brought to shame. The expectation of his own deliverance for which the psalmist prays was founded on the hope of a final deliverance and salvation that would, one day, be the lot of all the people of God.

The God of the covenant demands of a man only the total abandonment of himself to God, complete trust in the Almighty. When the trust is there God is bound to help, so argues the psalmist. Numerous other reasons for God's help are stated, such as acknowledgment of guilt and the performance of penance, which usually took the form of fasting and mortification. Then we have further as reasons for God's help, the inborn weakness of man, the short duration and feebleness of human existence, the promise that he will publicly give thanks, the trust the psalmist placed in Yahweh's faithfulness and in his commandments. Finally, there is the innocence of the psalmist. Not that he has never sinned but he declares emphatically his innocence of the particular misdeed of which he stands accused at the moment. He feels that Yahweh is bound to bring his innocence to light.[13]

The same four elements, namely invocation, petition, complaint, and reasons, are also to be found in the *communal psalms of petition,* but they are worked out differently. These psalms are not concerned with individuals but with the nation as a whole. Therefore the emphasis is placed on the ideas of covenant, of God's mighty acts in their nation's history, of his present and future judgment, of salvation and such themes, with greater stress than in the private psalms. The actual setting of these psalms is to be found in the national days of prayer and penance in Israel. These took place on the occasion of national disasters such as war, lost battles, drought, failure of the harvest, plague, the invasion of locusts, and other visitations of this sort. Furthermore such a "fast" could be prescribed to take place during the annual pilgrim celebrations but could also be fixed for a special occasion. All the nation came together then into the house of Yahweh,[14] not to feast and to enjoy a banquet, but to fast in sackcloth and ashes.[15] We find such a day of prayer described by the prophet Joel on the occasion of a great plague of locusts (Joel 1:13 to 2:17): "Gird on sackcloth and lament, O priests; wail, O ministers of the altar. Go in, pass the night in sackcloth, O ministers of my God ... Sanctify a fast, call a solemn assembly. Gather the elders and all the inhabitants of the land to the house of the Lord your God; and cry to the Lord. Blow the trumpet in Zion; sanctify a fast; call a solemn assembly; gather the people. Between the vestibule and the altar let the priests, the ministers of the Lord, weep and say, 'Spare thy people, O Lord, and make not thy heritage a reproach, a byword among the nations. Why should they say among the peoples: Where is their God?'"

Their ritual and historical contexts enable us to place these communal psalms of petition in their correct setting. In order to learn this setting we must examine the prayers of several great figures in Israel's history who interceded with God on behalf of their people. Moses prayed: "O Lord God, destroy not thy people and thy heritage, whom thou hast redeemed through thy greatness, whom thou hast brought out of Egypt with a mighty hand. Remember thy servants, Abraham, Isaac, and Jacob; do not regard the stubbornness of this people, or their wickedness, or their sin lest the land from which thou didst bring us say, 'Because the Lord was not able to bring them into the land which he promised them, and because he hated them, he has brought them out to slay them in the wilderness'. For they are thy people and thy heritage, whom thou didst bring out by thy great power and by thy outstretched arm" (Deut 9:25–29). In this strain, prayed also Joshua, Ezra, and Nehemiah,[16] while a prayer recited by the whole nation is set out for us in the First Book of Maccabees: "What shall we do with these? Where shall we take them? Thy sanctuary is trampled down and profaned, and thy priests mourn in humiliation. And behold, the Gentiles are assembled against us to destroy us; thou knowest what they plot against us. How will we be able to withstand them, if thou dost not help us?" (1 Macc 3:50–52.)[17] From these prayers we can get some idea of the treasury of thought that often found its way into the national psalms of petition. We sense a deep consciousness of God, of Yahweh's faithfulness and compassion, of his call to his people, of the living intercourse with Yahweh. We see also in these prayers a confession of faith, an acknowledgment of guilt. The accent is laid everywhere on the fact that these ideas were the possession of each and every member of God's chosen people, in whom the conviction was very strong that their prayer was sure to be heard because they could say, in effect: It is your affair, Yahweh.

Thou hast sold thy people for a trifle. (44:12)

Remember thy congregation, which
thou hast gotten of old. (74:2)

> O God, the heathen have come into thy inheritance;
> they have defiled thy holy temple. (79:1)

> Have regard for this vine,
> the stock which thy right hand planted. (80:15)

Following on this emphasis, which is placed upon the knowledge of their election as the chosen people of God comes the remembrance of favours bestowed upon Israel:

> Lord, where is thy steadfast love of old,
> which by thy faithfulness thou didst swear to
> David? (89:49)

> I consider the days of old,
> I remember the years long ago. (77:5)

> We have heard with our ears, O God,
> our fathers have told us,
> what deeds thou didst perform in their days,
> in the days of old. (44:1)[18]

The theological themes that are most prominent in this group of psalms of petition, communal as well as private, are varied in character and extensive. That of the problem of suffering meets the eye at once. Owing to the limited range of this book we shall confine ourselves to the discussion of this one theme. Over and above this problem of suffering, we should, if we were to make our study complete, discuss that of sin. Then we might also talk about the psalmist's unlimited trust in God, which is grounded on Yahweh's promises, and therefore not to be shaken. There would still remain God's faithfulness and compassion and many other themes that appear in these psalms to claim our attention. The pág 127 THE PSALMS OF PETITION

question, however, that we are going to try to answer runs: "How did the people of Israel regard the problem of suffering? How should the believer, whether he be Israelite or Christian, turn towards God in the time of suffering? What attitude ought we to take towards suffering itself?" Using the psalms as our starting-point we shall try to solve this problem.

Gunkel says in his introduction to the psalms: "We find no opinion about the blessing of suffering or of its object offered in the psalms of petition themselves. They are too immediate, too direct, for that. They are not sufficiently permeated by reflections upon the subject."[19] We shall see later to what extent we can agree with this statement. In any event, it is true that the problem of individual suffering, as such, remained initially in the background of the Israelite mind, because of their tremendous experience of God's deliverance. What *God* did was for them the most important point: Israel's religion was strongly theocentric. The sovereign works of God were the all-important factor, the results of these works, both for the individual and for the nation, were of secondary importance. Moreover, suffering as a problem remained in the background because the Israelites thought collectively. The interests of the whole community of the people of God held the central position in their thought; the fact of personal suffering and the interests of any particular section of the community counted for practically nothing. Indeed a man could never consider himself innocent, for, as a member of the community, he was responsible for the wrong-doing of all the other members. Even if an individual got no return at all for his work here on earth, and thus no return anywhere, according to Israelite thought, it remained true that the community, the nation, lived on and would experience again the favour of God. The individual disappeared largely in the community.

The people of God knew what suffering was. From the time of the oppression in Egypt to the upheaval of the Babylonian captivity a whole series of national calamities and threats to Israel's existence were experienced. This suffering was soon interpreted as punishment for Israel's sins or as a discipline to ensure for God an obedient nation. The final purification of the nation would, however, take place on the great "day of affliction" when the troubles of Israel would have reached their climax and God would intervene as their deliverer. In this way the suffering of the individual takes the same path as does that of the whole nation. Him too God puts in difficult straits through persecution by his enemies, or illness, or danger of death. But his prayer is also heard by God and his personal deliverance from anxiety and pain is regarded as a personal history of salvation and an image of that of the whole nation of Israel. From this fact "that the experience of the psalmist is not considered as something apart, but as a particularly clear example of what occurs in general",[20] it follows that in these psalms of petition there is a certain flatness in any description, together with an absence of bright colouring and of definite and personal detail.

Suffering began to be regarded as a problem in the days of the prophets who branded illness, defeat, deportation, and other afflictions, as punishment for sin. This was especially so in the time of Jeremiah when as a result of the deuteronomic reform of the law, divine recompense for good and evil was impressed upon the people. The strict application of this principle that suffering is a punishment for sin, the result of God's wrath, and that prosperity and all earthly blessings are a reward for a good life, led to great difficulties. The repercussion of these difficulties can be found in the imprecatory psalms and in the book of Job. This principle had an unfavourable influence on the idea of God. The idea of a justice that retaliates replaced that of a merciful God. The course of history was no longer considered to be the result of God's free and willing intervention, but was conceived as being regulated according to the laws of retribution. Their hope for the future was a rich and prosperous Israel as a result of their own merits. Moreover, the collapse of the national community at the time of the captivity brought the idea of the significance of the individual very much more to the fore. God proved his faithfulness no more to the nation, as such, for this had been wiped from the earth, but he manifested it to individuals, to those who were true to his covenant.

How were they then to explain the sufferings of the righteous man? How indeed, when the idea of retribution in the hereafter was still unknown? Why did such men have to suffer? The idea of retribution for good and evil did not give adequate explanation; they had to find some other solution. They turned to the idea that suffering was a great means of education that Yahweh used to purify his chosen ones. The prophet Hosea puts into the mouth of Yahweh the words: "They shall return to the land of Egypt, and Assyria shall be their king, because they have refused to return to me" (Hos 11:5), while Amos prophesies: "I smote you with blight and mildew; I laid waste your gardens and your vineyards . . . yet you did not return to me, says the Lord" (Amos

4:6–11). If this solution was true for the nation as a whole then it must also be accepted as true for the individual. A man's suffering was considered as an instrument in Yahweh's hands for the building up of his kingdom. In psalm 22 the account of the psalmist's pains ends in a vision of world dominion:

> All the ends of the earth shall remember
> and turn to the Lord;
> and all the families of the nations
> shall worship before him.
> For dominion belongs to the Lord,
> and he rules over the nations . . .
> Posterity shall serve him;
> men shall tell of the Lord to the coming generation.
>   (22:27–30)

They found a further solution of their problem by taking refuge in the experience of Yahweh's nearness as expressed in psalms 73 and 16.

It goes without saying that the righteous man must suffer, "many are the afflictions of the righteous" (34:19), he walks "in the midst of trouble" (138:7), he knows the time of need and the day of trouble (37:39; 50:15). But God delivers him from all these things. "May those who sow in tears reap with shouts of joy" (126:5). Suffering leads to happiness, sadness to joy. Therefore suffering takes on some meaning, because it expiates sin, because it purifies and acts as a means of education. It also opens up a man's heart for God. Perhaps we can say that God only really becomes our own through the testing experience of suffering. In any case, Israel made acquaintance with this, both for the nation and the

individual, through her ruin as a nation and her scattering
and humiliation in the Babylonian captivity. Then she
discovered her God anew in a deeper and more spiritual
sense; from that time on the personal relationship of
men to God was much more in evidence.

Now we can go yet a step further in our study of the
meaning of suffering. The poor, the *'anawim* are frequently referred to in the psalms.[21] These *'anawim* are
"humble and pious Israelites from all classes of society,
perhaps especially from the middle group, who were not
particularly blessed with this world's goods, yet were
not poor in the strict sense of that word".[22] They were
men who through suffering and affliction were tested
and matured, who through their suffering and trials had
found proper submissive relation to Yahweh. "Indeed
human misfortune points to sin, but is it not still more the
painful means used by God to bring a man to complete
self-surrender, to a sort of analysis of himself before
God's presence, to a dramatic purification of his belief
which leads him to utter the cry, 'Out of the depths
I cry unto thee, O Lord'?"[23] Suffering is no longer
considered here as a punishment, no longer as a means
of education but as a positive good in itself. It is
considered to have real value because it induces patience
(patientia), the "waiting upon the Lord". It is from the
experience of suffering that the cry first arises in the
Old Testament:

> Create in me a clean heart, O God,
> and put a new and steadfast spirit within me.
> (51:10)

Out of distress also comes the deep and sensitive
meditation of psalm 139.

A man waits patiently for God. That is to say, waits for him with perseverance and, full of hope, clings to God. Not that everything becomes clearer by so doing: "Evil remains a riddle also in biblical thinking. But ... the mystery of evil is placed in relation with revelation, and thus there comes the possibility of acceptance in faith of the incomprehensible secret."[24] In suffering we realize the nearness of God, so that we can say with the psalmist:

> The Lord is near to the broken-hearted,
> and saves the crushed in spirit. (34:18)

> Prove me, O Lord, and try me;
> test my heart and my mind. (26:2; 139:23)

> But thou, O God my Lord,
> deal on my behalf for thy name's sake;
> because thy steadfast love is good, deliver me!
> For I am poor and needy. (109:21–22)

And they knew also that the comfort of God is meted out according to the measure of suffering:

> When the cares of my heart are many,
> thy consolations cheer my soul. (94:19)

Jesus Christ is the perfect example of the poor and suffering man. When describing the passion and death of Jesus the four evangelists were clearly under the influence of texts from the psalms of petition. They either quote literally or allude to psalms 22, 31, 38, 69, and 88.[25] In the words of the psalms of petition the early Church heard Christ speak to his Father and, whereas other psalms referred to or prayed to Christ, they heard in these psalms the voice of Christ himself. In these songs the Passion of Jesus is depicted before our eyes, here also lives his unshakeable adherence to the Father, the "waiting upon the Lord" of the Old Testament. Here lives the faith in the new creation and the expectation of God's coming at the Judgment.

After Passion Sunday in the Church's liturgy there remains but one psalmist, one cantor, Jesus himself; and we notice that psalms such as 22, 42, 43, 69, and 102 are especially prominent.[26] Jesus is presented to us in these psalms of petition as the true David, the true King, as *the* Man, *the* suffering One, the poor Man, and the righteous One. In the light of his passion, death, and resurrection, these psalms of petition become more richly filled with life and acquire a deeper meaning.

For, "Was it not necessary that the Christ should suffer these things and enter into his glory?" (Lk 24:26). He certainly knew suffering. But by his self-sacrificing and loving acceptance of all the consequences of assuming our unregenerate nature and by the taking on himself of the results of our sin and enduring them to the end as one of us, he brought honour and glory to the Father in the name of us all. Because of this loving acceptance he was glorified and exalted as Lord (Kyrios) (Phil 2:2–11). This mystery of Christ's passion and death, of his desolation and love, is brought to life again for us when we make use of the psalms of petition. Moreover, many of these psalms widen our view of all that this glorification means by their proclamation of God's promises and the coming of his kingdom, and by their bearing witness to God's nearness and his saving inter-vention. All the central events of the history of our salvation are brought to life again in the psalms. This revival is not merely a matter of remembrance, but, in a certain sense, it is a genuine renewal in so far as these songs serve as a framework for the sacramental celebration of the passion and death of Jesus during the mystery of the Mass.

In imitation of Jesus the true Christian is also a man of sorrows: "Through many tribulations we must enter the kingdom of God" (Acts 14:22). But these tribulations are not only a consequence of, and a punishment for sin, nor are they only a means to be used for our enlightenment and purification. They form a fundamental ingredient of the Christian life; indeed, they may be said to be half of it. For the Christian to live means to be made into the image of the dying and risen Lord (Rom 8:17, 29; Phil 3:10–11). The following of Jesus means to be taken out of the world (Jn 15:19, 17:16); it means breaking with pride and rapacity, so that we live our manhood, our creature-hood, and our condition of fallen humanity in the same spirit of love and dedication that Jesus did in his sinless life on earth. Suffering need not have existed, for it is simply the fruit of sin, but just in so far as we accept suffering as Jesus did with full determination and love as penance for the sins of all men, we conquer sin itself. Suffering becomes valuable in itself, it unites us to God and forms us into the likeness of Jesus. However, the ability to endure suffering in this way is only possible for us when we follow in faith and love him, who is the Man of Sorrows and who comes to meet us in the psalms.

With the redeeming work of Jesus began "the last days", the days of great need and oppression in which God's kingdom will be born. Therefore Christian suffering, whether of one man or the whole of God's people, the Church, has an eschatological force. It is the pain, the suffering of "the last days". The need itself shows that we are in the final period and that full salvation is at hand. So, in the Revelation we read: "These are they who have come out of the great tribulation; they have washed their robes and made them white in the blood of the Lamb" (Rev 7:14). But once the fullness of the kingdom has arived, there will be no more suffering. "He will wipe away every tear from their eyes, and death shall be no more, neither shall there be mourning nor crying nor pain any more, for the former things have passed away" (Rev 21:4). Then the word of the psalmist, himself one of the *'anawim*, will be fulfilled:

> Many are the afflictions of the righteous;
> but the Lord delivers him out of them all. (34:19)

When praying the psalms of petition we come in contact daily with the mystery of suffering, both of individuals and of the nation in Old Testament times and with the Passion of Jesus, with the suffering of his Mystical Body, the Church, and with our own suffering. We can easily understand the lamentation, the description of the emergency; on certain days we can readily make this our own. But in these psalms, through and above the complaint, rings out trust, dedication, and loving acceptance of the suffering, especially on the lips of Jesus. Our praying of the psalms must gradually awaken us, as members of the Mystical Body of Jesus, to the true vision of, and the true attitude towards, suffering as we can find them in the psalms when we pray them in the light of Jesus' suffering and death. His passage through the depths

of agony and death has opened up for us the possibility
of doing the same.

Before bringing this chapter to an end we shall briefly
consider some of the smaller groups of psalms that are
very closely related to the psalms of petition.

First, there are the four psalms of trust (psalms 4,
16, 62, and 131), especially marked by confidence in
God. We have already seen how trust plays an
important part in this category of psalms, as a motive
for God's hearing them. A good example of this may
be seen in psalm 27, and in psalm 11 (which lays
emphasis, too, on God's intervention in judgment), and
also in psalm 23 where gratitude is the predominant
theme. Because of the stress laid upon trust the above-
mentioned four psalms make up a distinct group of
their own, in which confidence in God is the distinguishing characteristic.[27]

Next to this group of psalms of trust we may pick
out another group that treats of the problem of suffering
and that has much the same literary characteristics as the
psalms of petition. They do not, however, reflect any
personal reaction to the problem, either as regards an
individual or in relation to the people of Israel. The
presence of such a reaction would have called for
their inclusion among the psalms of petition. They deal
with the problem of suffering in its broadest sense, as
a universal phenomenon, as something that must
promote, even more, man's search for God. They do
not envisage a concrete or pressing need or threat, though
these may be as it were distantly sensed. They deal
rather with common and universal occurrences that
always produce questioning and doubts and that call
insistently for an answer. Why does evil exist? Why is

there a power for evil? Why does not God intervene?
What is really true happiness on this earth? — And
suchlike questions.

One of the forms under which the mystery of evil was
especially prominent in the Old Testament and one which
was especially scandalous was the corruption that was
frequently rife among judges and other officials. Two
of the psalms, those concerned with unjust judges,
describe in vivid terms the existing corruption and call
upon God to intervene. Psalm 58 contains both an
accusation and a prayer which demands of God some
form of divine intervention, basing its claim upon the
plea that the righteous man may be thereby further
strengthened in his faith in Yahweh. Psalm 82 represents
Yahweh as sitting in judgment in the heavenly court,
and opens with an accusation:

> God has taken his place in the divine council;
> in the midst of the gods he holds judgment:
> "How long will you judge unjustly
> and show partiality to the wicked?
> Give justice to the weak and the fatherless;
> maintain the right of the afflicted and the destitute.
> Rescue the weak and the needy;
> deliver them from the hand of the wicked."
> They have neither knowledge nor understanding,
> they walk about in darkness;
> all the foundations of the earth are shaken.
>   (82:1–5)

Thereafter follows the divine judgment and by way
of conclusion, the psalmist's prayer to God to intervene
effectively in the way already suggested in the court-scene.

Lastly, there remains a group of seventeen psalms that

we have styled the psalms about the just man and the
sinner. Other writers prefer to call these the wisdom
psalms, and it is clear that the reflections of wise men
have had a marked influence upon this group of psalms.[28]
This wisdom may be interpreted as a philosophy of life,
a reflection upon life and events of the sort that became
customary from the time of Solomon's accession to the
throne of his father David. During a period of development, of cultural progress, and of religous reflection,
wisdom of this kind is concerned chiefly with a description of the rules for a just and correct life, in the form
of aphorisms and of poems replete with the spirit of
wisdom. As soon, however, as a period of transition
appears and there are signs of division and of decadence,
the situation becomes more complicated, and vital
questions of how and why call for an immediate solution.
In Israel it was the task of wisdom to serve the covenant.
The blessings and the happiness of the covenant are
praised in a joyous and youthful spirit. But when, during
the troubles bred by a degenerate royal house, the
covenant is itself being threatened, and when Yahweh
himself is being reminded of his former pledges, we
observe how the wise men of Israel begin, to ponder the
need for a more serious application of till then generally
accepted ideas about human conduct and divine retribution. It is the theme of the good and evil elements
in the national life that is met with in the psalms
about the righteous and sinners.

Wisdom often adopts a didactic and improving tone;
we have already met with examples of this in the more
moralizing passages of the thanksgiving psalms. Instruction here confines itself to contrasting the fates of good
and evil members of the nation.[29]

It is worthy of note how these psalms have from a
literary standpoint a mixed character, so that we meet
in particular with some moralizing, with portions of
hymns, and with descriptive passages (dealing with
the comparison between the fate of believers and of
sinners). But above all we encounter the distinctive
features of the psalms of petition, such as complaints,
invocations, imprecations, expressions of trust, and so
forth. These characteristics proper to the psalms of
petition are so pronounced that, from a literary point
of view, these psalms may well rank, with some reser-
vations, with the psalms of petition. One must not,
then, be astonished that psalm 119 has also been brought
into this group, since as literature it is closely related
to the psalms of petition.[30]

The situation which gave rise to these psalms was the
critical position in which the adherents to Israel's
covenant were placed through the reckless conduct of
sinners. These psalms betray various reactions to this
most troublesome state of affairs. Some of the psalms
show a radical conviction on this subject, yet in a
peaceable manner, so that, while they often refer to evil
people, they are careful to add: "We trust in Yahweh;
all happiness is from him! He is the source of all that
is good!"[31] In psalms 126 and 127 the covenant's blessing
alone is described in a poetical and proverbial style.

Here we are once more confronted with psalm 119,
and at this stage it is necessary to point out how
reverence for the Law developed vigorously among the
Jews of the post-exilic period. Since there was no longer
a nation, a king, a temple, or an ark of the covenant,
the Law — which comprises both the written and the
spoken word of Yahweh — became for them the most

vivid symbol of Yahweh's presence among his people. Israel's religious thinking now concentrates upon the reflections of wise men and priests over Yahweh's utterances, and this devotion to God's word, as manifested in his revelation and his Law, which in practice is contained in essence in the five books of Moses, is most clearly expressed in psalm 119, to which may be added psalm 1 and the second part of psalm 19.[32]

Other psalms of this group show more violent reaction to the critical situation. They not only express confidence in Yahweh, but insistently demand Yahweh's intervention in favour of devout Jews and the destruction of sinners.[33]

> His mouth is filled with cursing and deceit and
>   oppression;
> under his tongue are mischief and iniquity.
> He sits in ambush in the villages;
> in hiding-places he murders the innocent...
> Arise, O Lord; O God, lift up thy hand;
> forget not the afflicted.
> Why does the wicked renounce God,
> and say in his heart, "Thou wilt not call to
>   account"? (10:7–13)

It will strike the reader that in several of these psalms there is a strong prophetical influence to be noticed, as is clear at once in psalms 12, 14, 49, and 75. We have truly arrived at what Gunkel has called the *Mischformen* in which there is a blending of themes and of influences.

Three of these wisdom-songs or psalms regarding the just man and the sinner go still further. While they assuredly confirm trust in God's presence and assistance, they also call for his intervention in the weakening and disintegrating state of the covenant. Further, they accentuate a vital problem by raising the all-important question about the retribution of good and evil.[34]

The question as to how God's justice could be reconciled with the often striking prosperity of the wicked on the one hand, and with the undeniable misfortunes of just men on the other, had been an acute problem in Israel for many generations. The Book of Job poses this question in an impressive manner and declares that current solutions are of no avail. Job himself does not know the answer to the problem, though he perseveres in refusing to take over such answers to the question as seem to him to be no answers at all. By his doubting and somewhat startling denials he believes that he is serving God better. The fact that to the Israelites the problem was so acute and in appearance so unsurmountable must be ascribed mainly to the absence of any exact knowledge about the existence of future life. For them contact with God was confined to this life, in which God's favour was manifested in terms of material prosperity. This was for Yahweh the only opportunity for bestowing his favours; the idea of some purely spiritual reward had not yet entered their minds. There was no prospect of an after-life. Limited as they were by an earthly horizon the Israelites had put up with the lack of a settlement of good and evil, and this was for all of them an anxious and painful problem.

The author of psalm 37 does not, therefore, know the answer. Like Job's friends he can do no more than offer the reflections of a wise and mature man, who repeats again and again that there will be happiness for the just man and misfortune for the sinner at some time or other. This one thing at least is certain.

In psalms 49 and 73, however, some searching for a practical solution to the problem appears to have developed. The answer to the riddle will lie in another life, or at least in some form of survival after death. The whole issue is well depicted in the lovely Asaph psalm (73):

> But as for me, my feet had almost stumbled,
> my steps had well-nigh slipped.
> For I was envious of the arrogant,
> when I saw the prosperity of the wicked.
> For they have no pangs;
> their bodies are sound and sleek.
> They are not in trouble as other men are ...
> All in vain have I kept my heart clean
> and washed my hands in innocence ...
> But when I thought how to understand this,
> it seemed to me a wearisome task,
> until I went into the sanctuary of God ...
> How they are destroyed in a moment,
> swept away utterly by terrors ...
> Nevertheless I am continually with thee;
> thou dost hold my right hand.
> Thou dost guide me with thy counsel,
> and afterward *thou wilt receive me to glory* ...
> My flesh and my heart may fail,
> but God is the strength of my heart
> and my portion for ever.

Psalm 49, which is a prophetically inspired, instructional psalm about the vanity of riches, contains some striking verses wherein faith is expressed in deliverance from a vague sheol, separated from God.

Like sheep they are appointed for Sheol;
Death shall be their shepherd;
straight to the grave they descend,
and their form shall waste away;
Sheol shall be their home.
But God will ransom my soul from the power of
     Sheol,
for he will receive me. (49:14–15)

In these two psalms (as also in Ps. 16:10) we detect an attempt to discover a new formulation of Israel's faith: God is the source of eternal, immortal, and imperishable life, and to him I submit myself unreservedly.[35]

Before this chapter on the psalms of petition is brought to a close, something should be added about the so-called "cursing" or imprecatory psalms, which are especially numerous in this group. Time and again Christians are made uneasy when reading passages from these "cursing" psalms, since they consider it impossible to justify such sentiments. Personally I must confess that these passages have become less of an obstacle for me, since I became better acquainted with the psalmists' mentality and the nature of their faith. To begin with, one should certainly not interpret these expressions as being a sign of violent personal hatred on the part of the psalmist. Rather, one should try to imagine the real situation and the world of thought in which he lived. He is a man in peril, enemies are threatening his life. How may he escape them? In normal circumstances the application of existing laws would help to resolve the dilemma, but this was not at all easy — if indeed it was possible at all — in ancient Israel with its rather primitive code of law, which later was frequently misapplied, owing to the corruption and intrigues of both judges and litigants. The only instrument at the disposal of the psalmist was the word, which had a position of great importance in the Israelite mind, and possessed real power, even the power of life and death. It was effective and would not return fruitlessly to its utterer. This was true both of a curse and of a blessing. A curse is a curse and will effect condemnation; a blessing is a blessing and will effect favours. The numerous blessings recorded in the Old Testament are more than pious wishes; they are considered to bring about an actual reward. Similarly, curses are not merely expressions of anger or disappointment. They actually effect misfortune. Hence, if an Israelite were in a desperate situation, he could do no more than intend that the misfortune which was to befall him should reverse its course and come down unexpectedly upon his enemy. The psalmist wishes to be freed from misfortune and to be saved. Hence he asks for the application of the *lex talionis* (the law of retaliation in kind). Wherever a phrase occurs such as, "May all this evil come down upon my enemy", one may well presuppose on the psalmist's part sincerity and a quiet conscience and interpret the words as meaning: "Save me! Deliver me from my peril!" A loud and emphatic utterance of words of maximum efficiency, pronounced in the heightened and exaggerated manner so common with Orientals would appear to the psalmist as his ultimate chance of saving himself.

Moreover, we observe that these curses are in many instances an explicit prayer to Yahweh. To God belongs anger; he is the just judge. While the psalmist prays that his enemies may be brought to shame (and indeed his prayer is often emphatically expressed) his petition is essentially that God will intervene in the very personal situation in which, without any culpability on his part, he happens to find himself. Now it is for Yahweh to judge, since in him the psalmist puts his trust. If we are prepared to make an effort to understand the actual situation in the world of the Old Testament and under the conditions of life that existed in ancient Israel, we may introduce these imprecatory psalms into our own prayers as the Jewish equivalent of cries for help and expressions of trust addressed to Yahweh who alone is the just judge of all men.

At this stage of history men had not yet fully apprehended the new order of love that we meet with in the New Testament, where Christ our Lord speaks of forgiveness of injuries and love of our enemies. "But I say to you, Do not resist one who is evil. But if any one strikes you on the right cheek, turn to him the other also" (Mt 5:39). "But I say to you, Love your enemies and pray for those who persecute you" (Mt 5:44). A prayer, such as we find in the Old Testament, that one may be freed from evil and that one's enemy may be unmasked is not necessarily a prayer uttered with evil intent. From the rather limited viewpoint of a believing Jew in Old Testament times such a prayer would appear sufficiently normal. Just as we must accept sundry other limitations in the Old Testament outlook and must try to view them in the living and factual setting of Israel's faith, so we ought here to be prepared to interpret in a positive way these so-called "cursing" or retaliation psalms.

CHAPTER 8

The Pilgrim Psalms

The Pilgrimages of Israel and the special circumstances that accompanied them were an incentive to the writing of new psalms. Songs that were used during the pilgrimages already existed from quite early times. Psalm collections like the one we possesses in the "psalms of ascent" or gradual psalms (120–134) were used. This chapter will not discuss those psalms of Israel's past that were used subsequently to their composition during the pilgrimages and were collected together for the benefit of pilgrims, but will consider only those psalms that actually grew out of the pilgrimages themselves.

A great place was given to pilgrimages to the sanctuaries of the gods in the outward demonstration of the religions of antiquity. In pre-Israelite Canaan such pilgrimages were already known. Moses also commanded pilgrimages to the house of Yahweh: "Three times a year all your males shall appear before the Lord your God . . . They shall not appear before the Lord empty-handed" (Deut 16:16; Ex 23:17, 34:23). This command concerned Easter, Pentecost, and the Feast of Tabernacles. The Easter feast, lasting for seven days, was the festive start of the harvest, in which the first sheaves of barley were offered to God. Seven weeks after Easter, when the wheat harvest was well under way, came the great harvest feast Pentecost. The Feast of Tabernacles celebrated the end of the fruit and wine harvest in the seventh month of the Jewish year, *Tishri*. All three of these great feasts had an agricultural origin but they had, at the same time, a very stong religious flavour in Israel. Easter was the great festival of deliverance, which celebrated in particular the Exodus from Egypt. The Feast of Tabernacles was the memorial of the sojourn in the desert, and the tents made of branches in full leaf were the symbols used to remind the people of this event. At the same time this feast celebrated all God's benefits to the people of Israel. Finally, the feast of Pentecost was associated with the celebration of the giving of the Law on Mount Sinai though at a date long after this event. The pilgrimages that accompanied the annual repetition of these feasts deepened in the minds of the Israelites their consciousness of belonging to the chosen people of God. This common celebration of God's acts of deliverance by the whole community strengthened the close links of friendship among themselves and enforced the ties that bound them as a chosen nation.

It is not an enemy who taunts me,
then I could bear it;
it is not an adversary who deals insolently with me,
then I could hide from him.
But it is you, my equal,
my companion, my familiar friend.
We used to hold sweet converse together;

within God's house we walked in fellowship.
(55:12–14)[1]

Behold, how good and pleasant it is
when brothers dwell in unity! (133:1)

However, the consciousness of God's saving intervention
in the affairs of men and the truth "that all earthly
existence is rooted in the saving grace of God"[2] was
firmly anchored in the minds of the Israelites by the
splendid pilgrim feasts. And as from ancient times
judgment had been given in the holy places (1 Sam 7:16;
8:1), so the pilgrimage was the occasion for transacting
legal business and bringing lawsuits. Thanksgiving
ceremonies were often postponed to these occasions, when
the people were already assembled around God's sanctuary. At such times the priests also gave instruction
in their national history and in the Law of Moses. They
answered questions or solved problems about the observ-
ances of the Law (Deut 17:8–12). Many Jews used this
opportunity also for doing business. Great markets were
held. By reason of all this the emphasis began to be laid
upon external things, and the spiritual purpose of the
pilgrimage tended to fall into the background. No
wonder then that we hear from the prophets, whose
duty it was to defend the inwardness of God's service,
unfavourable expression about these pilgrimages. "When
you come to appear before me, who requires of you
this trampling of my courts? Bring no more vain offerings ... I cannot endure iniquity and solemn assembly"
(Is 1:12–14). And ironically: "Come to Bethel, and
transgress; to Gilgal, and multiply transgression; bring
your sacrifices every morning, your tithes every three

days ... for so you love to do, O people of Israel"
(Amos 4:4).[3]

The principal pilgrim feast was the Feast of Tabernacles. This took place after the harvest, so that it was
for the agrarian population of the promised land the
most suitable time to leave home and go up to Jerusalem.
For the ordinary man this was the best beloved of the
festivals; it was the feast of feasts. Every seven years
the Law had to be read aloud to the people (Deut
31:10–13); perhaps a renewal of the covenant took place
at the same time. As the date of one of the festivals drew
near a messenger went from one village to another, so that
the people could prepare themselves. Later, when the
time came to leave the holy city, the psalmist reminded
himself of the pleasure he had felt at the call: "I was
glad when they said to me, 'Let us go to the house of
the Lord!'" (Ps 122:1). Jeremiah prophesied: "For there
shall be a day when watchmen will call in the hill
country of Ephraim: 'Arise, and let us go up to Zion,
to the Lord our God'" (Jer 31:6). "Now the Passover
of the Jews was at hand, and many went up from the
country to Jerusalem before the Passover, to purify
themselves" (Jn 11:55). On the occasion of the Feast
of Tabernacles in the period after the harvest the pilgrims
marched over bare and dried up fields; but the arid
season of the year was coming to an end, and one of
the objects of the pilgrimage was to pray for and obtain
the soft autumn rains that made the soil suitable for
ploughing and sowing. "And if any of the families of
the earth do not go up to Jerusalem to worship the King,
the Lord of hosts, there will be no rain upon them.
And if the family of Egypt do not go up and present
themselves, then upon them shall come the plague with

which the Lord afflicts the nation", says the prophet
Zechariah (Zech 14:17–18). One of the psalms describes
how the ground became already moist and soft under the
feet of the pilgrims:

> As they go through the valley of Baca
> they make it a place of springs;
> the early rain also covers it with pools. (84:6)

During these pilgrimages songs echoed and flutes were
played. There was joy in the hearts of all because they
were on their way "to the mountain of the Lord, to the
Rock of Israel" (Is 30:29). When they arrived in Jerusalem they saw on all sides groups of pilgrims coming
together to pay homage to God and to celebrate his acts
of deliverance. This vision of the crowd streaming in
from all sides inspired some of the prophecies of Isaiah.
He writes for example: "It shall come to pass in the
latter days that the mountain of the house of the Lord
shall be established as the highest of the mountains, and
shall be raised above the hills; and all the nations shall
flow to it, and many peoples shall come and say: 'Come,
let us go up to the mountain of the Lord, to the house
of the God of Jacob'." (Is 2:2–3)[4]

When the pilgrimage arrived in the holy city the first
visit to the temple took place at once; the first ceremonies
were held at the temple gate.[5] From the second book of
Chronicles we learn how Jehoiada, the guardian of the
little Joash "stationed the gatekeepers at the gates of
the house of the Lord so that no one should enter who
was in any way (ritually) unclean" (2 Chron 23:19).
The pilgrims approached the gate and were welcomed
by the levites or priests on duty. They then received

the blessing of the priests and manifested their joy at
being permitted to enter God's house.

> How lovely is thy dwelling place.
> O Lord of hosts!
> My soul longs, yea, faints
> for the courts of the Lord ...
> Even the sparrow finds a home,
> and the swallow a nest for herself,
> where she may lay her young,
> at thy altars, O Lord of hosts,
> my King and my God.
> Blessed are those who dwell in thy house,
> ever singing thy praise!

And the priests answer:

> Blessed are the men whose strength is in thee,
> in whose heart are the highways to Zion. (84:1–5)

At the same time, however, the pilgrims felt a certain
amount of diffidence and fear and asked the levites who
actually might enter into this holy place. In reply the
levites summed up the various qualities required, and
encouraged the pilgrims to true holiness of life. During
this summing-up they liked to choose illustrations from
certain features of Israel's history. Various psalms, which
grew out of this actual situation, or have it as their
literary setting, give us a picture of these dialogues at
the temple gate. Psalm 24 begins with a hymn, the last
echo of the song which the pilgrims have sung on their
way through the streets of Jerusalem:

> The earth is the Lord's and the fullness thereof,
> the world and those who dwell therein;

> for he has founded it upon the seas,
> and established it upon the rivers.

Then follows the question:

> Who shall ascend the hill of the Lord?
> And who shall stand in his holy place?

The answer comes:

> He who has clean hands and a pure heart,
> who does not lift up his soul to what is false,
> and does not swear deceitfully.
> He will receive blessing from the Lord,
> and vindication from the God of his salvation.

And once more the pilgrims reply:

> Such is the generation of those who seek him,
> who seek the face of the God of Jacob. (vv. 1–6)

Psalm 15 also gives instruction, in the form of a dialogue, about the qualities that distinguish the true worshipper of God. One who wants to be the privileged guest of Yahweh must be convinced that a pilgrimage is no question of magic or formalism. The only important question is the inner attitude, sincerity, faithfulness towards the covenant. Liturgical worship and daily life are one. Sometimes there is a dialogue between the priests and a very important pilgrim, as we see for example in psalm 91. Before the procession is allowed to enter the temple yet another stimulus is given to real faith, inward faith. While the hymns were echoing with the words: "Come, let us rejoice before Yahweh, let us shout and give thanks; let us worship and bow down before the Lord; let us kneel down before Yahweh who made us;

for he is our God and we are the people of his pasture",
all at once the voice of a prophet or a priest rang out,
as interpreting Yahweh's words:

> O that today you would hearken to his voice!
> Harden not your hearts, as at Meribah,
> as on the day at Massah in the wilderness,
> when your fathers tested me,
> and put me to the proof, though they had seen my
>   work.
> For forty years I loathed that generation
> and said, "They are a people who err in heart,
> and they do not regard my ways." (95:7–10)

By now the pilgrims were sufficiently prepared. Their
longings were aroused, the conditions demanded for
entrance to the holy place had been outlined and they
had had the necessity for faith and surrender to God
pointed out to them. Now they could actually enter the
temple itself, which they did during the singing of a song:

> Make a joyful noise to the Lord, all the lands!
> Serve the Lord with gladness!
> Come into his presence with singing!
> Know that the Lord is God!
> It is he that made us, and we are his;
> we are his people, and the sheep of his pasture.
> Enter his gates with thanksgiving,
> and his courts with praise!
> Give thanks to him, bless his name!
> For [The last verse is the people's refrain] the Lord
>   is good;
> his steadfast love endures for ever,
> and his faithfulness to all generations. (Ps 100)

Psalm 121 is one that does not exactly fit into this situation yet speaks of the holy sanctuary and of pilgrimage. The psalmist finds himself in great difficulties and therefore he wants to undertake a pilgrimage:

> I lift my eyes to the hills.
> From whence does my help come?

He looks round to the neighbouring hills, where he can see many of the Canaanite sanctuaries, the so-called "high places".[6] Or shall he go to the temple of Yahweh?

> My help comes from the Lord,
> who made heaven and earth.

He hesitates for a few moments and then finally comes the resolute, trustful answer; he will go on a pilgrimage to the house of the Lord:

> Behold, he who keeps Israel
> will neither slumber nor sleep.
> The Lord is your keeper;
> the Lord is your shade
> on your right hand . . .
> The Lord will keep you from all evil;
> he will keep your life.
> The Lord will keep
> your going out and your coming in
> from this time forth and for evermore. (121:4–8)

During the days that the pilgrims sojourned in Jerusalem many ceremonies took place. Psalms were sung, joyful and gay psalms of praise and thanksgiving. Each man performed his promised ceremony of thanksgiving and Yahweh was honoured as their king. They marched sometimes round in procession with the ark. These feasts provided at the same time the best opportunity for the priests of Jerusalem to make contact with the people from all parts of the country. They took the chance of instructing the people in the details of the service of God, while the people, on their side, had the opportunity of asking questions and explaining their problems. When, as we read in Isaiah 2:3, the nations prepare to go to the hill of the Lord, they say: "that he may teach us his ways and that we may walk in his paths. For out of Zion shall go forth the law, and the word of the Lord from Jerusalem." It was the task of the priests to give instruction in the Law of Moses (Lev 10:11). "For the lips of a priest should guard knowledge, and men should seek instruction from his mouth, for he is the messenger of the Lord of hosts" (Mal 2:7). No wonder that God himself encourages the people to "ask the priests to decide this question" (Hag 2:11).

Into this situation can be fitted many teaching poems, psalms that were used to instruct the assembled crowds of people.[7] The theme of the Exodus and the memory of the covenant on Mount Sinai play a great part in these songs. The people were led back in thought to the beginning of their history when God called the nation of Israel into being:

> Give ear, O my people, to my teaching;
> incline your ears to the words of my mouth!
> I will open my mouth in a parable;
> I will utter dark sayings from of old,
> things that we have heard and known,
> that our fathers have told us. (78:1–3)

Psalm 50 begins with a great theophany: Yahweh appears, and those "who made a covenant with me by sacrifice" (50:5) must come together:

> Hear, O my people, and I will speak,
> O Israel, I will testify against you.
> I am God, your God. (50:7)

On other occasions, as we have already seen in psalm 95, the jubilation of the hymns was interrupted by the appearance of a prophet or seer.[8]

> I hear a voice I had not known:
> I relieved your shoulder of the burden;
> your hands were freed from the basket.
> In distress you called, and I delivered you. (81:5–7)

In this way the people were instructed in the history of Yahweh's acts of deliverance. At the same time the Law was explained to them and they paid homage to it. That is why the "legal" psalms were frequently used on the occasion of the instructions in the temple. Psalm 19 shows all the characteristics of the joyful feasts of Israel. The God gives on every new day the law to the people of the covenant as he once did on Mount Sinai.

> The law of the Lord is perfect,
> reviving the soul;
> the testimony of the Lord is sure,
> making wise the simple;
> the precepts of the Lord are right,
> rejoicing the heart. (19:7–8)

In this way priests and people were linked together, for they had experienced a great deal together. We hear in psalm 134 how they reacted when the evening came and the pilgrims had to leave the holy city. At the hour of the sacrifice of the evening the pilgrims called out:

> Come, bless the Lord,
> all you servants of the Lord,
> who stand by night in the house of the Lord!
> Lift up your hands to the holy place,
> and bless the Lord!

From the sanctuary the priests answered:

> May the Lord bless you from Zion,
> he who made heaven and earth! (Ps 134)

Finally the pilgrims returned to their villages and fields. "On the twenty-third day of the seventh month he (Solomon) sent the people away to their homes, joyful and glad of heart for the goodness that the Lord had shown to David and to Solomon and to Israel his people" (2 Chron 7:10). The departure from Jerusalem was characterized by gladness, joy, and thankfulness. Their stay in the city which was at the heart of Yahweh-worship, in the midst of a cosmopolitan community, made a deep impression on the pilgrims. Psalm 87, which gives a picture of the Messianic Zion in much the same way as does Isaiah (Is 2; 54; 60; and 62), describes warmly how the pilgrim has found God in this city. He experienced Jerusalem as the city of God and learnt that God lives there. Being the city of God Jerusalem is the centre of mankind: every one has been born there. In the list of peoples which Yahweh holds, every one is said to have been "born in Jerusalem", since Jerusalem is the source of life for every man.

> Singers and dancers alike say,
> "All my springs are in you." (87:7)

Streams of living water issue from Zion (Joel 3:18; Ezek 47:1–12; Zech 14:8). It is there that the pilgrim feels the presence of God. This experience gives to his heart an abundant joy which animates his whole life.

> One thing have I asked of the Lord,
> that will I seek after;
> that I may dwell in the house of the Lord
> all the days of my life,
> to behold the beauty of the Lord,
> and to inquire in his temple.
> Thou hast said, "Seek ye my face."
> My heart says to thee,
> "Thy face, Lord, do I seek." (27:4, 8)

The psalmist of psalm 63 feeling himself as "a dry and weary land where no water is" reflects on his earlier experience of the temple:

> So I have looked upon thee in the sanctuary,
> beholding thy power and glory.
> For thou hast been my help,
> and in the shadow of thy wings I sing for joy.
>   (63:2, 7)

When the Jewish exiles in Babylon have been asked to sing their songs for their captors, they remember Zion in sorrow and longing:

> If I forget you, O Jerusalem,
> let my right hand wither!

> Let my tongue cleave to the roof of my mouth,
> if I do not remember you,
> if I do not set Jerusalem
> above my highest joy! (137:5–6)

Sometimes the stay in Jerusalem was particularly impressive, for example, when there had been a war from which Jerusalem had emerged unharmed:

> As we have heard, so have we seen
> in the city of the Lord of hosts,
> in the city of our God,
> which God establishes for ever . . .
> Walk about Zion, go round about her,
> number her towers,
> consider well her ramparts
> go through her citadels;
> that you may tell the generation
> that this is God,
> our God for ever and ever.
> He will be our guide for ever. (48:8, 12–14)

Jerusalem had been the ancient fortress of the Jebusites. When Israel entered Canaan they could not take the city. It was David who first breached the age-old fortifications and, because of its favourable geographical position, made it his residence and the symbol of national unity. When the ark had been transferred to Mount Zion within the city area and, later, Solomon's temple had been built, Jerusalem became the spiritual centre of the kingdom. The belief in God was indeed the foundation of Israel's national existence and of her unity as a nation. Jerusalem was above all the chosen city of Yahweh:

> But he chose the tribe of Judah
> Mount Zion, which he loves.
> He built his sanctuary like the high heavens,
> like the earth, which he has founded for ever.
>   (78:68–69)

> Why look you with envy, O many-peaked mountain,
> at the mount which God desired for his abode,
> yea, where the Lord will dwell for ever? (68:16)

In this town, on this holy hill Yahweh lived in the midst of his people. He was there as Emmanuel, "God-with-us". Every year the Israelite came up to this city, this permanent abode of his God and there enjoyed friendly contact with Yahweh. There he could experience the eternal reality of God's intervention on behalf of his people, the inexhaustible source of his immeasurable benefits. There at the same time he learned to know Yahweh as the hidden, exalted God, enthroned high above the cherubim in holy inaccessibility. Jerusalem was the pride and joy of every man of Israel: "For a day in thy courts is better than a thousand elsewhere" (Ps 84:10). But this pride and joy in the city was permitted only because Yahweh dwelt there among his people. A too wordly valuation of the holy city without any religious background was vain and meaningless. "Do not trust in these deceptive words: 'This is the temple of the Lord, the temple of the Lord, the temple of the Lord.' For if you truly amend your ways and your doings, if you truly execute justice one with another, if you do not oppress the alien ... then I will let you dwell in this place" (Jer 7:4–7).

The painful experience of the Babylonian captivity after the destruction of the temple and the city in 587 B.C. took away from the people all trust in false ideas and material things. The nation was banished, the people were taken far away from Zion, and the city of God became something to look back upon with longing. It was at this time that the Messianic desires and expectations grew very pronounced. Jerusalem must be the centre of a renewed people of God; then all nations would pour into the holy city (Is 60 and 66; Mic 4; Zech 8 and 14); streams from this chosen spot would flow out to make the country fertile (Joel 4; Ezek 47; Zech 14) and the renewed city of God would stand firm for ever: "For the Lord dwells in Zion" (Joel 3:21). Having come back from banishment, they found no ark of the covenant, as a symbol of God's presence, in the rebuilt temple. But Ezekiel taught the people of a more exalted presence of God who was not only *with* Israel but *within* them (Ezek 37:1–14). Yahweh himself "has been a sanctuary to them in the countries where they have gone" (Ezek 11:16).[9] God's word, the Law, was now the concrete symbol of God's nearness. The word that Yahweh speaks was the source of all blessing and good; the Law was the sign of his presence:

> He declares his word to Jacob,
> his statutes and ordinances to Israel.
> He has not dealt thus with any other nation;
> they do not know his ordinances. (147:19–20)

As appears from the writings of the New Testament, the infant Church saw in the person of Jesus Christ the fulfilment of the kingdom of God. In him God has come close to mankind. He is Emmanuel, the God-with-us (Mt 1:23). In him God's word lives (literally "spreads his tent") among us (Jn 1:14). He it is who has superseded the temple of the old covenant and replaced it by himself as the new dwelling-place of God (Jn 2:21). This was the great accusation brought against him before the Sanhedrin: "We heard him say, 'I will destroy this temple that is made with hands, and in three days I will build another, not made with hands'." (Mk 14:58) And never has God's word been so really present as in the one, perfect and complete Word that he uttered. Christ is *the* Word, *the* revelation of the Father's saving will, *the* Law (Heb 1:1).

The new temple in which God is present with us, where we can find him, is the temple of Jesus' body (Jn 2:21). But the body of Jesus is the Church.[10] The Church is the city "which has foundations, whose builder and maker is God" (Heb 11:10). She is the Jerusalem from on high (Gal 4:25), the heavenly, new and holy Jerusalem (Heb 12:22; Rev 3:12, 21:2, 10). In the Church God lives among us and the Law which is in force in the new Jerusalem is the law of the Spirit (Rom 8:2) which is love. God had already announced this through the mouth of Jeremiah, "I will put my law within them, and I will write it upon their hearts" (Jer 31:33). *Our* Jerusalem is the Church, our Law is love. Active love is God's commandment for all willing to serve him in the fellowship of the Church.

But this unity with God is not yet perfect. The Jerusalem which is the Church on earth is still only an image and anticipation of the final heavenly Jerusalem. The Church is God's people still on pilgrimage to the new Jerusalem (Rev 3:12). On her journey she prays and sings daily the old psalms that once were sung by the Israelites during their annual pilgrimages to the holy city and to God's house. In these songs she voices her desire to meet the Lord again and again. Zion and the temple form the old framework of the now spiritual meeting-place, in faith, word, and sacrament. The desire of the pilgrim-psalms stems from an authentic experience of faith. This same experience can now be ours, but in a deeper and more spiritual way. At the same time we find in these songs a real joy about the nearness of God. The original nearness in Jerusalem and the temple becomes fuller and deeper in the Church and will be completely realized at the end of time; they will be his own people and he will be with them: "And I saw the holy city, new Jerusalem, coming down out of heaven from God . . . and I heard a great voice from the throne saying, 'Behold, the dwelling of God is with men. He will dwell with them, and they shall be his people, and God himself will be with them'." (Rev 21:2 to 3)

CHAPTER 9

The Processional and Enthronement Psalms

The people of Israel had not only experienced the proximity of Yahweh in his intervention in the history of the
nation but they realized his continual presence with
them on his throne, the ark of the covenant, that was
always in their midst, either in the innermost holy
of holies or on the field of battle. The exact place of
God's presence was considered to be just above the ark
of the covenant over and between the cherubim, as it was
expressed in the fixed formula, "the Lord, who is
enthroned upon the cherubim".[1] Yahweh says to Moses
in the book of Exodus: "There I will meet with you,
from above the mercy seat, from between the two
cherubim that are upon the ark of the testimony, I will
speak with you of all that I will give you in commandment for the people of Israel" (Ex 25:22). In the book of
Numbers, chapter 7, verse 89, we read: "And when
Moses went into the tent of meeting to speak with the
Lord, he heard the voice speaking to him from above the
mercy seat that was upon the ark of the testimony, from
between the two cherubim."[2] It was this presence of God
which gave the ark its sacred character. The fact that

in the ark the two tablets of stone with the Law were preserved, in the same way as the heathen nations laid their contracts in a shrine under the idol, is of very little importance compared with the fact of God's presence.[3] The tablets of stone emphasized, indeed, that Yahweh was God of the covenant, but more than anything else they stood for the great fact, "Yahweh is here present". Thus the ark was simply "called by the name of the Lord of hosts" (2 Sam 6:2). When they lifted up or put down the ark they repeated the formula "Arise, O Lord", "Rest here, O Lord."[4] The ark testified to the nearness of Israel's God in the same way as the pillar of fire and the cloud of smoke had once done. The first reaction to the ark was a realization of the unapproachability and majesty of God. "Who is able to stand before the Lord, this holy God?" was their cry (1 Sam 6:20). On the other hand they referred to the ark as "the footstool of the Lord" (Pss 99:5, 132:7), so assured were they of his helpful presence and protection.

> In the shadow of thy wings I will take refuge,
> till the storms of destruction pass by. (57:1)

> Let me dwell in thy tent for ever!
> Oh to be safe under the shelter of thy wings!
>   (61 : 4)

> And under his wings you will find refuge;
> his faithfulness is a shield and buckler. (91:4)[5]

After its arrival in the promised land the ark was placed in Shiloh (1 Sam 3:3, 4:4). From Siloh it was taken to the field of battle against the Philistines (1 Sam 4:3–10),

and it was from there that the ark was captured and
brought by the Philistines to the temple of their god
Dagon in Ashdod (1 Sam 5:1–3). In psalm 78, verses 60
and 61, we read,

> He forsook his dwelling at Shiloh,
> the tent where he dwelt among men,
> and delivered his power (the ark) to captivity,
> his glory (the ark) to the hand of the foe.

Some time later the ark came, by way of Beth-shemesh,
to Kirjath-jearim (1 Sam 6). David transferred it to
Jerusalem (2 Sam 6), and we see it later on the field of
battle against the Ammonites (2 Sam 11:11). Finally
Solomon placed the ark in its permanent home in the
holy of holies of the newly-built temple (1 Kings 8).
This is the last we hear of the ark. It disappeared entirely
when Jerusalem was laid waste in the year 587 B.C.[6]
In the later temple of Zerubabel and in that of Herod
the holy of holies remained empty: Yahweh was no longer
seated "above and between the cherubim". It is only in
the heavenly temple, described in the book of Revelation,
that we see once again the ark of the covenant (Rev
11:19).

It is often suggested that King Solomon finally placed
the ark in the holy of holies and that it remained there
undisturbed until the destruction of the temple in 587 B.C.
From our study of the psalms we are led to draw
other conclusions: for in the psalms journeys and
processions are perhaps mentioned in which Yahweh
himself takes part and wherein he is referred to by
the name specifically associated with the ark, that is
"Yahweh, the Lord of hosts". It is probable, therefore,

that the psalms of which we are speaking are processional songs that were sung during the processions of the ark of Yahweh, the Lord of hosts. The immediate occasion for the writing of these songs was perhaps one of the historical occasions, referred to in the sacred writings, when the ark was transferred. Yet the later additions and the general perspective that they bring into view point to a regualar use of these psalms in the religious services of Israel.

The actual historical fact to which psalm 132 refers is the transfer of the ark from Kirjath-jearim to Mount Zion (2 Sam 6) referred to earlier:

> Lo, we heard of it (the ark) in Ephrathah,
> we found it in the fields of Jaar,
> Let us go to his dwelling-place;
> let us worship at his footstool!
> Arise, O Lord, and go to thy resting-place,
> thou and the ark of thy might. (132:6–8)

The commemoration of this event is bound up with the glorification of Yahweh's kingship and with the celebration of King David and his dynasty which is to continue for ever.

Other psalms describe how Yahweh comes up the mount of the temple. Above the heads of the crowd the ark is carried forward in solemn procession:

> With mighty chariotry, twice ten thousand,
> thousands upon thousands,
> the Lord came from Sinai into the holy place.
> Thou didst ascend the high mount,
> leading captives in thy train,

and receiving gifts among men ...
Thy solemn processions are seen, O God,
the processions of my God, my King, into the
    sanctuary,
the singers in front, the minstrels last,
between them maidens playing timbrels:
"Bless God in the great congregation,
the Lord, O you who are Israel's fountain!"
There is Benjamin, the least of them, in the lead,
the princes of Judah in their throng,
the princes of Zebulun, the princes of Naphtali.
    (68:17–27)

The whole of this psalm, which is one of the most difficult and, at the same time, one of the most beautiful of the songs in the Psalter, deals with a procession in which God's deliverance in the past is celebrated. It celebrates also his presence among the people in Zion and rejoices over a future world empire.[7]

Such a procession must have been the setting of psalm 47 where the ascent to Mount Zion is also referred to:

God has gone up with a shout,
the Lord with the sound of a trumpet.
Sing praises to God, sing praises!
Sing praises to our King, sing praises! (47:5–6)

The procession arrived finally before the gate of the temple. A priest spoke while the crowd remained silent:

Lift up your heads, O gates;
and be lifted up, O ancient doors!
that the King of glory may come in.

From within the temple they asked:

> Who is the king of glory?

And the answer rings out:

> The Lord, strong and mighty,
> the Lord, mighty in battle!

When the doors do not immediately open, the cry is repeated:

> Lift up your heads, O gates!
> and be lifted up, O ancient doors!
> that the King of glory may come in.

Again came the question:

> Who is the King of glory?

Then came the full answer, announcing the name of the ark:

> The Lord of hosts,
> he is the King of glory! (24:7–10)

The doors opened wide and Yahweh passed into his holy place.

The symbolic and eschatological character of these processions is brought out clearly in such psalms as 149. There is here no question of the ark or of Yahweh himself taking part in the procession. It is a song of victory set to music, probably with dancers who go rejoicing up the holy mountain accompanied by armed warriors. God's anticipated victory over the heathen was celebrated symbolically in this song. Israel's glory would consist in helping God to found his kingdom by means of this godlike "act of vengeance":

> Let the faithful exult in glory;
> let them sing for joy on their couches.
> Let the high praises of God be in their throats
> and two-edged swords in their hands,
> to wreak vengeance on the nations
> and chastisement on the peoples,
> to bind their kings with chains
> and their nobles with fetters of iron,
> to execute on them the judgment written!
> This is glory for all his faithful ones. (149:5–9)

Most processional psalms refer explicitly to the kingship of God, his rule, and his kingdom.

While Yahweh is celebrated in the symbol of the ark of his presence, the wider background, his kingdom and rule, which are now in process of growing and await completion, are recalled at the same time. Some psalms are wholly dedicated to the theme of Yahweh's kingship; These are the so-called enthronement psalms. The use of this title will grow clearer later. First let us consider their different elements. The group consists of psalms 93 and 96 to 99 inclusive, together with psalm 47. The whole of this group is related in literary form to the psalms of praise and have sections that are purely hymn-like in nature, even more so than the processional psalms. The first noticeable feature is therefore, the *invitation* or *address:*

> Clap your hands, all peoples!
> Shout to God with loud songs of joy! (47:1)

> The Lord reigns; let the earth rejoice;
> let the many coastlands be glad! (97:1)

> Sing praises to the Lord with the lyre,
> with the lyre and the sound of melody!
> With trumpets and the sound of the horn
> make joyful noise before the King, the Lord!
>   (98:5–6) [8]

This invitation is always a call to praise God and joy in regard to the kingship of Yahweh. There follows at once the description of the king. Yahweh sits enthroned, full of awe-inspiring majesty, exalted, clothed with grandeur, and girdled with glory. "Thy throne is established from of old; thou art from everlasting" (Ps 93:2). [9] Clouds and darkness wrap him round as a mantle, his throne is established on justice and righteousness, he sits above the cherubim, high and exalted. "Moses and Aaron were among his priests, Samuel also was among those who called on his name" (Ps 99:6). God is described as a mighty prince ruling in splendour and unlimited authority:

> For God is the king of all the earth;
> sing praises with a psalm!
> God reigns over the nations;
> God sits on his holy throne.
> The princes of the peoples gather
> as the people of the God of Abraham.
> For the shields of the earth belong to God;
> he is highly exalted! (47:7–9)

God's kingship had been revealed and demonstrated to them in their own deliverance and in creation, and was repeatedly proclaimed anew in the liturgy of Israel. The third element in this group of psalms speaks of those very acts of God that indeed reveal his kingship. God is Israel's deliverer:

> He subdued peoples under us,
> and nations under our feet.
> He chose our heritage for us,
> the pride of Jacob whom he loves. (47:3–4)

> The Lord has made known his victory,
> he has revealed his vindication in the sight of the nations.
> He has remembered his steadfast love and faithfulness
> to the house of Israel. (98:2–3)

God is also the creator. Therefore he rules and the earth stands firm and fixed on immovable foundations. He conquers the darker elements of the primeval chaos:

> The floods have lifted up, O Lord,
> the floods have lifted up their voice,
> the floods lift up their roaring.
> Mightier than the thunders of many waters,
> mightier than the waves of the sea,
> the Lord on high is mighty! (93:3–4)

God revealed himself in the elements of nature and in the development and protection of his people as their ruler and king. He did so also by coming to live among them, a fact which was celebrated repeatedly, as we have seen, by the entry (or re-entry) of his ark into the temple. The kingship of Yahweh is revealed and accepted as an actual, present fact in the rites and ceremonies of Israel: hence the repeated cry, "God is the king" (or: "has become

king").[10] This kingship cry, as we may call it is repeated
five times over in these psalms. The kingship of Yahweh
over Israel was indeed celebrated as a present fact while,
at the same time, the people looked forward to the epoch
when that kingship would be complete over the whole
earth. This forms the fourth element of the enthronement
psalms, the universalistic outlook. The influence of
Deutero-Isaiah upon these psalms can be clearly seen
here. Yahweh is king of the whole earth, all generations
of the earth must give praise to him, all nations must
tremble before him:

> The heavens proclaim his righteousness;
> and all the peoples behold his glory.
> All worshippers of images are put to shame,
> who make their boast in worthless idols;
> all gods bow down before him.
> Zion hears and is glad. (97:6–8)

> Ascribe to the Lord the glory due his name;
> bring an offering, and come into his courts!
> Worship the Lord in holy array;
> tremble before him, all the earth!
> Say among the nations, "The Lord reigns"!
>   (96:8–10)

Yahweh comes in judgment to establish the reign of God
upon earth:

> Let the heavens be glad, and let the earth rejoice . . .
> before the Lord, for he comes,
> for he comes to judge the earth.
> He will judge the world with righteousness,
> and the peoples with his truth. (96:11–13)[11]

As in the case of the hymns so the background into which these enthronement psalms fit is that of the liturgical feasts of Israel. The special character of these enthronement hymns gives us reasons to suppose that they were originally designed for use in some more particular situation. By comparing different parts of these psalms with data which we already have from other sources — about such matters as the ascent to the throne and the coronation ceremony of the earthly kings of Israel and their exercise of power over the land — we can considerably clarify our ideas on this subject. We meet the "kingship cry" repeatedly in the sacred writings. When Absalom made himself king, couriers went round saying: "As soon as you hear the sound of the trumpet, then say, 'Absalom is king at Hebron'." (2 Sam 15:10) When Jehu was called to be king all the people took their cloaks and spread them on the stairway before him, blew their trumpets and shouted, "Jehu is king" (2 Kings 9:13). The new king was usually brought in solemn procession into the place where he took his seat upon the throne (1 Kings 1:32 ff.). Trumpets and the clapping of hands always accompanied these events: "So Jehoiada (the priest) brought out the king's son (Jehoash) and put the crown upon him, and gave him the testimony; and they proclaimed him king, and anointed him, and they clapped their hands, and said, 'Long live the king'." (2 Kings 11:12) The elders of the people then came up to the king and made a covenant with him (2 Sam 5:3), they brought gifts (1 Sam 10:27), and good wishes rang out: "As the Lord has been with my Lord the king, even so may he be with Solomon, and make his throne greater than the throne of my lord King David" (1 Kings 1:37–47). Messengers carried the good tidings of joy through the whole land that the new ruler had been crowned (Is 52:7). The people shouted while they clapped their hands: "He has become king. Long live the king!"

We find several of these particulars clearly set out in the enthronement psalms which deal with God's kingship. The subject matter of these psalms is sometimes the entry in procession into the temple, the actual enthronement, the royal garments, the sound of trumpets, the good wishes, the demonstration of loyalty by the members of the court, the army, the civil servants, and other subjects. The Norwegian biblical scholar, S. Mowinckel, was led by these data to conclude that there was an annual feast, dedicated to the enthronement of Yahweh, which took place on the first of the month Tishri. This was the Jewish New Year and fell shortly before the Feast of Tabernacles. Year after year Yahweh mounted his throne anew. The ceremonies that accompanied this feast were to a great extent derived by Mowinckel from the Babylonian Marduk feast. Other scholars do not feel moved to postulate a particular feast of enthronement on the basis of the enthronement psalms,[12] yet they stress emphatically the eschatological colouring of these songs. The universal empire of the future was specially celebrated in song during the feast of the kingship of Yahweh.[13] Again others point out that in fact the correct background of these psalms must be sought by studying a royal feast of Zion. Such a feast may be reconstructed from texts of the type of 2 Samuel chapters 6 and 7, and 1 Kings chapter 8, in which the Davidic dynasty and the fact of Zion's election were celebrated. This feast is supposed to have developed, during the exile, into a celebration of Yahweh's kingship.[14] Be this as it may, various details in these psalms point to a close connexion with the religious services of Israel. The Bible gives us no information about a festival to celebrate Yahweh's kingship; but it is understandable that the Hebrews would have celebrated in some form or other Yahweh's rule over Israel. This celebration may have been held regularly either on one of the great Israelite feasts, or in connexion with some particular historical events when Yahweh's kingship over Israel may have been specially commemorated. During this feast, as part of a still greater festival, the people glorified Yahweh as the king of Israel from the very earliest days, as the king of the members of the congregation present at the time, and finally as king of the universal empire that was to be established on the earth at some future date. "In this manner, history and eschatology became in the cultic ceremony a present reality of actual significance in which the festival congregation shares." [15]

Israel's religion moves upon three planes. So also in its liturgy, the present, the past, and the future are all bound together in a single religious exercise. The covenant, once entered upon, has its effect through all times. The generation of today joins itself to the covenant freely and consciously and with confidence looks for its full consummation when Yahweh shall be God and King of the whole earth. It is in a liturgy of this sort that we must look for the setting of the enthronement psalms.

God's immediate presence and God's kingdom are the great themes of these enthronement psalms. The focal point of the whole history of revelation is partnership between God and man. God comes close to man, he establishes his kingdom among children of men. The rule of God means that mankind is drawn into community with him. Yahweh is in fact king, but his kingship manifests itself to man only gradually. In the measure in which it was revealed, ever more and more clearly, in the history of God's chosen people, so gradually they began to understand it better. Yahweh was king because under his protection Israel has no further anxiety about its own persistence as a nation and of its victory over its enemies. The prophets say Yahweh's kingdom is realized in the kingdom of justice that they announced, in his "judgment" of Israel and of the heathen world. The later prophets visualized the creation by God of a new world where he would be always near at hand as king, while the apocalyptic writers saw the establishment of the kingdom of God take place by way of a series of world catastrophes. In the Wisdom literature God's kingdom is the fruit of gradual realization of his wise plans for the world. The New Testament proclaims the good tidings that the long-expected kingdom of God has come through the death and resurrection of Jesus, and that it is an interior kingdom, a kingdom of love. The Christian centuries live in expectation of the full revelation of God's kingdom at the end of time. All these truths are included in the single term "Kingdom of God". They are not opposed, not altogether different, and yet not identical. They hang together, and one idea leads to another. They are at the same time both announcements and fulfilments. They are a series of ever-increasing realizations of what is meant by companionship between God and man. They began in Israel and God now develops them still further in the Church.[16]

The psalms sing about God's nearness, about his kingdom. Israel knew Yahweh as its king from very early times. Already in the Song of Moses we read, "The Lord will reign for ever and ever" (Ex 15:18). The mysterious

prophet Balaam blessed Israel as the people over whom
Yahweh reigns (Num 23:21). The ancient war-cry was
"A hand upon the banner of the Lord! The Lord will
have war with Amalek from generation to generation"
(Ex 17:16), or "For the Lord and for Gideon" (Judg
7:18). When the Israelites desired that Gideon and his
sons and grandsons should reign over them, Gideon
answered: "I will not rule over you, and my son will
not rule over you; the Lord will rule over you" (Judg
8:23). In 1 Sam 8:7, Yahweh says to Samuel when
the nation asks for a king: "They have not rejected
you, but they have rejected me from being king over
them", so that Samuel on his retirement could say to
the people: "You said to me, 'No, but a king shall
reign over us', when the Lord your God was your king"
(1 Sam 12:12). All these texts show clearly that Yahweh's
kingship was accepted and experienced by Israel from
ancient times. It had for Israel immediate relevance to
the present but was, none the less, enduring and more
or less timeless. It is this real and actual kingship of
Yahweh that is celebrated in the psalms. Some few
examples must suffice:

> The Lord is king for ever and ever. (10:16)

> The Lord sits enthroned over the flood,
> the Lord sits enthroned as king for ever. (29:10)

> Yet God my King is from of old,
> working salvation in the midst of the earth. (74:12)

> The Lord has established his throne in the heavens,
> and his kingdom rules over all. (103:19)[17]

Yahweh's kingship was, however, still limited to and

bound up with Israel. He was present with his people; his presence was localized in the temple above the ark of the covenant. It was by this presence of Yahweh that Israel was held together as a nation apart. When they paid reverence to the ark they were celebrating the election of Israel as the chosen people of God, of Jerusalem, of Zion as the dwelling-place of God. God had chosen them before all other nations, he had chosen to dwell in these places. This intercourse between God and his people, the visible realization of the kingdom of God, was, however, only an image of another, inner and universal kingdom of God. Yahweh would not only dwell with the nation as a whole but with, and indeed in, every member of the covenant. Every man, and not only a descendant of Abraham, would be able to share in this covenant. It was the disaster of the Babylonian captivity that forced Israel to come to this point of view. When Yahweh's glory left the temple (Ezek 10:18 ff) the ark disappeared, and the temple was laid waste.

Yet even this terrible punishment proved to be a blessing in the loving hands of God. Amidst the ruins of a fallen theocracy a deeper and truer insight into God's mercy and faithfulness came to birth. Now the more spiritual Israel, with an understanding of God's inner and deeper manner of being present among them, began to develop. Jeremiah, Ezekiel, and Deutero-Isaiah prepared the nation for a truer coming of the kingdom after this pattern. The kingship of Yahweh was no longer just a present fact; it took on a future not limited to Israel alone but one that was to be for all nations. Jeremiah speaks of a new covenant: "I will put my law within them, and I will write it upon their hearts; and I will be their God, and they shall be my people . . . for

they shall all know me" (Jer 31:33 ff). Ezekiel prophesies: "Then I will make a covenant of peace with them;
it shall be an everlasting covenant with them; and I
will bless them and multiply them, and will set my
sanctuary in the midst of them for evermore" (Ezek
37:26). And, finally, we read in Deutero-Isaiah: "For
behold, darkness shall cover the earth, and thick darkness
the peoples; but the Lord will arise upon you, and his
glory will be seen upon you. And nations shall come
to your light, and kings to the brightness of your rising"
(Is 60:2–3). All the later prophets are full of this
universal expectation for the future and in the psalms
this future rule of Yahweh is sung:

> And all the families of the nations
> shall worship before him.
> For dominion belongs to the Lord,
> and he rules over the nations. (22:27–8)

> Because of thy temple at Jerusalem
> kings bear gifts to thee. (68:29)[18]

It is above all in the enthronement psalms that we find
references to the coming of the kingdom of God.[19] In
these psalms Yahweh himself is he who founds his kingdom on earth, but there is never a word about the
Messiah. God rules, clothed in might, he brings all good
with him, he is highly exalted, he has come to found his
kingdom upon earth. God's coming and the foundation
of his kingdom is at the same time an awe-inspiring
judgment. The psalms speak of Yahweh's terribleness,
the subjugation of peoples, of darkness, fire, and
lightening. Yet at the same time his coming means mercy
and all good fortune; he bestows on them their heritage:

it is the glory of Jacob whom he loves, and men must bear witness to his goodwill. He rules in justice and in peace and is mindful of his kindness and faithfulness. As a result of the conception of God's kingdom, as described by these psalms, come joy, great gladness with song and harp, joy in which the whole of creation must have its part: heaven and earth, seas, woods, trees and rivers, the fields and the mountains, all things must shout and sing, because Yahweh brings deliverance and establishes his kingdom upon earth.

We know that the kingdom of God came into being with the advent of Jesus. "From that time Jesus began to preach, saying, 'Repent, for the kingdom of heaven is at hand'." (Mt 4:17) In Jesus, God came among men, in him God established his rule among us. It was Yahweh himself who did this. In the person of Jesus of Nazareth God himself entered into world-history. It was the Father who raised Jesus from the dead, "whom God raised from the dead ... And there is salvation in no one else" (Acts 4:10–12). It is by this intervention that God has already laid the axe against the root of the tree, and the Messiah will go with his winnowing-fan in his hand to clear the threshing-floor (Mt 3:10–12). He comes in judgment but at the same time with help and salvation. He is set not only for the fall, but also for the rise of many, as Simeon, old and white-haired, had already prophesied (Lk 2:34). For "he who hears my word and believes him who sent me, has eternal life; he does not come into judgment" (Jn 5:24). No wonder, then, that the announcement of his coming is a gospel, glad tidings. Everything foretold in the enthronement psalms about the foundation of God's kingdom we see fulfilled in Jesus.

All this is also fulfilled in the life of the Church, in the inner loving presence of God to men of faith, in his indwelling in those living temples that are the faithful, in his real presence in the Eucharist compared to which the ark was no more than a faint shadow! In order to celebrate God's presence the Church daily makes use of Israel's time-honoured processional chants. She sings the enthronement songs which describe the joyous coming of God's kingdom. At the present time especially, when the peoples of Asia and Africa are becoming conscious of themselves, the Church is becoming more and more aware of her mission and is being forced to wrestle with tremendous missionary problems. Now more than ever we hear in these songs the call to take our share in the foundation of God's kingdom. The Church looks forward impatiently to the full revelation of the kingdom of God. In the enthronement psalms the joy of all created things is accompanied by the sighs and groans of all creation in labour and travail up to the present hour (Rom 8:21–22). The Church prays for a new heaven and a new earth. "Then comes the end, when he delivers the kingdom to God the Father ... When all things are subjected to him, then the Son himself will also be subjected to him who put all things under him, that God may be everything to every one" (1 Cor 15:24–28). As the enthronement psalms have sung for centuries, when God has judged the world and delivered mankind through his Son Jesus Christ, the whole of creation will share in the joys of the kingdom of the heavenly Father.

> All the ends of the earth have seen
> the victory of our God. (98:3)

CHAPTER 10

The Royal Psalms

We have seen that the future kingdom which is celebrated in the enthronement psalms is the reign of Yahweh. He has founded this empire and he is its ruler. When, however, we examine the actual manifestation of Yahweh's kingship in the theocracy of Israel and in the Messianic kingdom other regal figures appear alongside the figure of Yahweh. These are the earthly king of Israel and the Messianic king. Yahweh had appointed them as his representatives and in them, at one and the same time, his power as ruler, and his peaceful guidance, are embodied. Various songs in the book of psalms mention this royal figure, Israel's earthly King. He is described as the king's son, Yahweh's king, the anointed of Yahweh, and so on.[1] Eight psalms are entirely devoted to this kingly figure and show traces of a common background. The present chapter deals with these chants.

In order to put these royal songs in their correct setting we must identify them not so much with Yahweh's temple and Israel's religious ceremonies, as with the court of Israel's kings. There also great ceremonies and feasts took place, and, along with worldly splendour and pomp, religion at all times had a prominent place. Israel after having demanded a king to govern them like all the nations (1 Sam 8:5), had not been given a king of the same type as the kings of the surrounding nations. Israel's king was the prince in a theocratic kingdom and was not an autonomous ruler. Yahweh was the real king. His earthly representative was "the anointed of Yahweh", the one who was particularly dear to Yahweh, chosen out to reign over Israel (1 Chron 28:5). He was to walk before Yahweh "in simplicity of heart and uprighteousness" as David had done (1 Kings 9:4; 2 Chron 7:17). When the people paid homage to the king on his coronation day, or on his birthday or on the anniversary of his anointing, when they celebrated his wedding or his triumphal entry after a victory, he remained always the anointed one of Yahweh; thus through him they celebrated Yahweh. When they prayed for his recovery from an illness or for his success in a new campaign he was still endowed with a glorious promise of salvation. He was not only a military or political leader. On the contrary, Yahweh's love and care were concentrated, as it were, on him. Through him the promise of salvation for the people would be realized.

We can imagine that on occasions such as the above, in the palace or in the temple royal, songs were sung. The king and other great personages of the kingdom were present. Sometimes the king himself spoke the words, as in the case of the "speech from the throne" in psalm 101 or the prayer of psalm 144. On most occasions, however, the ruler's glory and integrity were sung by others (Pss 21 and 72). An oracle was made known to him (Pss 2; 20 and 110), or good wishes were expressed (Ps 45). Each one of these different kinds of royal psalms should be considered as yet another separate literary genre. They bear some relationship to the psalms of petition and also to the psalms of thanksgiving, the oracles, and so on. Yet, in spite of their resemblance to other groups, these eight songs form a group apart. They concentrate on the person of the king and they spring from a milieu quite different from that of the other groups. Thus a quite individual stamp was set upon them.

This unique character of the royal psalms can be clearly seen from the specific elements of which they are composed and which are repeated again and again. As the particular occasion which caused these psalms to be written was in each case different, we cannot arrange these elements together into one fixed pattern. Since, however, the general background of these psalms must be looked for in the milieu of the court, the same group of ideas come repeatedly to the fore. The first element we meet is the description of the ruler in all his splendour as it is given in psalm 45:

> You are the fairest of the sons of men;
> grace is poured upon your lips . . .
> In your majesty ride forth victoriously
> for the cause of truth and to defend the right . . .
> Your divine throne endures for ever and ever.
> Your royal sceptre is a sceptre of equity . . .
> your robes are all fragrant with myrrh and aloes
>   and cassia . . .
> at your right hand stands the queen in gold of
>   Ophir . . .
> The princess is decked in her chamber with gold-
>   woven robes;
> in many coloured robes she is led to the king,

with her virgin companions, her escort, in her train.
With joy and gladness they are led along ...

It is most striking that in this psalm the king throughout
holds a central position. The psalmist extols and glorifies
the king without giving a description of the marriage
feast as a whole. The king is a man of handsome
appearance; he is a warrior-hero; he proclaims truth
and justice; he is to occupy his throne for ever (which in
court parlance means a very long time); to be his wife
is a great honour for the bride; those who are in power
will make a bid for his favour; he will leave behind
him a great and puissant line of succession. A similar
description occurs in all the royal psalms. Psalm 2
emphasizes his kingly rule in Sion; Yahweh had delivered
the power of ruling into his hands. Psalm 110 enlarges
upon this still further; he will be victorious over his
enemies, and he will be the priestly mediator between
Yahweh and his people. At a special solemn feast of the
ruling monarch psalm 21 speaks of the rich blessings
received by the king, and about a crown of pure gold
that Yahweh has placed on his head, while a prayer for
the new monarch in psalm 72 describes the ideal king:
he will accomplish the covenant; he will bestow its gifts
upon all the people of Israel, and will be careful to give
a share to the poor and needy; he will reign for a long
while; his kingdom will grow and increase; foreign
potentates will bow before him; and his people will
enjoy great prosperity.

We see how in these royal psalms the king of Israel
is described just in the terms in which his people loved
to think of him and imagine him — buoyed up, as they
were, by living faith. He is the representative and the

most privileged of Yahweh's sons; he exercises as it were
a divinely bestowed power of ruling.

Yet another striking feature is revealed. All the
blessings and the prosperity enjoyed by the king are
explained by and attributed to Yahweh's divine favour.
Yahweh sets the king upon his throne in Zion (Ps 2)
and places him at his right hand (Ps 110). Yahweh
bestows on him a share in his ruling power, and, because
of the special task and offices held by the king in
Yahweh's name and as his presentative, he even calls the
king his son. On the day of the king's ascent to the
throne, Yahweh is said to bring forth his son, who is
born to enjoy honours that are specially sacred (Pss 2:7
and 110:3). All that the king owns is regarded as
Yahweh's gift to him; as king he is anointed with the
oil of gladness; he is chosen from among and set above
his companions; he is victor over his enemies (described
in the concrete in the thanksgiving psalm of a king,
Ps 18); he is ready and armed for battle, so that psalm
21 can truthfully sing:

> For thou dost meet him goodly blessings;
> thou dost set a crown of fine gold upon his head.
> He asked life of thee; thou gavest it to him,
> length of days for ever and ever.
> His glory is great through thy help;
> splendour and majesty thou dost bestow upon him.
> Yea, thou dost make him most blessed for ever;
> thou dost make him glad with the joy of thy
>   presence. (vv. 3–6)

The king is the beloved of God, as was also David the
prophet-king, ancestor of the Davidic house. This

accounts for the fact that so often an appeal is made on the king's behalf in the name of David, who is regarded as a guarantor that all the rulers of his house will be blessed.[2]

A third characteristic feature of these psalms consists in prayers and good wishes for the king. There are prayers at the beginning of his reign, prayers before battle is joined, and prayers too for a peaceful reign:

> May he send you help from the sanctuary,
> and give you support from Zion! (20:2)

> Give victory to the king, O Lord. (20:9)

> Give the king thy justice, O God,
> and thy righteousness to the royal son!
> May he judge thy people with righteousness,
> and thy poor with justice! (72:1–2)

For this reason they now offer the king their good wishes:

> May he grant you your heart's desire,
> and fulfil all your plans! (20:4)

> Let your right hand teach you dread deeds. (45:4)

In psalm 144 we hear the king himself at his prayers. He prays: "Deliver me from the hand of aliens", and then continues:

> May our sons in their youth
> be like plants full grown,
> our daughters like corner pillars
> cut for the structure of a place;
> may our garners be full,
> providing all manner of store;

> may our sheep bring forth thousands
> and ten thousands in our fields;
> may our cattle be heavy with young,
> suffering no mischance or failure in bearing;
> may there be no cry of distress in our streets!
> (vv. 12–14)

Then the king for his part promises Yahweh that he will himself live a virtuous life and practise social justice towards his entourage and his people (Ps 101). At the end of psalm 45 the singer, deeply moved by what he sees, prays that the king's posterity be numerous and powerful:

> Instead of your fathers shall be your sons;
> you will make them princes in all the earth.
> I will cause your name to be celebrated in all
> generations;
> therefore the peoples will praise you for ever and
> ever. (45:16–17)

Another no less outstanding feature of the royal psalms, which is their fourth characteristic, is the oracular utterance addressed to the king,[3] which appears again and again like an echo of the famous prophecy of Nathan to David (2 Sam 7:11–16; 1 Chron 17:11–14). The whole of psalm 2 resembles a prophetic address to all the nations and rulers of the earth, calling on them to acknowledge the king appointed by Yahweh. Verse 6 quotes Yahweh's actual words:

> "I have set my king
> on Zion, my holy hill."

There follows immediately the text of the oracle that Yahweh made known to the king as token of the latter's complete sovereignty:

> He said to me, "You are my son,
> today I have begotten you.
> Ask of me, and I will make the nations your
>   heritage,
> and the ends of the earth your possession.
> You shall break them with a rod of iron,
> and dash them in pieces like a potter's vessel."
>   (2:7-9)

Related to this is the oracular utterance of psalm 110 in which the king is solemnly assured that he may have his throne next to Yahweh's, and as victor may place his foot upon his enemies' necks while they prostrate themselves before him as his footstool.

Another oracle reserves to the king of Israel the office of mediator:

> The Lord has sworn
> and will not change his mind,
> "You are a priest for ever
> after the order of Melchizedek." (110:4)

Next to these oracles that refer to the kingship itself and that firmly portray the influence of the ancient East we find in psalm 20 an allusion to an oracle in which the king is promised victory in battle. The establishment and maintenance of the Davidic line was a religious event. It was the fulfilment of promises made by Yahweh, the realization of the destined gifts of the covenant

(20:7–9). There still remain a few more oracles bearing a relation to the kingship. One prophecy is expressly quoted, namely that of Nathan to David, in psalm 89:19 to 37, sometimes known as the people's psalm of petition, which implores Yahweh's help in the difficult situation with which both people and royalty are faced. A quotation of, or allusion to the same oracle occurs four times in psalm 132, namely in verses 1–2, 10, 11–12, and 17, as part of a prayer for the king and his people during a procession. The appeal to the promises made to David is made as to a perpetual guarantee of help and blessings: Yahweh will be true to his promise. We shall later on hear about the content and meaning of Nathan's prophecy in 2 Samuel 7:1–17.

In this way the eight royal psalms bring before our minds the image of Israel's king, the image of a ruler specially blessed by Yahweh, on whose behalf they pray for peace, and who knows himself to be strengthened by the divine promises. All these songs relate to the kings of the Old Testament period. In them we read how the people regarded the kingship as being a religious vocation and responsibility. As a national figure the king embodies in his own person all the qualities of the chosen people. He is the elected one, he enjoys the special favour of Yahweh, he is Yahweh's representative, and he is to give a tangible shape to, and realize the union of Yahweh with his people. In the very celebrations on the king's behalf the people were frequently reminded of their own election. When they were singing the royal psalms they did honour to their much-revered king precisely in so far as he was the anointed of Yahweh, and they experienced in his election a thrilling and conscious awareness of their own choice by God.

The king is habitually praised in the age-long fashion
of the East, and with expressions that savour of
ostentation. It is all part of the style customary in
Eastern courts, which recognize him as in a special sense
a son of Yahweh. Expressions such as "eternal", "the
whole earth", "generation after generation", and the like,
should not be taken too literally. Under the influence
of the ideas prevalent in the ancient East, such terms
are certainly admissible when addressed to Israel's king.
Many examples show that such terms, including even that
of divine sonship, were used and were meant to express
the people's conviction about their king's mission and
his relation with the deity. It would have been very
natural, to say the least, for the Israelites to adopt
expressions of this kind, if only because they desired
to retain a conspicuous place for the kingship among
the chosen people of God. It is therefore not at all
necessary to find Messianic allusions in the formularies
of the royal psalms. They are songs about Israel's earthly
kings.[4] Admittedly the Israelite kingship has already,
to some extent, of its own nature a Messianic dimension,
as we shall see later on. Still less are we obliged to
conclude that some of the royal psalms may be poems
of a later date, which according to the writer's intention
were meant to speak in the ancient symbolic language
of a primitive dynasty about the spiritual kingdom of
God, and which were directly employed as descriptions
of Messianic expectation in the future. The direct
meaning of those songs is concerned with the Israelite
king as he reigned on earth, who is praised and extolled
on the day of his accession to the throne, on the day of
his wedding feast, and on the day of his going forth to
battle. They are royal psalms which have preserved for

us the highlights of the religious and national experience of Israel, songs in which a strong faith is alive in God's presence among his people in the figure of the king.[5]

As we saw in the previous chapter Yahweh himself was the king of Israel. Yet the people, regardless of this, began when they were well and truly established in the promised land, to beg for a king such as other nations had (1 Sam 8:5). This king was at first refused to them, since the danger that the Israelites would like other nations range themselves behind a national leader and no longer acknowledge Yahweh as their king, was too great. When they did get a king it was more in the nature of a concession on Yahweh's part to the stupidity of his people than the gracious bestowal of a precious gift. Later Yahweh could still say, "I have given you kings in my anger, and I have taken them away in my wrath" (Hos 13:11). Yet kingship was truly a great gift from Yahweh to his people but one that, at the time, they were scarcely able to appreciate. Henceforward, Israel possessed in its leader "the anointed of Yahweh", the king of Israel was seated "upon the throne of the kingdom of the Lord" (1 Chron 28:5). He was not only great and "godlike" as were all the other kings of the ancient East. He was the chosen one of Yahweh, an instrument in the hands of the living God who wished to establish his reign upon the earth. Especially after the everlasting covenant that Yahweh entered into with the house of David, respect for the Israelite kingship was increased and its meaning was more clearly understood. The prophet Nathan had said to David, when the latter wished to build a temple to Yahweh: "Moreover the Lord declares to you that the Lord will make you a house. When your days are fulfilled and you lie down with your fathers, I will raise up your offspring after you, who shall come forth from your body, and I shall establish his kingdom. He shall build a house for my name, and I will establish the throne of his kingdom for ever; I will be his father, and he shall be my son. When he commits iniquity, I will chasten him with the rod of men; with the stripes of the sons of men; but I will not take my steadfast love from him, as I took it from Saul, whom I put away from before you. And your house and your kingdom shall be made sure for ever before me; your throne shall be established for ever" (2 Sam 7:11–16).

Yet the royalty of Israel fell in ruins. The kings proved faithless to their mission in a theocratic state by their taking to themselves powers that belonged to Yahweh alone, the real king,[6] the national royal line came to grief in the catastrophe of the year 587 B.C. Isaiah had foretold, however, that a sapling should spring out of the hewn-off trunk of Jesse (Is 11:1). This trunk had been cut down, but David's house would rise up again, purified and spiritualized in the Messianic ruler who would be appointed in God's kingdom. Many of the prophets speak of the new David who would rule in a coming kingdom of peace, justice, and mercy. "In that day I will raise up the booth of David that is fallen and repair its breaches, and raise up its ruins, and rebuild it as in the days of old" (Amos 9:11). "And I will set up over them one shepherd, my servant David, and he shall feed them: he shall feed them and be their shepherd. And I, the Lord, will be their God, and my servant David shall be prince among them; I, the Lord, have spoken" (Ezek 34:23–24).[7]

Because the faithful community of Israel was at a

certain moment incarnated in the structure of a state and a kingdom, the Bible speaks, after the exile and still in Christian times, about our salvation in metaphors which came into existence in this former kingdom. Even in our time we talk about "the kingdom of God"; the man who establishes his kingdom in God's name we call a king; he is the promised son of David. When Israel, after the Babylonian exile, sings the old royal songs in its liturgy, it sings them with a new accent and colour. These songs about God's presence, about his help and his blessings are now directed to the future, are now sung with a view to a coming time, full of hope and desire. The royal songs are now "prayers of hope".[8] They are now read with the eyes of Is 9, 11, and 32. The old expressions are now "eschatologized".[9] But gradually Israel forgot the relation of these songs to the wonderful acts of Yahweh's intervention. In spite of the spiritual features that were acknowledged in these songs by both the people and the prophets, especially by Isaiah, concerning the expected king and the kingdom over which he was to rule, the Jews after the captivity and in the time of the Maccabees held firmly to the expectation of an earthly Jewish empire that should centre round the person of a hero in the cause of freedom to whom at some future date the rulership of the world would be given. The kingship of the expected deliverer was more and more strongly stressed. He was going to be Yahweh's anointed one, the Christ, the Messiah who should come to liberate the nation, in a political sense.

Jesus is the Christ, the Messiah. In him God founds his kingdom upon earth. He is the king in that kingdom.[10] Yet Jesus laid no stress upon the title of king. He preferred to show that in him the prophecies of Isaiah about the "servant of Yahweh" were fulfilled (Lk 4:18–19). He allowed himself to be called "son of David" yet when the people would make him their king he withdrew alone into the mountain (Jn 6:15). At the entry into Jerusalem Jesus allowed himself to be honoured as a king and so the prophecy of Zechariah was fulfilled. "Lo, your king comes to you; triumphant and victorious is he, humble and riding on an ass, on a colt the foal of an ass" (Zech 9:9; Mt 21:5). But Jesus was always apprehensive lest the people should transfer their false ideas about the kingship of the expected Messiah to his own kingship.

He was not a Jewish national hero in the struggle for earthly freedom. When, in the Passion story, he could not avoid mention of his kingship he added immediately: "My kingdom is not of this world" (Jn 18:36).[11] Already during his public life Jesus had said that in himself psalm 110 was fulfilled: "How is it then that David, inspired by the Spirit, calls him (Christ) Lord, saying, 'The Lord said to my lord, Sit at my right hand, till I put thy enemies under thy feet'?" (Mt 22:41–46). The son of David is yet superior to David: he, Jesus, is the Lord proclaimed to the end of time.

The early Church always considered Jesus as king. The title with which they especially liked to refer to him was Lord, *Kyrios,* and they preferred to avoid using the title of king.[12] But when Paul and Silas proclaimed the Gospel in Thessalonica and a crowd of people dragged Jason and others of the brethren before the magistrates the accusation was, "they are all acting against the decrees of Caesar, saying, that there is another king, Jesus" (Acts 17:7). Psalm 2 played a great part in early Christianity as the foundation of the New Testament teaching about the lordship of Jesus. The same can be said of psalm 110, in which, as well as the enthronement at God's right hand, the triumph over all enemies is stressed. This triumph of Jesus was for them again prophesied in psalm 8 where it is said of, and about, man:

> Thou hast given him dominion over the works of
>   thy hands;
> thou hast put all things under his feet. (8:6)[13]

The confirmation of the lordship of Jesus was seen by the early Church in his Glorification on the occasion of his resurrection and ascension. There followed his enthronement by which he was installed as king, and whereby there came to pass a new aspect of lordship (Acts 2:36).

In the first chapter of the letter to the Hebrews, where the sublimity of Jesus is described, several passages from the royal psalms 2, 45, 110 follow one other. We see here how early Christian exegesis, contrary to that of Judaism which is built up primarily on the five books of Moses, looks back to the prophetic writings to which the psalms of the king and prophet David belong.[14] Is not Christ himself revealed most clearly and distinctly there? The books of the New Testament are full of the interpretation, inspired by the love of Christ, of the old texts. No wonder that already the faithful in the early Church read into psalm 72 the description of the life of the Church, in psalm 21 they found the triumph of their king described, and in psalm 45 they saw the glory of God's Son for whom the Church is as a bride (Eph 5:25–27), and in psalms 2 and 110 the might and final victory of their Lord.

The Messianic kingdom is only a sort of realization, a stage in the development of the kingdom of God. Jesus must be king "until he (the Father) has put all his enemies under his feet" (1 Cor 15:25).[15] As soon as everything has been made subject to him, then also the Son himself will surrender his kingdom to God the Father when he shall have brought to naught all other rule, so "that God may be everything to every one" (1 Cor 15:24–28). The theocracy of Israel is a thing of the past, the Davidic dynasty has born fruit in Christ and his kingdom at a spiritual and universal level; this Messianic kingdom will pass over into the heavenly kingdom, where God the Father rules as king for ever and ever.

In connexion with the royal psalms we shall now deal with the possible Messianic oracles that may be contained in the Book of Psalms.[16] The first question must be: "What really is Messianism?" We speak of Messianism in the strict sense of the word only, when the texts are concerned with the final redemption of man, and also with the king of those last days who will bring about this redemption. The texts must, therefore, have reference to that last king of all who will either establish the kingdom of God, or, in any event, will reign as Yahweh's representative. Apart from such texts, there exist also many eschatological writings which could be styled Messianic, but in a much broader sense, in which there is question of God's future dealing with men in the course of history (as, for example, in the enthronization psalms) or in which one can perceive evidence of certain expectations, such as those of the Davidic dynasty. An accurate analysis of the royal psalms has proved for certain that nowhere can we find in them any trace of the last king of all who will reign at the end of time. They are concerned with the earthly kings of David's line and not with the person of the Messiah. For this reason the royal psalms cannot be classed as directly Messianic. The original, literal meaning is centred upon the Israelite kings as they reigned in the earthly Zion. Yet a king of this lineage is connected with the Davidic dynasty upon which Messianic expectation was focussed (in terms of the Nathan-oracle recalled in psalms 89 and 132), so that every king of that dynasty in some sense participated in that expectation. What the royal psalms intended to make known was not so much the external course of Israel's kingly line as the deep religious meaning of God's condescension to his people in the person of the reigning monarch, so that God's power is present through the intermediacy of the king. The aim is the establishment of justice as the ideal covenant; the purpose is also the setting-up of Yahweh's sovereignty in and through the king. Since all existing opposition comes from the powers of evil, it is the king's task to gain the victory over the enemies of God's kingdom. Among his various functions is that of priest and mediator. We are here dealing once more with a vision inspired by a faith that is founded on the actual experience of ancient Israel. But this vision is still valid for later generations in similar circumstances, and the earlier wording of these psalms still continues to express what they experience in later times.

The realities of God's kingdom are throughout incarnated in a human and earthly manner. The post-exilic believers expressed their hope in a restoration and a new diffusion of God's kingdom by means of those royal texts that had already been in use in earlier centuries, and the early Christian Church did not hesitate to express in terms of these texts her own religious experience of Jesus and of his claim to be God's own representative. The dimensions have now altered, there is no longer a question of an earthly kingdom, of political enemies, of external weapons to be used against them. But the mystery is basically one and the same, even though it is now proclaimed in clearer and more explicit language. Through our Lord's death and resurrection the scene has completely changed, so much so that Jesus is now seen to be the fulfilment of those ancient royal texts. Now these texts are predicated of him, as we have already seen at an earlier stage. Jesus is the king, crowned, albeit with thorns (Mk 15:16–20) and acclaimed as king in an almost ironical manner in the inscription set by Pilate upon the Cross (Mk 15:26; Jn 19:18–22). This does not imply, however, that we should now interpret *all* New Testament texts as so many fulfilled prophecies of the Old Testament Scriptures. But the deepest and fullest interpretation (founded on one and the same sense of faith) — that God had established the kingdom by means of a king — now reveals the hidden meaning of those texts, formerly present only implicitly and in embryo. Even though we are unable in these or other psalms to discover a strictly Messianic reference, and must be content with Messianism in a much wider sense, we shall still be obliged to concede that Jesus had fulfilled and has given the most profound meaning to many passages in the psalms, in particular to those of the royal psalms and of many psalms of lamentation. All this is made possible because the ancient texts voice a similar experience of one and the same salvation. This living experience of God's saving power has had all through the ages the same inward objective, because it was always related to the dealings of the one God, ever identical in himself, with a similar child of Adam and a similar people of God. In so far as God revealed himself more, so the fashion of his dealings with men became clearer and more explicit. Although we do not consider the royal psalms to be Messianic in the strictest sense, we can, nonetheless, with ample justification ascribe to them a deeper and a truly Christian meaning.

In Appendix VIII may be found a list of all the New Testament quotations from the psalms, as they are given in the Dutch Willibrord Bible.[17] The passages here listed have, according to the interpretation of the New Testament authors, acquired a Christian meaning. No doubt the question remains open whether the quotation of a psalm in the New Testament, in its christological sense, should be regarded as a genuine exegesis of the text or whether it should be considered as no more than a use of the accommodative ones, as this is explained in the introductory handbooks to Scripture. Our personal view is that, in most instances, it is merely a question of arriving at a methodically exact and deeper understanding of the Scriptures. There are, moreover, many more psalms or parts of psalms that are not quoted in the New Testament, and that, when viewed in the light of Christ's revelation, are patient of a different and more profound meaning. We are aware of the extent to which the Fathers of the Church practised this type of Christian interpretation of the Old Testament. Because of their deep love for Christ our Lord, and their whole-hearted appreciation of his revelation, they were led to interpret the whole Psalter in a christological sense. Jesus himself had already made known to his disciples after his resurrection what had been written about the Son of Man "in the law of Moses and the prophets and the psalms" (Lk 24:44).[18] Thus Christian interpretation of the psalms was worked out more thoroughly by the Fathers. The fact that Christ made use of the psalms for his own prayers especially stimulated their interest. Such terms as the Man, the Just One, the Man of Sorrows, the Root of David, all these are so many prototypes of Christ in whom they were fully realized, and who in his own person most amply experienced being the Man, the Just One, the Man of Sorrows, and the heir to David's throne. The psalms thus understood become the voice of Christ praying to his heavenly Father. In them one may also hear the voice of Christ in his Church. The Old Testament community, the oppressed nation, the redeemed people of Israel, all these are a figure of the Church.

Apart from this ever-growing identification of the ancient consciousness of faith and of the new one, there was yet another way in which the psalms were interpreted.[19] Thus theological texts became christo-logical texts. This means that whatever part of the psalms was related to God, that is to Yahweh, was now understood as relating to Christ. Christ is the Lord *(Kyrios)*, the creator, the redeemer; he is even the Father, in the sense in which we address the Godhead as "Our Father". The psalms are no longer simply the voice of Christ praying to the Father. They are the voice of the Church, and the soul who addresses herself to Christ. This christo-logical interpretation of the psalms as it has been applied throughout the Christian centuries, was no doubt often exaggerated with a too individual and over-specific emphasis. On the other hand the continuation of the typological reference "from down below" (psalmist-Christ) and "from on high" (Yahweh-Christ) is based on a sound principle that is already adopted by the New Testament authors, and that may help us to recover a Christian vision of the psalms.

When praying the psalms in a truly Christian spirit one should be at pains to avoid a search for a fully detailed application that is not based on the religious experience of Israel. Rather, one should try to appreciate the text against the background of the Old Testament religion, and in union with the living consciousness of Israel's faith. Out of an appreciation of this kind of Old Testament mystery of faith, there may emerge a more developed experience of the New Testament. Because we consider as present in the Old Testament the promise, the expectation, and the anticipated realization of Christ in his mysteries, we should carefully distinguish the greater themes, the central events, and the actual Israelite institutions (such as the kingship), in order to attain to a sound Christian exegesis. It is evident that we must not limit ourselves to the Old Testament alone, but it is clearly imperative that we must not, at any time, attempt to force the meaning of the holy Scriptures.

CHAPTER 11

The Old and New Covenants

The Bible bears witness throughout to one thing, that there is a direct spiritual contact and association between God, the Holy One, and man. God has revealed himself to man, has shown himself and let himself be seen. He has come down to meet man in order to teach him to know God. The ultimate meaning of this revelation of God is to establish the relationship between God and man in the kingdom of God; that is indeed its whole purpose.

The certainty that this association between God and man exists is the foundation of the whole witness of the Bible in both the Old and the New Testaments. We must not think that in the Old Testament God is shown only as the hard despot, the God of fear, who knows nothing of the love that seeks personal contact. Just as the God of the New Testament is, and remains, not only a merciful Father and God of love but also, at the same time, the Holy One who is to be approached with awe: so also is the God of the Old Testament not only a God of fear but also Yahweh whose love *(ḥesed)* led him to make a covenant with his people. Throughout the Old Testament we find continued reference to the fellowship between God, the Holy One, and man. It is the central witness of the whole of the Sacred Writings and of each and every book of the Scriptures. It is round this association that all the psalms also centre.

Yahweh revealed himself to Israel in particular in all the events of history, in all his dealings for the benefit of his people. First of all we see the moulding and training of this heterogeneous group of people into a nation by means of the wonderful works of the Exodus from Egypt and their sojourn in the wilderness. Yahweh revealed himself in these events as a personal God who saves and redeems his people who have established friendship with him in the bond of the covenant at Mount Sinai. He revealed himself as a living God, ever present with his people and yet at the same time the holy and distant God. "There are always these two aspects to his activity: it is majestic and it inspires confidence."[1]

Whenever God reveals himself man's first reaction is terror, fear, awe, and trembling; in short, the fear of the Lord. God is holy, he is the sovereign majesty, the altogether pure, the unapproachable who is different and apart from all others. He, and he alone, is God. "That God is holy means, thus, that he is the absolutely perfect One, who is unapproachably great and far above and beyond all created things."[2] When the Holy One comes down to meet mankind, man experiences the greatness of God. When Yahweh spoke to his people from Mount Sinai and they experienced the awe-inspiring signs of that theophany, they trembled and stood a distance shuddering: "And they said to Moses, 'You speak to us, and we will hear; but let not God speak to us, lest we die'." (Ex 20:19) Yet God, in all his majesty, appeared precisely in order to enter into a covenant with Israel. "Israel's Holy One really concerns himself with the earth. He really intervenes in the lives of the individual and the nation."[3] He wishes to form together with Israel a family circle, a community. Thus is Israel absorbed into God's circle of life, is given a part in the terrible holiness of God and becomes a holy nation. "You shall be holy, for I the Lord your God am holy" (Lev 19:2 ff.). Israel is to be God's heritage, God's possession, bound to him and dependent on him. Yahweh makes the rules that must be observed within their community. If Israel obeys them it is sanctified. If Israel discards them then it is disloyal and refractory; yet, Yahweh, on his side, will never break the covenant. He will maintain the community life even if it is only with a "remnant". This covenant brings with it for the nation joy, trust, and certainty. The people know themselves to be God's people under his protection.

"This communion does not, however, do away with the holiness of God, the respect and distance between him and man. It is precisely in God's revelation that it becomes evident how God, who seeks communion with man yet remains God! Even as the God of the covenant he remains inscrutable in holiness for his people. God does not reveal himself to man in such a way that man could see through him, that man could enter into his thoughts; on the contrary, when he reveals himself he rather makes him conscious of his glory, and brings him to adoration, not only when he acts in his judgments, but also in his work of salvation. His exceptional eternal goodness emphasizes his majesty."[4]

Yes, we can almost say that, just because of his transcendence, God is so inescapably near. He surrounds

and permeates our whole life, he is the basic element in
every human heart. He is more intimate with us than
we are with ourselves. Just because he is the creator
who is so "immeasurably above created things he can enter
into their deepest heart".[5]

> For I am God and not man,
> the Holy One in your midst,
> and I will not come to destroy. (Hos 11:9)[6]

The totality of Israel's life and belief revolves upon these
two truths, the majesty and the love of God, Yahweh,
his immeasurable distance and his inescapable nearness,
his transcendence and his immanence. And all this has
taken shape in the covenant between Yahweh and Israel,
and the spiritual climate in which the psalms are set is
precisely this idea of a covenant. Yahweh has chosen
Israel from all other nations, Israel is Yahweh's people.
We find every possible reaction, both in the individual
human heart and in the nation's life, to this intervention
of God put into words in the psalms and then expressed
in song.

As we survey the various groups of psalms in the way
we have done in this book we can enumerate their themes,
their principal ideas such as creation, deliverance, the
people of God, God's kingdom, sin, suffering, the city
of God, kingship, the Messiah, the temple, and the Law.
All these themes are focussed upon the idea of the
covenant, which is their point of departure. God's
nearness in the covenant gives joy to the heart. Man
knows himself to be in very truth a beloved creature,
as redeemed and as a member of God's people. The
nation obtained from Yahweh a king, a city, a temple,

and a Law. Because of this they exulted and rejoiced greatly in the psalms of praise and of thanksgiving. They sang their psalms in procession and on royal occasions and shouted: "Yahweh is our God; he blesses us, he saves and redeems us, he takes us into his own community." But at the same time they were well aware, through experience, that Yahweh was not only near at hand but that he was the Holy One, the distant, unapproachable One who seemed to grow more remote in proportion to a man's faithlessness and self-will which disturb the pure relationship of the covenant. Thence comes the pain of man's inadequacy, man's sinfulness, by reason of which there is suffering and injustice in the world. The covenant is not yet perfected, the communion with God is still incomplete and not guaranteed to last. The people expressed and gave vent to their feelings about their own miseries in the psalms of petition, which express as a prayer the nation's and the individual's cries for pity. The knowledge of his wealth and his povertry dwelt side by side in the heart of the Israelite: on the grounds of what he might already claim to possess and of what he still lacked, he fixed his hopes on the day in which God would give still more of himself, would draw man still nearer to himself. He looked forward to the time when there would be a still deeper communion with God and when God would give him a greater share in his glory. In the enthronement and royal psalms the psalmist sang of this future happiness, and looked forward to the reign of God, to the new king, to re-creation and salvation, to what Jeremiah calls "the new and everlasting covenant", the full communion with the Holy God. To put it briefly, the covenant was his kingdom and at the same time his torment. This first association with God that was given to Israel was its greatest happiness, but at the same time it exhibited man's poverty and sinfulness. "Some bottomless depths of the soul of man are exposed by the burning light of revelation." [7]

The idea of the covenant provides a coherent explanation of the psalms. Therefore Arthur Weiser has quite rightly made an attempt to see all the psalms from this point of view. He even thinks he can conclude that there existed a feast of the covenant in Israel and brings almost all the psalms into relationship with such a feast. [8] This celebration of the covenant has not been reconstructed according to the Babylonian model as was done by S. Mowinckel for the feast of a king's accession to the throne; nor has it been centred round the human figure of Israel's king as was the royal feast of Sion by H. J. Kraus. This feast of the covenant was purely Israelite and its central point was Yahweh and his pact with the people of Israel. The appearance of Yahweh on Mount Sinai was remembered and so far as was possible staged by means of scriptural readings, clouds of incense, trumpet blasts, and such-like.

Be this as it may, it sounds in no way improbable that a renewal of the covenant took place at regularly repeated intervals in the temple of Jerusalem and that many of the psalms we know were sung there in their original setting. The Scriptures themselves give us in various places indications of the existence of such a covenant feast. In Deuteronomy, chapters 26 to 30, Moses swore to the people that the covenant would be kept, not only by those then living, but by all the generations of Israel. In chapter 24 of the book of Joshua we read about a formal renewal of the covenant in Shechem after the death of Joshua. The second book of Chronicles, chapters 29 to 31, speaks about the reforms under King Hezekiah, about a new dedication of the nation to Yahweh, while chapter 23, verses 1 to 3 of the second book of Kings and chapter 34, verses 29 to 33 of the second book of Chronicles, report the renewal of the covenant under King Josiah. We are told that from the time of Ezra a reading of the Law took place with expressions of assent on the part of the people (Neh 8). Instructions for a frequent revival of the proclamation of the Law are already given at the time of the deuteronomic reform (Deut 31:10–13). If the covenant was to be renewed and strengthened from time to time then the gatherings and celebrations of pilgrims in Jerusalem bear witness to this, and we find here a setting in which the psalms were to be sung.

In any event we reach the following conclusion: the psalms were born out of the experience of a nation living under the Old Testament covenant with all the tensions caused by the two apparently opposed facts of God's holiness and his nearness, which were a result of this covenant. They celebrated in song the great spiritual wealth and need of men who had been drawn into the holy community of God.

"In these last days God has spoken to us by his Son" (Heb 1:2). "Jesus Christ is God's epiphany in a living form. In him the hidden God stands fully revealed in history."[9] This ultimate and definitive revelation of God is in its turn intended to bring all mankind into a circle of communion with God. It is especially God's "love", "goodwill", and "love of mankind" (Tit 2:11, 3:4) that became perceptible; the revelation in Christ is the revelation of Love. God approaches near to us, the God-made-man is our Emmanuel, our God-with-us. God is our Father, and we are his adopted children. Jesus Christ, who "pitched his tent amongst us", is our brother. And the living law of love, which is the Holy Spirit, dwells within us. Here, indeed, we have an altogether new type of revelation! Here God has really and truly entered into the community of man. Now most certainly the accent has fallen on goodness, love, and trust!

Yet it remains true that the God, who draws us into his own circle of life, is the Holy God of an awe-inspiring majesty. The accent on love that we find in the New Testament is placed against the background of the Old Testament idea of the holiness of God. "Before this last and definitive revelation that God is Love a period was allowed to precede it in which the image of the Holy God was deeply imprinted and experienced, and this idea has become so profoundly rooted that it would be impossible to eliminate it." [10] God's approach to us must never lead to too great a familiarity on our part. We need a pure and true idea of God, the *sens de Dieu*. How easily can it happen that God becomes in some way commonplace so that we lose the appreciation of his holiness! "A Christianity which had ceased to be aware of this ultimate fact of the opposition between God and his creatures, would have lost that note of absolute urgency without which the Gospel entrusted to it can never be other than unthinking and superficial." [11] It is striking how the real spirituality of Christian monks, as it comes to us, for example, in the seventh chapter and innumerable other places in the rule of St Benedict, is firmly established on reverence, on awe for God's transcendent majesty, on the Old Testament "fear of the Lord". Even if love does exclude servile fear and the heavenly vision banish the childish dread of separation, still reverence, trembling awe, and holy fear in the presence of God's infinity will always be present.

Christian faith knows both the terrible majesty of God *and* his love, his complete otherness and his nearness. Yes, the new, startling and final thing about the New Testament revelation is precisely this blending together of the altogether Holy with real and perfect Love. The transcendent Absolute is here made into the living and concrete by Love. Love, on the other hand, becomes fuller, deeper and more real through the Infinite and the Absolute.[12] The descent of God is now made concrete in the community which God has founded in Jesus' blood of the new covenant (Mt 26:28). The deliverance described in Exodus, which was an image and a preparation, has been followed by the salvation that has come through the death and resurrection of Jesus. This is the kingdom of the new covenant; God delivers us, we have the right of access to him, we are his children, we live in Christ and have received the Holy Spirit. The early Church instinctively appreciated the unbroken continuity between the Old and New Testaments. She took the psalms as the best interpretation of her joy in her salvation.

But the new covenant has also its reverse side. It means our fellowship with the Holy God. In spite of the fact of his deliverance man is still in bondage. He is sinful and unfaithful. Suffering and sin are his daily bread, and death awaits him at the end. But the Church has been given an interpretation of this anguish of mind, uncertainty, and pain in the songs of penance and lamentation of Israel. It is of both the riches and indigence of her children that the Church sings in her psalms, voicing all the trust and the despondency that membership of the community of God brings with it for man's unstable nature. And as Israel, the people of the covenant beloved by Yahweh, looked forward to the coming of the Messiah and the fullness of the kingdom of God, so does the Church, the bride of Christ and the new people of God, look forward to the coming of Christ in glory and the heavenly fellowship in the vision of God. It is the psalms that can interpret these longings, this forward-looking hunger as it is expressed in the New Testament, in the same way as they did for the people of the Old Testament period.

The faithful bear witness to their great riches, their immense need and their expectation, all products of the New Testament communion with God, most especially when they are called together to celebrate the covenant in the liturgy. Therefore the psalms must take a great place in liturgical celebration. We have just spoken about a feast of the covenant, if such there was in the Old Testament, when the covenant was renewed. That was possible, and almost probable, in Old Testament times; it is a full reality and a certainty in the New Testament. We find celebration and renewal of the covenant in our liturgy, especially in the celebration of the Eucharist, when Golgotha becomes present among us sacramentally. Just as the psalms were used in an Old Testament renewal of the covenant, so the Church brings them into her breviary prayers and her choir chants in union with the daily presentation of Christ's sacrifice in the holy Mass. In the Mass and in the sacraments God continues his work of salvation among us. There the Holy God enters into communion with sinful man, there we celebrate our salvation brought to us by the death and resurrection of Jesus, there we look forward to the full communion at the end of time, and it is there also that the psalms have their rightful setting, for the Christian.

In this book we have tried to discover the religious themes of the psalms. We must endeavour to place these themes in their right perspective, namely, in the light of the covenant in which man's life is absorbed into that of God. That covenant, brought to perfection by Jesus, the Church celebrates and lives out in her daily worship, especially in the mystery of the Eucharist. It is with the psalms that the Church prepares herself for the repeated meeting with God in the sacrifice of Christ. It is with the psalms that she thanks God when he has fortified and developed anew his fellowship with her. In the phase in which we are now living the psalms come fully into their own, because they are concerned with God's actions in the mystery of the holy Mass. They are sung by the Church now when she comes to meet him who is both holy and present, now when she experiences the riches of salvation and the neediness of the pilgrim state, now when she looks forward with longing to the full communion with God in heaven, where all the uncertainty of man's life on earth shall be at an end. The psalms are the songs of the New Covenant!

Author's Notes

References to the abundant literature have been kept to a minimum in view of the nature of this book. References in the Notes to works listed in the Bibliography at the beginning of the book are by author and short title only. English translations are preceded by the abbreviation, E. T.

1. The Psalms as Christian Prayer

[1] Rule of St Benedict, end of ch. 19.

[2] Origen's Commentary on St John 13:60, Migne, PG 14, 517; *Series super Matth.* 79, PG 13, 1729.

[3] Strictly speaking, the Old Testament runs from the time of Abraham to the time of Christ.

[4] See H. Renckens, *De Godsdienst van Israel,* Roermond (1962), pp. 63–66. Also Grelot, *Sens chrétien,* pp. 426–7 and 458.

[5] "The author of the Letter to the Hebrews reads the whole of the Old Testament with Christian eyes. For him it has become the Christian Bible and is no longer only the Jewish one. Nor can it be otherwise; a Christian must necessarily read it differently from a Jew." "The existence of this fuller significance *(sensus plenior)* has as its basis the harmony that God has willed to exist between the two Testaments, which are related to each other as the imperfect to the perfect." J. van der Ploeg, OP, in *Revue Biblique* 54 (1947), pp. 227–8.

[6] *Acta Apost. Sedis* (1950), 551; *Enchiridion Biblicum* (1954), 599.

[7] Charlier, *Christian Approach*, p. 247.

[8] Kraus, *Psalmen*, tries in his commentary under "Ziel" to transpose the theological theme of every psalm to the New Testament plane. George, *Prier*, gives also a Christian interpretation of the psalms discussed. T. Worden, *The Psalms are Christian Prayer,* London (1962), deals with several themes out of the Book of Psalms, and strongly emphasizes their Christian meaning. The Lutheran scholar, N. Müller, published a very instructive monography about the meaning of the psalms in the liturgy: *Die liturgische Vergegenwärtigung der Psalmen,* Munich (1962).

2. The Origin of the Book of Psalms

[1] That Yahweh was replaced by Elohim appears, for example, from a comparison of psalm 14 with psalm 52 and psalm 40 with 70. This is also clear from the expression "God, my God" which originally appeared as "Yahweh, my God". See 43:4; 45:7; 50:7, for examples.

[2] G. Bouwman, in *Heilige Land* 6 (1953), pp. 24–27 41–44.

[3] R. Tournay, OP, *Les Psaumes (Bible de Jérusalem),* Paris (1950), p. 16.

[4] Doxologies, or the praises of God, are found in psalms 41:13; 72:18, 19; 89:52; and 106:48.

[5] A. Arens, *Die Psalmen im Gottesdienst des Alten Bundes,* Trier (1961), pp. 160–216.

3. Hebrew Poetry

[1] On the power of the Hebrew word-accent, see T. H. Robinson, *The Genius of Hebrew Grammar,* London (1928), p. 8, where it is compared to the crash of a great wave on a beach: "You have from the start the same hurrying movement, almost impatient of the obstacles present by the intractable pure long vowels, surmounting such as may lie in its way and speeding eagerly till it nears the tone, and then the whole hangs for a moment in suspense in the immediate

pre-tone before it falls with all its crashing force of sound and sense upon the great word-accent."

For fuller details of Hebrew poetic usages, consult Robinson's *The Poetry of the Old Testament,* London (1947), ch. 2, "The Forms of Hebrew Verse" — Editor's note.

[2] Knowledge and study of the Hebrew metrical system is important because it sometimes indicates corrections, changes, or displacements in the text of verses or half-verses; it can be a valuable aid in studying these old, often poorly transmitted texts.

4. THE VARIOUS TYPES OF PSALMS

[1] H. H. Rowley, *The Growth of the Old Testament,* London (1950), Introduction.

[2] Gunkel is followed by, among others, H. Schmidt, A. Weiser, F. Böhl, H. Kraus, and in the Catholic camp by E. Vogt SJ, J. Steinmann, E. Podechard PSS, A. Descamps, G. Castellino, and A. George, while A. Robert PSS and R. Tournay OP go more or less their own way, even though they make use of several results of Gunkel's system. See the bibliographical survey of J. Coppens, *Études récentes sur le Psautier,* in *Le Psautier,* (Louvain (1962), pp. 1–79.

[3] *Enchiridion Biblicum,* 556–9. See the translation of the encyclical in *Biblical Studies,* Catholic Truth Society, London, pp. 39–42.

[4] *Les Questions liturgiques et paroissiales* 35 (1954), p. 252.

[5] W. Grossouw in *Gedenkboek Thijmgenootschap,* Amsterdam (1954), p. 44.

[6] Encyclical *Mediator Dei.* See *Christian Worship,* Catholic Truth Society, London, pp. 176–7.

[7] See, for example, Deut 5:3; 6:20 ff.; 26:5, 16–19; Ps 95:7–8.

[8] R. Guardini, *Vom Geist der Liturgie,* Freiburg (1957), pp. 61 ff.

[9] The following psalms are alphabetic: 9; 10; 25; 34; 37; 111; 112; 119, and 145.

[10] W. Grossouw, in *Gedenkboek Thijmgenootschap,* p. 43.

[11] Therefore it would be imprudent to try to give at this stage a summary of the development of the psalms and the different types

of psalms within the religious and literary history of Israel. For this reason we shrink from agreeing with the conclusions of R. Tournay OP in his recent articles in the *Revue Biblique*, about the post-exilic origin of many psalms. Some new commentaries already try to fix a date for several of the psalms. The study of P. Bonnard, *Le Psautier selon Jérémie*, Paris (1960), examines thirty-three psalms for their affinities with the book of Jeremiah.

5. THE PSALMS OF PRAISE, OR HYMNS

[1] See the psalms: "Clap your hands, all peoples!" (47:1) and with poetic licence, "Let the floods clap their hands" (98:8).

[2] See, for example, Ps 118:1–4; and 136. In Hebrew this cry is *"Ki le 'olam ḥasdo"* short with two ictus and thus easy for the people to shout together.

[3] As is sometimes the case now, poets and musicians only get recognition after their death.

[4] Compare in the psalms: stretching out of hands, 28:2; 77:2; 134:2; 141:2, bowing down and prostration, 5:7; 29:3; 86:9; 95:6; 96:9; 138:2, kneeling, 95:6.

[5] "Heaven" is a roundabout way of saying the name Yahweh which in later days was considered too holy to be uttered. Thus in the same way in the Gospel "Kingdom of Heaven" is nothing other than "God's kingdom" and does not indicate in this context "the heavens".

[6] In the Revised Standard Version the name of Yahweh has been translated as the Lord.

[7] This invitatory formula would seem to be the original, the primitive form of the later psalms of praise. See Gunkel, *Einleitung*, p. 43.

[8] See further, for example, 47:2, 7; 95:3; 98:1, 9; 135:3–4.

[9] See further, for example, 103:3–5; 147:7–9. Hebrew participles are often translated through English relative or independent clauses.

[10] See further, for example, 135:19–21; 136:26.

[11] For the application of what has been said up to now about the psalms of praise as a class, see the schemes in Appendix II.

[12] Gunkel, *Einleitung*, p. 58.

[13] A. Weiser, *The Psalms*, p. 55.

[14] The idea of creation and of God as Creator and Lord of nature is the governing theme of psalms 8; 19; 29; 33; 104; and 148. References to the creation occur in 135; 136; 145; and 146. The idea of deliverance predominates in 105; 135; and 136. In psalms 111; 145; 146; 147; and 148, and especially in the pilgrims' psalms, the processional hymns, and the enthronement psalms, we find pronounced references to deliverance.

[15] Vriezen, *An Outline*, p. 187.

[16] Renckens, *Israel's Concept*, p. 60.

[17] G. Wright.

[18] Eichrodt, *Theology*, I, p. 431.

[19] For further examples see, Amos 3:1; Jer 2:6; Deut 13:5.

[20] Six psalms of petition (44; 74; 77; 80; 83, and 106), four psalms of praise (105; 114; 135, and 136), three pilgrim psalms (78; 81, and 95), one processional psalms (68) and one psalm of thanksgiving (66).

[21] Compare the prophets Hos 2:16–18; Is 43:16 ff.; Jer 31:31–34; and others.

[22] See chapters 8–9 and 15–16.

[23] Compare also Rom 3:24; 1 Pet 2:9–10.

[24] W. Förster, *Theologisches Wörterbuch zum N. T.* III, 1005, art. κτίζω; see too the rest of the article, 999–1034.

[25] Renckens, *Israel's Concept*, p. 62.

[26] P. Schoonenberg, *Het Geloof van ons Doopsel* I (The belief of our baptism) 's-Hertogenbosch (1955), p. 60.

[27] The hemistich in brackets is not found in the Hebrew masoretic text, but occurs in the Septuagint Greek, and is easily restored according to Ps 104:14 — Editor's note.

[28] For further examples, see Ps 33:13 ff.; 104:27 ff.; 113:5–9; 145:13b–20; 146:7 ff.; and 147.

[29] Compare Ps 121:2.

[30] Further, see especially Ps 19 a, 104, and 148:5–6.

[31] Renckens, *Israel's Concept*, p. 90.

[32] The "fear of the Lord" is, in the first place, the reaction of a man to the revelation of the Holy God: he is filled with reverence

and awe. But for the total experience, in the Old Testament sense, this reaction is unthinkable without the resulting strict observance of God's will; just so, in reverse, the numinous fear of the Holy God must be active in us as the groundwork of every experience of the Law of God. In most cases the "fear of the Lord" means what we call piety, devotion, and dedication. A God-fearing man is a believing man, a dedicated man, an upright man.

[33] Renckens, *Israel's Concept,* p. 88.

6. THE PSALMS OF THANKSGIVING

[1] See also Ps 111:1; 71:15–18, 22–24.

[2] Deut 16:11, 14; 26:11; 1 Sam 9:13, 22, 23, etc.

[3] E. Vogt, SJ, in *Biblica* 34 (1953), pp. 195–211.

[4] A. Weiser, *The Psalms,* p. 85.

[5] Ps 41:4; 116:11; Is 38:10; Jon 2:4. Compare Ps 30:6; 31:22.

[6] See M. Delcor, *Les Hymnes de Qumran, Hodayot,* Paris (1962), pp. 19 ff.

[7] See psalms 3; 6; 13; 26; 28; 31; 52; 54; 56; 57; 61; 69; 71; 86; 109.

[8] Such a prophetic oracle we find in psalms 12:5 and 62:11. See also Chapter 8, note 8 and Chapter 10, note 3.

[9] *The Psalms,* p. 79. For the application of what has been said up till now to particular psalms of thanksgiving, see the schemes set out in Appendix III.

[10] Gunkel, *Einleitung,* p. 272.

[11] So psalms 9; 92; 105; 107; 111; 118; 136; 138 begin with the Hebrew verb *hodah* rendered in the new Latin translation mostly by *celebrare* but in the Vulgate by *confiteri* which is to be preferred because it includes the motion of bearing witness.

[12] A. Weiser, *The Psalms,* p. 84.

[13] See further, Ps 32:6; 34:11 ff.; 40:4; 51:14; 58:11; 107:42–43; 145:11–12.

[14] For the use of the psalms 22, 31 and 118 in the New Testament, see Appendix VIII. See also Grelot, *Sens,* pp. 463, 471.

[15] Compare Heb 2:12.

[16] Rom 1:8; Col 3:17.

[17] L. Bouyer, "Psaumes et Catéchèse" in *La Maison Dieu* 33, p. 18.

[18] J. Daniélou, "Le Psaume 22 (23) et l'initiation chrétienne" in *La Maison Dieu* 23, pp. 54–69.

[19] The phrase *"praeclarum calicem"* (Ps 23) appears in the Canon of the Mass; the expression *"calicem salutaris"* (Ps 116) is found in the Offertory prayer and in the Communion prayer.

[20] See further, Ps 9:11; 18:49; 138:4–6.

[21] See the schemes in Appendix III.

7. THE PSALMS OF PETITION

[1] Compare Job 7:6, "My days are swifter than a weaver's shuttle."

[2] Is 8:19; 29:4. Compare Is 14.

[3] Ps 6:5; 30:9; 88:10–12; 115:17; Is 38:18.

[4] See psalms 16:9; 30:3; 49:15; 86:13; 89:48.

[5] See further, psalms 31:11–13; 35:15–16; 109:22–25.

[6] See Jer 5:26; 22:3; Amos 5:12; among others.

[7] Ps 7:15; 54:5; 55:15–23; 57:6; 64:8; 69:22–28, for example. We find the classic formulation of the *lex talionis* in its broadest significance in Ex 21:23–25, a text out of the *"Book of the Covenants of Moses."*

[8] Ps 122:5, "There thrones for judgment were set, the thrones of the house of David."

[9] Hunters, Ps 7:12–13; 35:4–6; 57:6; 64:5; 140:5; Robbers, 17:9 to 11; 56:5–6; Dogs, 59:14–15; Snakes, 58:4–5; Lions, 7:2; 17:12; 57:4; 58:6. Here we must mention also the attestations of innocence (Ps 7:3–5; 17:1–5; 26:2–6; 35:7; and so on), which look sometimes like a hymn on the greatness of Yahweh, who searches and knows man (Ps 139:1–18). Also the appeal to the right of asylum in the temple (Ps 27; 36; and 57). The above-mentioned is a means to get justice from Yahweh. See also Deut 17:8–13. For details about

justice and processes, see R. de Vaux, *Les Institutions de l'Ancien Testament*, I, Paris (1958), pp. 221–50, E. T. *Ancient Israel: its life and institutions*, London (1961).

[10] See, for example, Num 11:11–15 (Moses); Josh 7:7–9 (Joshua); 1 Kings 17:20 (Elijah); Jer 15:17–18; 20:7 (Jeremiah).

[11] Vriezen, *An Outline*, p. 173.

[12] Renckens, *Israel's Concept*, p. 95.

[13] For schemes of private psalms of petition see Appendix IV, A.

[14] 1 Kings 8:33 ff.; 2 Chron 20:9; 1 Macc 4:37.

[15] 1 Sam 7:6; 1 Macc 3:47; Jud 4:8 ff.

[16] Josh 7:7–9; 2 Chron 20:6–12; Ezra 9:6–15; Neh 9:6–37; 1:5–11.

[17] Further, for example, Bar 1:15 to 3:8.

[18] See the schemes of communal psalms of petition set out in Appendix IV, B.

[19] Gunkel, *Einleitung*, p. 238.

[20] Gunkel, *Einleitung*, p. 185.

[21] For example, Ps 9; 10; 25; 34; 37; 22:26; 69:32–33; 74:19; 85:1–2; 132:15; 149:4.

[22] J. v. d. Ploeg, *Oud testamentische Studien* 7 (1950), p. 265.

[23] A. Gelin, *Les pauvres de Jahwe*, Paris (1953), p. 57.

[24] W. Grossouw, *Bijbelse Vroomheid*, Utrecht (1954), p. 200.

[25] See Dodd, *Scriptures*, pp. 96–101; Grelot, *Sens*, p. 436.

[26] See H. Duesberg, OSB, "Le psautier en Carême" in *La Maison Dieu* 31, pp. 102–31.

[27] See Gunkel, *Einleitung*, pp. 254–6.

[28] G. Castellino gives in his commentary an excellent description of these psalms. He calls them "wisdom-psalms" and groups them together in almost the same manner as we do here. See *Libro*, pp. 728–31.

[29] "A favourite subject is the instruction about *the destinies of good and evil people* as in psalms 1 and 112." S. Mowinckel in "Psalms and Wisdom" in *Supplements to Vetus Testamentum*, III (1955), p. 214.

[30] Compare A. Descamps in *Mélanges Robert*, Paris (1955), p.

196 on psalm 119 "où dominent les thèmes de la complainte individuelle."

[31] Compare psalms 1; 52; 112; 119; 127; and 128.

[32] On psalm 119 compare the extensive commentary by A. Deissler, *Psalm 118 (119) und seine Theologie*, Munich (1955). In his analysis of this psalm Deissler rightly makes use of the so-called anthological method.

[33] Compare psalms 10; 11; 12; 14; 53; 75; 94, and 125.

[34] See psalms 37; 49, and 73.

[35] See J. Coppens, *Het Onsterfelijkheidsgeloof in het Psalmboek* (The belief in immortality in the Psalter), Brussels (1957). For schemes of the group of psalms discussed above, see Appendix IV, C and D.

8. THE PILGRIM PSALMS

[1] Compare Ps 42:4.

[2] Eichrodt, *Theology* I, p. 212.

[3] See further, Amos 5:5, 21; 8:10, 14; Is 29:13.

[4] See further Is 60:1 ff. "The mountain of the house of the Lord" is of course, Mount Zion, the site of the temple.

[5] These gates were not simply doors but complete buildings. See Jer 7:2; 36:10; Ezek 40:6–37 among other sources.

[6] Jer 3:2; Ps 78:58: "For they provoked him to anger with their high places; they moved him to jealously with their graven images."

[7] Psalms 50; 78; 81; 115; and 134 show a clear connexion with the cult. They probably came into being for use in Israel's worship of God. Psalms 1; 19b, and 119 show no signs of being connected with the cult; they were thus merely made use of in the liturgy in later ages.

[8] See Is 1:11 ff.; Jer 7; Amos 7:10. We find traces in psalms 46:10; 50:7 ff.; 60:6–8; 75:4–5 81:6 ff.; 85:8–9; 87:4; 91:14; and 95:8 ff. See also Chapter 6, note 8, and Chapter 10, note 3.

[9] See also Y. Congar, *The Mystery of the Temple*, London (1962).

[10] Together with the building of the Body of the Church we find, in Eph 2:21–22, reference to the building of the spiritual temple which is the Church; also the individual believer is God's temple, in him is God also present. See 1 Cor 3:16; 6:19; 2 Cor 6:16.

9. THE PROCESSIONAL AND ENTHRONEMENT PSALMS

[1] 1 Sam 4:4; 2 Sam 6:2; 2 Kings 19:15; Ps 80:1; 17:11; Dan 3:55; etc.

[2] For a description of the ark, see Ex 37:1–9. The mercy seat on the ark was the place of God's presence, the empty throne: on the great Day of Atonement the mercy seat ἱλαστήριον was sprinkled with blood by the high priest (Lev 16:14). As the blood is the life (Lev 17:11), it has always been considered to have a uniting force; it restores the living bond between God and his people. St Paul in Romans 3:25 calls Christ our ἱλαστήριον: "whom God put forward as an expiation". Compare Heb 4:14 ff.

[3] The urn containing manna (Ex 16:33) and the staff of Aaron (Num 17:10; Heb 9:4) were also kept in the ark, according to a later tradition.

[4] Compare Ps 68:1 and Num 10:35.

[5] See also Ps 36:7 and 63:7.

[6] In the Scriptures we read that the prophet (Jeremiah) had, at God's command, given orders that the tabernacle of the covenant and the ark should be carried after him when he climbed the mountain up which Moses had gone to see the promised Land; and that when Jeremiah had arrived there he found a rocky cavern to which he had the tabernacle, the ark, and the altar of incense brought, and whose entrance he blocked. When some of his companions later climbed up in order to memorize the route they could not find it any more (2 Macc 2:4–6).

[7] Opinions concerning the date of this psalm are instructive: 100 B.C. (Duhm); 170 B.C. (Wellhausen); in the period after the captivity (Pfeiffer 1941); from the reign of David or Solomon (Cassuto 1941), (Eerdmans 1947); many fragments from tenth to thirteenth centuries B.C. (Albright 1950). Recently the psalm is dated: very old (Weiser 1950), out of the time of Josiah, seventh century B.C. (Castellino 1955); 320 B.C. (Podechard 1949 and George 1960). See also H. Kraus in his commentary (1961), who distinguishes three stages or levels in this psalm.

[Mgr. E. Kissane (1953) quotes Kirkpatrick as writing (1921) "Every conceivable date has been suggested from the age of Joshua to that of the Maccabees." He himself favours a date "towards the end of the Exile or shortly after". See *The Book of Psalms*, I, Dublin (1953), p. 288.] — Editor's note.

[8] For further examples see Ps 47:6; 96:11–12; 99:3, 5, 9.

[9] According to the Targum: "from everlasting thou art God".

[10] The formula in Ps 47:7 agrees with Is 52:7 and means rather "has become king"; the formula in Ps 93:1; 96:10; 97:1; 99:1, which agrees with Ex 15:18, means "is king". This points to an enduring condition, whereas "has become king" indicates specific occurence.

[11] Ps 96:11–13. For the scheme of the processional and enthronement psalms, see Appendix VI.

[12] For the sake of convenience we have labelled the psalms in question "enthronement psalms" although some such name as "songs of God's kingship" or "songs about the establishment of the Kingdom" would be better.

[13] To some extent according to H. Gunkel and A. Feuillet.

[14] H. J. Kraus. His argument, against Mowinckel's hypothesis are concisely set out in the first volume of his *Psalmen*, under Excursum 7 to Psalm 24, pp. 197–205.

[15] A. Weiser, *The Psalms*, p. 375.

[16] L. Bouyer, *La Bible et l'Évangile*, Paris (1951), p. 232.

[17] For further examples see Ps 5:2; 24:7 ff.; 44:4; and 145:1, 11.

[18] For further examples see Ps 48:2; 87:4.

[19] See A. Feuillet's article in *Nouvelle Revue Théologique 73* (1951), pp. 352–62.

10. The Royal Psalms

[1] Kings son: Ps 72:1; Yahweh's king: Ps 2:6; 18:50; Anointed of Yahweh: Ps 2:2; 28:8; 84:9; 132:10.

[2] See psalms 144:10; 89:19–37; 132:11–18.

[3] For oracles, see Ps 2:7–9; 20:7–9; 89:3–4, 19–37; 110; 132:11–18. See also Chapter 6, note 8, and Chapter 8, note 8.

[4] See Grelot, *Sens*, p. 335, note 1. He quotes Podechard, Mowinckel, Weiser, Kraus, Castellino, von Rad, Auvray, de Vaux, and others, for this opinion.

[5] See Appendix VII for the scheme of the royal psalms.

[6] "Except David and Hezekiah and Josiah they all sinned greatly, for they forsook the law of the Most High; the kings of Judah came to an end..." Sir 49:4.

[7] See further Hos 3:5; Jer 30:9; Ezek 37:24.

[8] A. George, *Prier*.

[9] P. Grelot, *Sens*, p. 488.

[10] Mt 13:41; 25:31-34; 1 Cor 15:24; Rev 19:16.

[11] Compare Mk 15:9 ff.; Mt 2:2; Jn 19:3; 19:21.

[12] Dodd, *Scriptures*, p. 120.

[13] Concerning psalms 2; 8; and 110, see Appendix VIII.

[14] *Recueil Lucien Cerfaux*, Gembloux (1954), II, pp. 211-12.

[15] Compare psalms 110 and 8.

[16] See especially J. Coppens, *De Messiaanse verwachting in het psalmboek*, Brussels (1955); P. Grelot, *Sens*, pp. 488-90; and A. George, *Prier*, pp. 149 ff.

[17] Catholic Biblical Foundation (1961).

[18] One may notice the allusion to the threefold division of the Old Testament Scriptures: the Law, the Prophets, and the Writings. In this text the last group is represented by the psalms — Editor's note.

[19] See B. Fischer, "Le Christ dans les psaumes" in *La Maison Dieu* 27, pp. 86-109.

11. The Old and New Covenants

[1] Vriezen, *An Outline*, p. 136.

[2] J. Beek, *Verbum* 17 (1950), p. 29.

[3] Renckens, *Israel's Concept*, p. 75.

[4] Vriezen, *An Outline*, pp. 234-35.

[5] Renckens, *Israel's Concept*, p. 65.

[6] This line is also translated as "... and I will not come into the city."

[7] H. de Lubac SJ in *Recherches de Science Religieuse* 36 (1949), p. 118.

[8] Weiser, *The Psalms*, pp. 35–52.

[9] R. Guardini, *Freiheit, Gnade, Schicksal*, Munich (1956), p. 74, E. T. *Freedom, grace, and destiny*, three chapters in the interpretation of existence, London (1961).

[10] J. Beek, *loc. cit.*, p. 28.

[11] W. Eichrodt, *Theology*, pp. 276–7.

[12] "L'Absolu vivifié par l'Amour, l'Amour magnifiée par l'Absolu", L. Bouyer, *Le Sens de la vie monastique*, Turnhout (1951), p. 173.

Appendixes

The general descriptions of the different groups of psalms which have been given in this book could be applied with advantage to each individual psalm. This will help the reader to obtain a clear insight into the literary structure and original meaning of the psalms that go to make up the different groups. In order to further this examination of the individual psalms the following appendixes give a schematic analysis of the psalms belonging to each group. Both grouping and analysis are, of course, to some extent subjective, but I feel convinced that in the main they are reliable.

The Grouping of the Psalms

TABLE A

17 Psalms of praise:

8; 19; 29; 33; 104; 105; 111; 113; 114; 117; 135; 136; 145; 146; 147; 148; 150

17 Private psalms of thanksgiving:

9; 18; 22b; 23; 30; 32; 34; 40a; 41; 63; 66b; 92; 103; 107; 116; 118; 138

8 Communal thanksgiving psalms:

46; 48; 65; 66a; 67; 76; 124; 129

42 Private psalms of petition:

3; 5; 6; 7; 13; 17; 22a; 25; 26; 27; 28; 31; 35; 36; 38; 39; 40b; 42; 43; 51; 54; 55; 56; 57; 59; 61; 64; 69; 70; 71; 86; 88; 102; 108a; 109; 120; 130; 139; 140; 141; 142; 143

16 Communal psalms of petition:

44; 60; 74; 77; 79; 80; 83; 85; 89; 90; 106; 108b; 115; 123; 126; 137

4 Psalms of trust:

4; 16; 62; 131

2 Psalms against unjust judges:

58; 82

17 Psalms about the righteous and the sinner:

1; 10; 11; 12; 14; 37; 49; 52; 53; 73; 75; 94; 112; 119; 125; 127; 128

14 Pilgrim psalms:

15; 24a; 50; 78; 81; 84; 87; 91; 95; 100; 121; 122; 133; 134

10 Processional and enthronement psalms:

24b; 47; 68; 93; 96; 97; 98; 99; 132; 149

8 Royal psalms:

2; 20; 21; 45; 72; 101; 110; 144

TABLE B

Psalms of Praise	Psalms of Thanksgiving Priv.	Psalms of Thanksgiving Commun.	Psalms of Petition Priv.	Psalms of Petition Commun.	of Trust	against Judges	on the Righteous and Sinners	Pilgrim Psalms	Processional and Enthronement Psalms	Royal Psalms
			3		4		1			2
			5							
			6							
8	9		7				10			
							11			
			13				12			
19	18		17		16		14	15		20
	22b		22a							21
	23		25					24a	24b	
			26							
			27							
29	30		28							
33	32		31							
	34		35							
			36				37			
			38							
			39							
	40a		40b							
	41	46	42–43	44					47	45
		48	51				49	50		
							52			
			54				53			
			55							
			56							
			57			58				
			59	60						
	63		61		62					
		65	64							
	66b	66a								
		67	69						68	
			70							
			71	74			73			72
		76		77			75	78		
				79						
				80		82		81		
				83				84		
			86	85				87		
			88	89						
	92			90			94	91	93	
								95	96	
									97	
									98	
104	103		102					100	99	101
105	107			106						
			108a	108b						
111			109				112			110
113										
114	116			115						
117	118		120				119	121		
		124		123			125	122		
				126			127			
		129	130		131		128	133	132	
								134		
135										
136	138		139	137						
			140							
			141							
			142							
145			143							144
146										
147										
148										
150									149	

The Psalms of Praise

Psalm 8 *Praise of the Creator of the universe and man*

1a   Introductory refrain

1b–8   Body of the psalm: God's majesty in the night sky (2–3); man as the crown of creation (4–8)

9   Concluding refrain

Psalm 19 *Praise of the Creator and Lawgiver*

No introduction

1–10   Body of the psalm: the universe declares God's glory (1–6); praise of God's law (7–10)

11–14   Psalmist's final prayers

Psalm 29 *The voice of Yahweh in the thunderstorm*

1–2   Call to praise

3–9   Body: description of the storm above the sea (3–4); above Lebanon (5–6); above the wilderness (7–9)

10–11   Concluding prayer

Psalm 33 *Praise to the Creator and Sustainer of the world*

1–5   Call to praise

6–19   Body: God as Creator, Sustainer, and Source of all grace

20–22   Trustful final prayer

Psalm 104 *Praise of the Creator*

1a   Call to praise

1b–30   Body: the majesty of God (1b–4); he created and ordered the earth (5–9); cares for drinking-water and dwellings for animals (10–18); regulated sun and moon (19–23); created the sea with everything therein (24–26); all living creatures depend on him (27–30)

31–35   Ending: summary and exhortation to praise

Psalm 105   *Praise of the Deliverer*
   1–6   Call to praise
   7–14 Body: covenant with the fathers (8–11); Joseph
         (12–22); Egypt (23—38); description of the Exodus
         (39–41)
   42–45 Ending: summary and stimulation to praise

Psalm 111   *Alphabetic psalm of praise*
   1   Call to praise
   2–9 Body: several reasons for praise are combined
   10   Ending: stimulation to praise

Psalm 113   *Praise of God's goodness*
   1–3 Call to praise
   4–9 Body the great God (4–6); he pays attention to the
        poor (7–9)
        No ending

Psalm 114   *The wonders of the Exodus*
        No characteristics of a psalm of praise; it is a piece
        of old poetry and has probably inspired the writing
        of psalm 115 with which 114 became combined in
        the Septuagint. See Appendix IV, B

Psalm 117   *An Israelite hymn in its simplest form*
   1   General invitation to praise
   2   Body: liturgical formula

Psalm 135   *Praise of the one true God*
   1–4   Call to praise
   5–18 Body: Yahweh is the one true God, Lord of nature
         (5–7); Friend and Helper of Israel (8–14); stronger
         than all the idols of other nations (15–18)
   19–21 Ending: a renewed call to praise

Psalm 136   *A sung litany* (with second half-verse as refrain)
   1–3   Call to praise
   4–25 Body: God's good deeds in nature (4–9); in Israel
         (10–22); to everybody in need (23–25)
   26   Ending: renewed call to praise

Psalm 145 *Alphabetic psalm of praise*
- 1–2 Call to praise
- 3–20 Body: The psalmist praises the greatness and goodness of Yahweh
- 21 Ending: a renewed call to praise

Psalm 146 *Praise of divine providence*
- 1–2 Call to praise
- 3–9 Body: description of divine providence
- 10 Ending

Psalm 147 *Praise of Yahweh, the mighty Creator, the Deliverer of Israel*
- 1 Call to praise
- 2–6 Body: Yahweh, the mighty, the Deliverer of Israel from oppression
- 7 Call to praise
- 8–11 Body: Yahweh, the Creator who takes particular care of the faithful
- 12 Call to praise
- 13–20 Body: Yahweh the Creator, who reveals himself in a special way to Israel

Psalm 148 *A call to praise the Creator*
- 1–6 Call upon the heavens to praise (for the reason given in 5 and 6 — the power of Yahweh)
- 7–14 Call to the earth to praise (for the reasons given in 13 and 14 — the glory of Yahweh and of his people)

Psalm 150 *Liturgical invitation to praise Yahweh*
(final doxology of the Book of Psalms)

APPENDIX III

The Psalms of Thanksgiving

A. PRIVATE PSALMS OF THANKSGIVING

Psalm 9 *Thanks for deliverance*

- 1–2   Declaration of gratitude
- 3–6   Narrative
- 7–11   God's justice described to the bystanders
- 12–16   Narrative
- 17–20   Ending

Psalm 18 *Thanksgiving of the king*

- 1–3   Declaration
- 4–19   Narrative: description of distress (4–5); of supplication (6); of divine intervention (7–19)
- 20–24   Explanation addressed to the bystanders
- 25–30   Expression of trust in Yahweh
- 31–45   Continuation of the narrative in the form of a prayer
- 46–50   The proper thanksgiving

Psalm 22b *(22–31): Thanksgiving of the poor*

- 22–23   Declaration
- 24   Narrative (very short, perhaps because verses 1–22 can be considered as the narrative)
- 25–26   Description of the meal of thanksgiving
- 27–28   Call to universal thanksgiving
- 29–31   The proper thanksgiving

Psalm 23 *Psalm at a sacrificial meal of thanksgiving*

- 1–4   Thanksgiving and trust in Yahweh
- 5   Description of the thanksgiving meal
- 6   Thanksgiving and trust

Psalm 30 *Thanks for deliverance from deadly danger*

- 1   Declaration
- 2–3   Narrative
- 4–5   Call to the bystanders to give thanks

6–11   Narrative
12   Thanksgiving

Psalm 32   *Thanksgiving for a cure from illness*

1–2   Declaration
3–5   Narrative
6–11   Expressions of trust in Yahweh and exhortation of the bystanders

Psalm 34   *Alphabetic psalm of thanksgiving*

1–3   Declaration and call to thanksgiving
4   Narrative
5–22   Exhortation of the bystanders (by a priest or wise man?) as a result of the benefit received

Psalm 40a   *Prayer of a man who is falsely prosecuted*

(This part of psalm 40 has the character of a psalm of thanksgiving, and provides the motive for petition in the second part, 40b; see Appendix IV A.)

1–3   Narrative
4   Conclusion drawn for the bystanders
5–10   Proper thanksgiving

Psalm 41   *Thanksgiving after the cure of a serious illness*

1–3   Lesson for the bystanders: Yahweh sustains the poor
4–12   Narrative: renewal of his past petition (4–10); story of his cure (11–12)
13   Doxology of the First Book of Psalms

Psalm 63   *Thanksgiving for a favour received*

1–2   Declaration
3–6   Description of his thankful mood
7–8   Narrative
9–11   Expression of his certainty for the future

Psalm 66b   *Thanksgiving sacrifice* (of an important person)

13–15   Declaration
16–19   Story and lesson for the bystanders
20   Thanksgiving

Psalm 92   *A song of thanksgiving*

   1–3   Declaration (in the form of a hymn)

   4–9   General reflection: the unhappiness of fools who do not acknowledge God's power

 10–11   Narrative

 12–15   Counterpart to verses 4–9; The happiness of the just

Psalm 103   *Thanksgiving for God's mercy* (very similar to a hymn of praise)

   1–2   Declaration

   3–5   Narrative

   6–9   General reflections on God's mercy

 10–14   Narrative

 15–19   General reflections

 20–22   Concluding hymn

Psalm 107   *A combined ceremony of thanksgiving*

   1–3   Declaration

   4–9   Narrative about the travellers

 10–16   Narrative about the prisoners

 17–22   Narrative about those who had been ill

 23–32   Narrative about the seafarers

 33–41   General summing-up of God's favours

 42–43   Call to the bystanders to be thankful

Psalm 116   *Thanksgiving for deliverance from danger*

   1–2   Declaration

  3–11   Narrative, interrupted in 5, 6, and 7 by reflection on God's bounty

 12–19   Description of the thanksgiving sacrifice

Psalm 118   *A psalm for a thanksgiving service*

  1–20   Before the door of the temple: Opening of the ceremony (1–4); Narration of the deliverance, interrupted by applause from those present, vv. 8, 9, and 15 (5–18)

 19–20   Dialogue at the door of the temple

 21–29   In the temple: Proper thanksgiving (21); Reaction of those present (22–25); Blessing from a priest over those giving thanks and over the people, and the

answer of the people (26–27a); Summons from the
priest to bring offerings (27b); Personal thanksgiving
of the psalmist (28); Response from the people (29)

Psalm 138 *Thanksgiving hymn in the temple*
- 1–2 Declaration of gratitude
- 3 Narrative
- 4–6 Effect of God's intervention upon the great kings
of the earth
- 7–8 Effect on the psalmist himself: trust

B. COMMUNAL THANKSGIVING PSALMS

Psalm 46 *Thanks for the salvation of Jerusalem*
- 1–3 First couplet: We trust in Yahweh; narrative in
verse 1
- 4–7 Second couplet: God protects Jerusalem; narrative
in verse 6
- 8–11 Third couplet: Be thankful; narrative in verse 9

Psalm 48 *Thanksgiving for the relief of Jerusalem*
- 1–3 Call to praise in the form of a hymn
- 4–7 Narrative
- 8–14 Proper celebrations: exclamations of thanksgiving
of the pilgrims (8–11); appeal to the pilgrims to
trust in God (12–14)

Psalm 65 *Thanksgiving for rain and a good harvest*
- 1–4 Proper celebrations
- 5–8 Hymn to God as Creator and Sustainer
- 9–13 Narrative: abundant rain and a rich harvest

Psalm 66a *Liturgy of thanksgiving*
- 1–7 Hymn to God, Creator of heaven and earth, the
God of Israel
- 8–12 Narrative

Psalm 67 *Liturgy of thanksgiving for a good harvest*
- 1–5 Proper celebrations: blessing by a priest (1); call
to all peoples to praise (2–5)
- 6 Narrative: good harvest

7 Prayer for further blessings

Psalm 76 *A song of thanksgiving for the miraculous deliverance of Jerusalem*

1–9 Narrative

10–12 Call to all peoples to recognize Yahweh's kingship

Psalm 124 *Thanksgiving of Israel*

1–5 Narrative

6–8 Expression of thanksgiving (verse 7, narrative)

Psalm 129 *Thanksgiving*

1–4 Narrative

5–8 Glimpse into the future

The Psalms of Petition

A. PRIVATE PSALMS OF PETITION

Psalm 3 *Trustful prayer in the midst of enemies*

  1–2   Address to God and lament
  3–6   Argument: psalmist's trust
  7–8   Prayer of petition; certainty of being heard

Psalm 5 *Fugitive's prayer of petition at the morning sacrifice in the temple*

  1–3   Address to God and prayer of petition
  4–6   Argument: injustice is not pleasing to God
  7   Argument: God loves the just (who may enter his temple)
  8–11   Prayer of petition and lament
  12   Argument: God blesses the righteous

Psalm 6 *Lament of a sick person*

  1–4a   Address to God and prayer of petition
  4b–5   Argument
  6–7   Complaint
  8–10   Prayer and the certainty of being heard

Psalm 7 *Prayer of one persecuted at law*

  1–2   Address to God and prayer of petition
  3–5   Oath of innocence
  4–9a   Prayer of petition
  4b–16   Argument: God knows the innocence of the psalmist; he saves the good and punishes the wicked
  17   Promise of thanksgiving

Psalm 13 *Lament of a pious man*

  1–2   Address to God and a bitter lament
  3–5a   Prayer of petition and arguments
  5b   Promise of thanksgiving

Psalm 17 *Prayer of one persecuted in a lawsuit*

  1–2   Address to God and a prayer of petition

3–5	Declaration of innocence
6–9	Prayer of petition
10–12	Lament and description of the enemy
13–14	Moving prayer of petition
15	Expression of trust

Psalm 22a *Prayer of a poor man*

(perhaps meant as narrative after being answered, see Appendix III A)

1–10	Address to God and lament
11	Prayer of petition
12–18	Renewed lament
19–21	Prayer of petition

Psalm 25 *Alphabetical prayer of petition*

1	Address to God
2a	Argument: trust in Yahweh
2b–3	Prayer of petition
8–15	Argument: God saves those who fear him
16–22	Lament and prayer of petition

Psalm 26 *Prayer of one who is falsely accused*

1	Address to God and prayer of petition
2–8	Argument: psalmist's innocence
9–12a	Prayer of petition
12b	Promise of thanksgiving

Psalm 27 *Trustful prayer of one falsely accused*

1–6	Expression of trust
7	Address to God and petition
8–10	Argument: trust in Yahweh
11–12	Earnest petition and lament
13–14	Expression of trust

Psalm 28 *Prayer of a sick man*

1–3	Address to God and prayer of petition
4–5	Prayer for the destruction of evil enemies
6–7	Thanksgiving (after being answered?)
8–9	Prayer for the king and people

Psalm 31 *Psalm of a sick man, threatened by friend and enemy*

1–8 Address to God, prayer of petition, and expression of trust

9–13 Lament

14 Expression of trust (argument)

15–18 Prayer of petition

19–24 Thanksgiving (after being cured?) with characteristics of a thanksgiving psalm: proper thanksgiving (19–20); narrative (21–22); exhortation of bystanders (23–24)

Psalm 35 *Moving prayer of petition from a person falsely accused*

1–6 and 8 Address to God and prayer of petition

7 and 9 Declaration of innocence; appeal to God, the protector of the poor

10–16 Lament

17–27 Prayer of petition

18 and 28 Promises of thanksgiving

Psalm 36 *Prayer of a poor man who takes refuge in Yahweh*

1–4 Description of the presumptous enemies

5–9 Description of the happiness and the protection which the pious find in the temple

10–12 Prayer for protection against the wicked

Psalm 38 *Prayer of a sick man*

1 Address to God and prayer of petition

2–12 Lament: Description of his sickness (3–11); deserted by his friends, threatened by his enemies (12–13)

13–16 Trust in Yahweh (argument)

17–20 Renewed lament

21–22 Prayer of petition

Psalm 39 *Prayer of a very sick man in despair*

1–6 Bitter lament

7 Expression of trust (argument)

8–13 Prayer of petition

Psalm 40b *Prayer of a guiltless, persecuted man*

(The first part of psalm 40 is a psalm of thanksgiving (see Appendix III A) which is used as an argument in the following petition: see vv. 9–10)

9–10 Argument for being heard
11–12 Address to God and lament
13–16 Prayer of petition
17 Certainty of being heard

Psalms 42 and 43 *Prayer of an exile*

1–4 Address to God and lament: Comparison of previous happiness (1–14) and present trouble (6–10)
5 Psalmist encourages himself (in place of an argument)
6–10 Lament (see above)
11 see verse 5
43:1–3 Prayer of petition
1–3 Prayer of petition
4 Promise of thanksgiving
5 see 42:5

Psalm 51 *Prayer of petition for forgiveness of sins and inner renewal*

1–2 Address to God and prayer of petition
3–6 Confession of guilt as argument for being heard
7–12 Prayer for inner renewal and to obtain God's spirit
13–17 Promise of thanksgiving
18–19 Petition for restoration of Jerusalem (later addition)

Psalm 54 *Prayer in the midst of enemies*

1–2 Prayer of petition and address to God
3 Lament
4 Certainty of being heard
5 Prayer for deliverance from enemies
6–7 Promise of thanksgiving

Psalm 55 *Prayer of one unjustly persecuted and betrayed by his friend*

1–2 Address to God and prayer of petition
3–15 and Lament over the fear which has seized the psalmist
18b–21 (3–9); over the injustice in the city (10–11); over his friend's disloyalty (12–15 and 18b–21)

16–18a and 22 Expression of trust (argument)
23 Prayer of petition

Psalm 56 *Trustful prayer of a man in danger from his enemies*

1–2 Address to God and lament
3–4 Expression of trust (argument)
5–6 Lament
7–9 Prayer of petition with argument
10–11 Expression of trust
12–13 Promise of thanksgiving in the certainty of being heard

Psalm 57 *Trustful prayer of an accused man who takes refuge in the temple*

1–3 Address to God, petition, and expression of trust
4 Lament
5 Prayer of petition, identical with v. 11
6 Expression of trust (Yahweh shall punish evildoers)
8–10 Promise of thanksgiving
11 Prayer of petition, identical with v. 5

Psalm 59 *Prayer from someone threatened by enemies*

1–3 Address to God and petition
3–4a Lament
4b–5 Prayer of petition
6–7 Lament
8–10 Certainty of being heard (argument)
11–13 Prayer of petition
14–17 Certainty of being heard (argument) and promise of thanksgiving

Psalm 61 *Prayer of an exile*

1–2 Address to God and prayer of petition
3–5 Argument for being heard (trust)
6–7 Prayer for the king
8 Promise of thanksgiving

Psalm 64 *Trustful prayer of a man persecuted by his enemies*

1–2 Address to God and prayer of petition
3–6 Lament
7-8 Certainty of being heard (argument)

9–10   Effect on the pious of God's intervention (argument)

Psalm 69   *Prayer of a pious man, suffering because of his faithfulness to Yahweh*

1–4   Call on God and lament
5–9   Argument: The psalmist's innocence; he suffers for

God's sake
10–12   Lament
13–18   Prayer of petition
19–21   Lament
22–29   Prayer of petition: punishment for his enemies
30–33   Promise of thanksgiving
34–36   Addition made by the exiles

Psalm 70   *Prayer for help*

1–3   Address to God and prayer of petition
4–5   Argument and prayer of petition

Psalm 71   *Prayer of an old man threatened by enemies*

1–4   Address to God and prayer of petition
5–8   Argument for being heard
9–13   Prayer of petition and lament
14–21   Expressions of confidence and other arguments for being heard
22–24   Promise of thanksgiving

Psalm 86   *Prayer of a pious man*

1–7   Address to God, prayer of petition and argument
8–10   Argument: God's greatness
11   Prayer of petition
12–13   Promise of thanksgiving
14–17   Prayer of petition and argument

Psalm 88   *Bitter lament from a sick and forsaken man*

1–2   Call on God and prayer of petition
3–9   Lament
10–14   Argument
15–18   Lament

Psalm 102   *Prayer of a sorely tried person*

(Perhaps verses 12–22 and verse 28 were added

afterwards because Israel saw in this sick person an image of herself)

1–2	Call on God and prayer of petition
3–11	Lament
23–28	The eternity of God in contrast to the transitoriness of man (argument)

Psalm 108a *See psalm 57:7–11*

Psalm 109 *Prayer of a man falsely accused*

1–5	Call upon God, lament, and declaration of innocence
6–19	Lament: narration of what the enemies address to him during the sitting of the court
20–21	Prayer of petition that the imprecations return on the accusers themselves
22–25	Lament: description of his own miserable state as refutation of the accusation
26–29	Prayer of petition (implicitly in answer to the accusation)
30–31	Promise of thanksgiving

Psalm 120 *Prayer of petition from an Israelite among foreign people*

1–2	Address to God and prayer of petition
3–4	Execration of his enemies
5–7	Lament

Psalm 130 *Prayer of a sinner*

1–2	Call upon God
3–6	Expression of trust
7–8	Israel hopes for salvation

Psalm 139 *Prayer of a man who is falsely accused*

1–18	Declaration of innocence by an appeal to: the omniscience of Yahweh (1–6) the omnipresence of Yahweh (7–12) God's formation of man, whom he knows thoroughly (13–18)
19–22	Declaration of innocence and rejection of the behaviour of the wicked

23–24 Declaration of innocence

Psalm 140 *Prayer of petition from a person threatened by enemies*

  1–5 Address to God and lament
  6–7 Expression of trust (argument)
  8–11 Prayer of petition for the destruction of enemies
12–13 Certainty of being heard

Psalm 141 *Prayer of a pious man for strength under temptation*

  1–2 Address to God and prayer of petition
  3–7 Prayer for patience
  8–10 Trustful and earnest petition

Psalm 142 *Prayer from one whose life is threatened by enemies*

  1–4 Lament
  5–6 Call upon God and prayer of petition
    7 Argument: promise of thanksgiving

Psalm 143 *Urgent prayer from one oppressed*

  1–2 Call upon God and prayer of petition
  3–6 Lament
    5 Argument: God's help in former times
  7–12 Prayer of petition mingled with arguments

B. COMMUNAL PSALMS OF PETITION

Psalm 44 *Prayer of petition after a defeat*

  1–8 God's care for Israel (argument)
  9–16 Lament
17–22 Constancy of the people (argument)
23–26 Earnest prayer of petition

Psalm 60 *Liturgical service of petition after a defeat*

  1–5 Call upon God and lament
  6–8 Oracle from a cultic prophet (?): certainty of being heard
  9–12 Prayer of petition and arguments

Psalm 74 *Lament over the destruction of the sanctuary*

  1–11 Call upon God and lament

| 2 and 12–18 | Arguments: predestination of Israel and Sion (2); Yahweh is insulted (18); creative and redeeming power of Yahweh (12–17) |
| 19–23 | Prayer of petition |

Psalm 77 *Lament of an Israelite over the troubles of his people*

| 1–6 | Lament |
| 7–20 | Argument: appeal to Yahweh's help in former times |

Psalm 79 *Lament over the destruction of Jerusalem*

| 1–5 | Call upon God and lament |
| 6–13 | Prayer of petition with argument |

Psalm 80 *Service of petition for the restitution of Israel*

1–3	Call upon God and prayer of petition
4–6	Lament
7	Prayer of petition
8–11	Argument: Yahweh's care for Israel
12–13	Lament
14–17	Prayer of petition
18	Argument: promise of loyalty and thanksgiving
19	Prayer of petition

Psalm 83 *Prayer of petition against the hostile peoples who threaten Israel*

1	Call upon God and prayer of petition
2–8	Lament
9–18	Prayer of petition, combined with arguments: appeal to Yahweh's former help (9–11); the glory of the Lord's name (16–18)

Psalm 85 *Prayer for complete deliverance after the return from exile*

1–3	Argument: return from exile
4–7	Prayer of petition
8–13	Pronouncement of an oracle by a cultic prophet (?): certainty of salvation

Psalm 89 *Lamentation over the seeming unfaithfulness of Yahweh to the Davidic promises*

| 1–38 | Arguments for being heard: |

God's faithfulness in general (2–3); Yahweh's power and faithfulness in the creation (6–15); Yahweh's former care for Israel (16–19); Yahweh's covenant with David's dynasty (4–5 and 20–38)

39–47   Lament: nothing remains of Yahweh's trust

48–52   Prayer of petition (v. 50, renewed appeal to the Davidic promise)

Psalm 90   *Prayer of Israel in a time of difficulties*

1–2   Argument: God's protection in the past

3–12   Argument: the transitoriness and the sinfulness of man, and the eternity and anger of God

13–17   Prayer of petition

Psalm 106   *Confession of sins made by the whole nation*

1–5   Liturgical summons and petition

6–14   Confession of sins in Israel's history:
The sins of their forefathers at the time of the Exodus in the desert and in the promised land (6 to 40); punishment and grace from Yahweh in the course of Israel's history (with allusion to the contemporary situation) (41–46)

47   Prayer of petition for the end of the dispersal

48   Doxology to the Fourth Book of Psalms

Psalm 108b   *See psalm 60:5–12*

Psalm 115   *Liturgical service of petition*

(psalm 114:1–8 is used as argument in psalm 115, see Appendix II)

1–2   Address to God, prayer of petition and lament

3–8   Satirical song on the idols to reinforce confidence

9–11   Exhortation of the people to trust in Yahweh

12–16   Blessing by the priests in response to the people's trust

17–18   Reaction of the people to this blessing

Psalm 123   *Prayer in distress*

1–2   Expression of confidence (as argument) by a precentor

3–4 Prayer of petition and lament

Psalm 126 *A prayer for complete restitution*

1–3 Argument: God's intervention in the return from exile

4 Prayer of petition for the present

5–6 Certainty of being heard in the form of self-exhortation

Psalm 137 *Lament over the afflictions of exile*

1–6 Lament over the afflictions of exile (1–3); over the mockery of oppressors (4–6)

7–9 Curses against Babylon and Edom

C. PSALMS OF TRUST

Psalm 4 *Rejoicing in Yahweh*

1 Prayer of petition

2–5 Exhortation of enemies to trust in Yahweh

6–8 Expression of trust

Psalm 16 *Yahweh the heritage of the pious*

1–2 Trustful prayer of petition

3–4 Denunciation of the deeds of the evil

5–9 Deep feeling of belonging to Yahweh

10–11 Certainty of deliverance from danger of death

Psalm 62 *In God alone is deliverance*

1–2 Expression of trust

3–4 Lament

5–7 Expression of trust

8–12 Exhortation of the bystanders

Psalm 131 *Childlike surrender to Yahweh*

1–2 Expression of trust

3 Exhortation to Israel

D. THE PSALMS AGAINST UNJUST JUDGES

Psalm 58 *Prayer against unjust judges*

1–5 Accusation against Israel's chiefs

  6–9   Prayer of petition
 10–11   Argument: the effect on the pious of God's inter-
         vention

Psalm 82   *The judges before the judgment-seat of God*

    1   The hearing begins
  2–5   The accusation
  6–7   The verdict of God
    8   Prayer of the psalmist for God's intervention

E. PSALMS ABOUT THE RIGHTEOUS AND SINNER

Psalm   1   *The happiness of the righteous and the punishment
               of the sinner*

  1–3   The behaviour and the prosperity of the righteous
  4–5   The lot of the sinner
    6   Summary

Psalm 10   *Prayer for help against the sinners*

  1–2   Call upon God and lament
 3–11   Lament: the presumption of the sinners
12–15   Prayer of petition: that Yahweh protect the *'anawim*
16–18   Certainty that Yahweh will procure justice

Psalm 11   *Trust in the judgment of God*

  1–3   Trust and lament
  4–7   Confidence in the righteous judgment of God

Psalm 12   *Prayer for judgment on the sinners*

  1–2   Lament
  3–4   Prayer of petition for the destruction of the wicked
    5   Declaration that Yahweh will procure justice
  6–8   Certainty that God will intervene

Psalm 14   *Corruption of the sinners and their punishment*

  1–3   Description of the sinners
  4–6   God will punish them
    7   Prayer of petition for God's people

Psalm 37 *Alphabetic and didactic psalm about the retribution*
In this psalm are mixed:
exhortations for good behaviour; description of
the behaviour and the lot of the righteous; description of the behaviour and the lot of sinners.

Psalm 49 *Didactic psalm about the vanity of riches*
1–4 Summons to listen
5–15 Death is the lot poor and rich alike, of wise and
foolish men
16–20 Conclusion: do not envy the rich

Psalm 52 *The lot of an oppressor*
1–4 Description of the oppressor
5 Punishment by Yahweh
6–7 Effect of the judgment on the just
8–9 The happiness of the righteous man who gives thanks

Psalm 53 *This psalm is the same as psalm 14*

Psalm 73 *The problem of the prosperity of the sinners*
1–3 The psalmist introduces the problem
4–12 The seeming happiness and the presumption of the
sinners
13–16 Temptation against faith
17–20 The reflection which recalls faith: the death of the
sinners
21–22 Repentance over the psalmist's foolish doubts
23–28 Prayer: my happiness consists in thy loving proximity

Psalm 75 *Oracle on the lot of the wicked*
1 Liturgical introduction
2–3 Oracle: God declares his judgment
4–9 Explanation of the oracle (by a cultic prophet?);
punishment of the sinners (4–8); salvation of the
righteous (9)
10 New affirmation by God himself

Psalm 94 *Prayer for the judgment of Yahweh*
1–2 Prayer for the intervention of Yahweh
3–7 Lament: description of the behaviour of the wicked

8–11   Appeal to the wicked to mend their ways

12–19   Trust in Yahweh who has given consolation and help

20–23   Certainty that Yahweh will give his judgment

Psalm 112   *Alphabetical psalm about the good fortune of the righteous*

1   Introductory blessing of the just

2–9   The good fortune of the righteous

10   Envy and ruin of the wicked

Psalm 119   *Meditation and prayer of a righteous man*

This psalm consists of twenty-two strophes, each of eight verses. Each strophe begins with a successive letter of the Hebrew alphabet in their usual order, and each strophe uses the eight recurring synonyms for "Law", namely: Law, promises (testimonies), word, statutes, commandments, ordinances, precepts. The psalm glorifies the gift of the Law of God, of his word, of his whole revelation in its living reality. As to the literary qualities, nine strophes are characterized by the literary rules of the individual psalms of petition, while in twelve other strophes a considerable influence from the psalms of petition can be seen (desire, confidence, protection against enemies, imprecation, petition, etc.)

Psalm 125   *Exhortation to a resolute faith in Yahweh's judgment*

1–3   Assurance of Yahweh's protection

4–5   Prayer for judgment of the righteous and the wicked

Psalm 127   *Yahweh blesses the family life of the righteous*

1–29   Yahweh blesses house and work

3–5   Sons especially are a sign of his blessing

Psalm 128   *The domestic happiness of the righteous*

1   Blessing: the requirement for this happiness

2–4   Description of this happiness

5–6   Blessing: the happiness of the individual is related to the lot of Jerusalem and the whole people of Israel

APPENDIX V

The Pilgrim Psalms

Psalm 15 *Conversation at the temple gate*

    1   Question put by the pilgrims

2–5a   Answer of the priests

  5b   Promise of Yahweh's support

Psalm 24a *On arrival at the temple*

        (for this psalm, see also Appendix VI)

  1–2   Hymn on Yahweh's glory

    3   Question put by the pilgrims: Who may enter?

  4–5   Answer of the priests

    6   Affirmation by the pilgrims: We are such

Psalm 50 *Prophetic warning to the pilgrims*

  1–6   Theophany: God appears (1–3) and calls for a hearing (4–6)

 7–21   Accusation: over the magic sacrificial cult (7–15; over the lack of observance of the law (16–21)

22–23   Final summing-up

Psalm 78 *Warning on the basis of the history of redemption*

  1–7   Call to listen to teaching from the past

 8–11   The disloyalty and stubbornness of the northern kingdom (lesson for the southern kingdom)

12–16   Yahweh's wonders during the Exodus

17–22   Israel's disbelief in the desert

23–31   Wonders in the desert

32–42   Disbelief in the desert

43–55   The wonders in Egypt and during the entry into the land of Canaan

56–58   The disbelief in Canaan

59–64   Punishment of Ephraim

65–72   The election of Judah, Mount Zion, and King David

Psalm 81   *Prophetic warning*

   1–5a   Hymn
    5b   Introduction to the prophetic oracle
  6–16   The prophetic oracle: recalling the deliverance from Egypt (6–12); exhortation to trust in Yahweh (13–16)

Psalm 84   *On arrival at the temple*

   1–4   Exclamations of the pilgrims: blessed are those who dwell here
   5–7   Answer from the priests: blessed are those who come here
  8–11   Prayer of the pilgrims and expression of their trust
    12   Final words (of one of the priests?)

Psalm 87   *Hymn of praise over the election of Zion*

   1–3   The city chosen by God
   4–5   The mother of all nations
   6–7   Explanatory statement: she is the source of life

Psalm 91   *A king makes a pilgrimage to the temple to obtain a divine oracle*

   1–2   Profession of faith of the pilgrim
   3–8   First promise of Yahweh's protection
    9a   New profession of faith of the pilgrim
 9b–13   Renewed promise of Yahweh's protection (meanwhile the pilgrim enters the temple)
 14–16   The oracle of God, the object of the pilgrimage

Psalm 95   *Liturgy on entering the temple*

  1–7a   Hymn and summons to prayer
    7b   Voice of a priest or prophet
  8–11   Oracle: the hardness of heart of their fathers, warning for the present generation

Psalm 100   *Procession into the temple*

   1–2   Hymn
     3   Exhortation
     4   Invitation to enter the courts
     5   Shouts of joy from the people on entering

Psalm 121   *Exhortation to make a pilgrimage*

  1–4   Question and answer: Where shall we go for a
        pilgrimage?
  5–8   Yahweh alone keeps us

Psalm 122   *Prayer over Jerusalem, on the arrival of the pilgrims*

  1–2   Expression of joy on going up to Jerusalem
  3–5   Hymn on Jerusalem
  6–9   Prayer for Jerusalem

Psalm 133   *Blessing over the people that are gathered in the
                temple*

Psalm 134   *Psalm at the evening sacrifice in the temple*

  1–2   The people call on the priests to bless Yahweh
    3   The priests bless the pilgrims that are present

The Processional and Enthronement Psalms

Psalm 24b *Temple entry with the ark of the covenant*
(To this very old fragment psalm 24a was later
added, see Appendix V: amplification of the dialogue
among the pilgrims present)

7 Request for the opening of the gate of the temple
8 Question from inside the temple
9 Renewed request for the opening of the gates
10a Question from inside the temple
10b The decisive answer, Yahweh is here

Psalm 47 *Celebrations of Yahweh's kingship*

1 Call to praise (universalistic)
2–5 Body: Description of the king (2); revelation of
his kingship in his works of redemption (3–4) and
in the present ascent of Zion (5)
6 Renewed call to praise
7–9 Body: the revelation of his kingship in the future

Psalm 68 *Processional psalm*

1–3 Introduction to the procession
4–6 Call to praise Yahweh (v. 7 concrete experience of
salvation as occasion for this celebration?)
7–23 Position of this experience in the entirety of Yahweh's
works of salvation: the gates through the desert
(7–10); conquest of Canaan (11–14); predestination
of Zion from where God protects his people (15–23)
24–27 Description of the procession
28–35 Prayers for salvation and universalistic hymn

Psalm 93 *Yahweh is king*

1–2 Description of Yahweh's kingship
3–4 Revelation of his kingship in nature (allusion to the
Exodus)
5 This mighty king lives here in the temple

Psalm 96 *Yahweh is king*

1–3 Call to praise (universalistic)

4–6   Description of the king

7–10   Universalistic perspective: call to all peoples (revelation of Yahweh's kingship in v. 10)

11–13 Call on all creation to praise Yahweh whose reign is coming

Psalm 97 *Yahweh is king*

1–6   Revelation of Yahweh's kingship (in the form of a theophany)

7   The effect of his judgment upon the wicked

8–12   The effect on the pious

Psalm 98 *Song of praise of Yahweh's kingship*

1a   Call to praise

1b–3   The revelation of Yahweh's kingship in his works of salvation

4–9   Universalistic perspective: call on all creation to praise

Psalm 99 *Yahweh is king*

1–2   Description of the king

3   Refrain: Call to praise God and answer of the people

4   Description of the king: his justice

5   Refrain (see verse 3)

6–8   Description of the king: a king who hears and forgives

9   Refrain (see verse 3)

Psalm 132 *Prayer for king and people on the occasion of a procession*

1–9   The oath of David: prayer for the king and argument for being heard (1–5); actual celebration: the transfer of the ark (6–9)

10–18 The oath of Yahweh: prayer for the king (10); oracle over the anointed and Zion (11–18)

Psalm 149 *Hymn on the establishment of the kingdom of Yahweh*

1–3   Call to praise

4   Revelation of Yahweh's kingship: the salvation of the poor

5–9   Eschatological outlook: Israel may help Yahweh in the establishment of his kingdom

The Royal Psalms, or Psalms of the King

Psalm 2 *On the occasion of a royal coronation*

    1–3   Rebellion of the vassal kings

    4–6   Nevertheless Yahweh will rule by means of his king

    7–9   The king relates the oracle which Yahweh announced to himself

    10–12   Exhortation to submission

Psalm 20 *Prayer for victory for the king*

    1–5   Prayer for the king in the form of well-wishing

    6–8   The response announced in an oracle

    9   Final prayer

Psalm 21 *Celebration of Israel's king*

    1–7   Thanks for Yahweh's favour shown to the king

    8–12   Well-wishing for the king: victory over his enemies

    13   Prayer to Yahweh to accede to the wish

Psalm 45 *Song for the king on his wedding day*

    1   Declaration of the singer

    2–9   He sings to the king: description of the royal majesty (v. 10, the king as bridegroom)

    10–15   Exhortation to the bride to become the wife of the king

    16–17   Good wishes for the king: a permanent dynasty

Psalm 72 *Prayer for a new king*

    1–4   May the king procure justice in the name of Yahweh

    5–7   May he give fortune and peace to his people

    8–11   May his kingdom grow

    12–14   The poor (*'anawim*) find there their good fortune

    15–17   Summing-up: may his reign be a golden period

    18–20   Doxology to the Second Book of Psalms

Psalm 101 *Aims of a good king*

    1   Address to God

    2–4   Principles for his personal life

    5–8   Care for social justice

Psalm 110 *Divine oracle about the king*

      1   First oracle: the proclamation of the king

    2–3 Elaboration of the oracle: rule over enemies, the king is son of Yahweh

      4   Second oracle: the king as mediator

    5–7 Further elaboration of the first oracle: victory and judgment

Psalm 144 *Prayer of the king for victory and prosperity*

    1–4 Call to God and argument for being heard: expression of trust (1–2); weakness of mankind (3–4)

    5–8 Prayer of petition

      9   Promise of thanksgiving

  10–11 Prayer for victory

  12–15 Prayer for the prosperity of the people

The Psalms in the New Testament

Psalms	New Testament	Psalms	New Testament
2:1–2	Acts 4:25–26	29:3	Acts 7:2
2	Rev 6:15; 11:15	31:5	Lk 23:46
1–5	Rev 11:18	24	1 Cor 16:13
7	Acts 13:33;	32:1	Jas 5:20
	Hebr 1:5; 5:5	1–2	Rom 4:7–8
8–9	Rev 2:26–27;	33:3	Rev 5:9; 14:3
	19:15	34:8	1 Pet 2:3
9	Rev 12:5	12–16	1 Pet 3:10–12
4:4	Eph 4:26	20	Jn 19:36
5:9	Rom 3:13	35:19	Jn 15:25
6:8	Mt 7:23; Lk 13:27	36:1	Rom 3:18
8:2	Mt 21:16	37:11	Mt 5:5
4–6	Heb 2:6–9	39:12	1 Pet 2:11
6	1 Cor 15:27;	40:6–8	Heb 10:5–9
	Eph 1:22	41:9	Jn 13:18
10:7	Rom 3:14	44:22	Rom 8:36
14:1–3	Rom 3:10–12	45:6–7	Heb 1:8–9
16:8–11	Acts 2:25–28	48:2	Mt 5:35
10	Acts 2:31; 13:35	51:4	Rom 3:4
18:49	Rom 15:9	55:22	1 Pet 5:7
19:4	Rom 10:18	62:12	Rom 2:6;
22:1	Mt 27:46;		Rev 2:23; 22:12
	Mk 15:34	68:18	Eph 4:8
7	Mt 27:39;	35	2 Thess 1:10
	Mk 15:29	69:4	Jn 15:25
8	Mt 27:43	9	Jn 2:17; Rom 15:3
13	1 Pet 5:8	21	Mt 27:34; 27:48;
18	Mt 27:35;		Mk 15:36; Jn 19:28
	Mk 15:24;	22–23	Rom 11:9–10
	Lk 23:34; Jn 19:24	25	Acts 1:20
21	2 Tim 4:17	28	Rev 3:5; 17:8;
22	Heb 2:12		20:12; 21:27
24:1	1 Cor 10:26	75:8	Rev 14:10

Psalms	New Testament	Psalms	New Testament
78:2	Mt 13:35	4	Heb 5:6; 7:17;
24	Jn 6:31		7:21
82:6	Jn 10:34	112:9	2 Cor 9:9
86:9	Rev 15:4	115:4–7	Rev 9:20
89:7	2 Thess 1:10	13	Rev 11:18; 19:5
27	Rev 1:5	116:10	2 Cor 4:13;
37	Rev 1:5; 3:14		Rev 11:18; 19:5
90:4	2 Pet 3:8	117:1	Rom 15:11
91:11–12	Mt 4:6; Lk 4:10	118:6	Heb 13:6
	to 11	22	Mt 21:42;
92:5	Rev 15:3		Mk 12:10;
94:1–2	1 Thess 4:6		Lk 20:17;
11	1 Cor 3:20		Acts 4:11;
14	Rom 11:1		1 Pet 2:7
95:7–8	Heb 4:7	26	Mt 21:9; 23:39;
7–11	Heb 3:7–11		Mk 11:9;
11	Heb 4:3		Lk 13:35; Jn 12:13
97:7	Heb 1:6	130:8	Tit 2:14
102:25–27	Heb 1:10–12	132:5	Acts 7:46
103:8	Jas 5:11	11	Acts 2:30
104:4	Heb 1:7	135:15–17	Rev 9:20
106:20	Rom 1:23	137:9	Lk 19:44
109:8	Acts 1:20	139:14	Rev 15:3
110:1	Mt 22:44; 26:64;	140:3	Rom 3:13
	Mk 12:36; 14:62;	141:2	Rev 5:8
	16:19;	143:2	Rom 3:20;
	Lk 20:42–43;		Gal 2:16
	22:69;	146:6	Acts 4:24; 14:15;
	Acts 2:34–35;		Rev 10:6
	1 Cor 15:25;	147:15	Acts 10:36
	Heb 1:13; 10:13		

Index of Biblical Quotations

1. THE PSALMS
(See also appendixes II–VII)

Psalms
Ps 1, *140, 222, 223*
Ps 2, *184, 186, 187, 189, 196, 197*
Ps 2:2, *28, 225*
Ps 2:6, *225*
Ps 2:7, *187*
Ps 2:7–9, *190, 225*
Ps 2:10, *28*
Ps 3, *220*
Ps 3:4, *29*
Ps 3–41, *18*
Ps 4, *136*
Ps 4:4, *165*
Ps 5:2, *114, 225*
Ps 5:7, *215*
Ps 6, *220*
Ps 6:1, *118*
Ps 6:5, *95, 221*
Ps 7:2, *118, 221*
Ps 7:3–5, *115, 221*
Ps 7:15, *221*
Ps 8, *64, 78, 197, 219, 226*
Ps 8–9, *219*
Ps 9, *22, 45, 90, 217, 220, 222*
Ps 9:3, *99*
Ps 9:11, *221*
Ps 9:13, *107*
Ps 9:14, *89*   [223
Ps 10, *22, 45, 217, 222,*

Ps 10:7–13, *140*
Ps 10:16, *179*
Ps 11, *136, 223, 225*
Ps 12, *140, 223*
Ps 12:5, *220*
Ps 13, *220*
Ps 14, *140, 223*
Ps 15, *152*
Ps 15–16, *219*
Ps 16, *130, 136*
Ps 16:9, *221*
Ps 17:1–5, *221*
Ps 17:8–13, *221*
Ps 17:9–11, *221*
Ps 17:12, *221*
Ps 17:15, *114*
Ps 18, *187*
Ps 18:5, *107*
Ps 18:49, *221*
Ps 18:50, *225*
Ps 19a, *219*
Ps 19, *140, 156, 219*
Ps 19:7–8, *156*
Ps 20, *184, 190*
Ps 20:2, *188*
Ps 20:4, *188*
Ps 20:7, *118*
Ps 20:7–8, *28*
Ps 20:7–9, *191, 225*
Ps 20:9, *188*
Ps 21, *186, 197*
Ps 21:3–6, *187*

Ps 22, *99, 130, 132, 133*
Ps 22:8, *119*
Ps 22:12, *119*
Ps 22:22, *99*
Ps 22:22–24, *220*
Ps 22:23–24, *83*
Ps 22:26, *84*
Ps 22:27, *101, 222*
Ps 22:27–28, *180*
Ps 22:27–30, *130*
Ps 22:27–31, *130*
Ps 23, *84, 93, 101, 136, 221*
Ps 24, *151, 225*
Ps 24:7 ff., *225*
Ps 24:7–10, *169*
Ps 25, *217, 222*
Ps 26, *220*
Ps 26:2, *132*
Ps 26:2–6, *221*
Ps 26:6, *43*
Ps 26:6–7, *84*
Ps 27, *136, 221*
Ps 27:4–8, *158*
Ps 28, *220*
Ps 28:2, *218*
Ps 28:8, *225*
Ps 29, *31, 219*
Ps 29:3, *218*
Ps 29:10, *62, 179, 218*
Ps 29:10–11, *77*

Ps 30, *45*
Ps 30:2, *109*
Ps 30:3, *99*
Ps 30:4, *83, 107, 221*
Ps 30:6, *220*
Ps 30:9, *221*
Ps 30:12, *95*
Ps 31, *98, 132*
Ps 31:11–13, *221*
Ps 31:13, *119*
Ps 31:22, *120, 220*
Ps 31:24, *98*
Ps 32:4, *109*
Ps 32:6–9, *76, 220*
Ps 32:9, *76*
Ps 32:10, *28*
Ps 32:11, *98*
Ps 33, *219*
Ps 33:3–9, *61*
Ps 33:13 ff., *219*
Ps 33:21, *118*
Ps 34, *45, 217, 222*
Ps 34:8, *84*
Ps 34:11, *98*
Ps 34:12 ff., *220*
Ps 34:16, *30*
Ps 34:18, *132*
Ps 34:19, *130, 135*
Ps 35:4–6, *221*
Ps 35:7, *221*
Ps 35:13–15, *110*
Ps 35:15–16, *221*
Ps 36, *221*
Ps 36:7, *224*
Ps 37, *45, 141, 217, 222, 223*
Ps 37:1, *28*
Ps 37:39, *130*
Ps 38, *109*
Ps 38:2, *108*
Ps 38:3, *109, 132*
Ps 38:12, *109*
Ps 40, *216*
Ps 40:1–2, *91*
Ps 40:2, *107*
Ps 40:5, *93, 220*
Ps 40:6–7, *88*
Ps 41:4, *109, 220*
Ps 41:5, *110*
Ps 41:12, *89*

Ps 41:13, *216*
Ps 42:4, *223*
Ps 42–49, *18*
Ps 43:4, *89, 216*
Ps 44, *219*
Ps 44:1, *126*
Ps 44:5, *225*
Ps 44:12, *125*
Ps 45, *184, 185, 189, 197*
Ps 45:4, *188*
Ps 45:7, *216*
Ps 45:16–17, *189*
Ps 46, *102, 103*
Ps 46:10, *223*
Ps 47, *168, 170*
Ps 47:1, *218*
Ps 47:2, *218*
Ps 47:3–4, *172*
Ps 47:5–6, *168*
Ps 47:6, *224*
Ps 47:7, *225*
Ps 47:7–9, *171*
Ps 48, *102, 103*
Ps 48:2, *225*
Ps 48:8, 12–14, *159*
Ps 48:9, *103*
Ps 49, *45, 140, 141, 142, 223*
Ps 49:14, *107*
Ps 49:15, *221*
Ps 49:19, *106*
Ps 50, *156*
Ps 50, *18, 223*
Ps 50:7, *156, 216, 223*
Ps 50:15, *130*
Ps 51:1, *118*
Ps 51, 19, *45*
Ps 51:10, *78, 131*
Ps 51:10–12, *122*
Ps 51:14, *220*
Ps 52, *220, 223*
Ps 52:3–5, *114*
Ps 52:18, *216*
Ps 53, *223*
Ps 54, *220*
Ps 54:1, *118*
Ps 54:5, *221*
Ps 54:6, *84*
Ps 55:12–14, *148*

Ps 55:15–23, *221*
Ps 55:25, *23, 105*
Ps 56, *220*
Ps 56:5–6, *221*
Ps 56:12, *84*
Ps 57, *220, 221*
Ps 57:1, *165*
Ps 57:6, *221*
Ps 57:4, *221*
Ps 58, *137*
Ps 58:4–5, *221*
Ps 58:6, *221*
Ps 58:11, *220*
Ps 59:14–15, *221*
Ps 59:16, *114*
Ps 60:6–8, *223*
Ps 61, *220*
Ps 61:2, *28*
Ps 61:4, *165*
Ps 62, *136*
Ps 62:11, *220*
Ps 63, *45, 158*
Ps 63:2, *89*
Ps 63:2, 7, *158*
Ps 63:4, *83*
Ps 63:7, *224*
Ps 64:5, *221*
Ps 64:8, *221*
Ps 65, *102*
Ps 65:4, *103*
Ps 65:8, *103*
Ps 66, *86, 90, 219*
Ps 66:1, *103*
Ps 66:1–5, *90*
Ps 66:13–15, *43, 82*
Ps 66:16, *83*
Ps 67, *102*
Ps 67:2, *98*
Ps 67:6, *103*
Ps 68, *39, 216*
Ps 68:1, *223*
Ps 68:16, *160*
Ps 68:17–27, *168*
Ps 68:29, *180*
Ps 69, *45, 132, 133, 220*
Ps 69:3, *120*
Ps 69: 10–12, *111*
Ps 69:14, *107*
Ps 69:14–15, *106*

Ps 69:22–28, *221*
Ps 69:26, *108*, *111*
Ps 69, 30–31, *89*
Ps 69, 32–33, *222*
Ps 69:35, *62*
Ps 70, *216*
Ps 71, *220*
Ps 71, 15–18, *220*
Ps 71:22–24, *220*
Ps 72, *184*, *186*, *197*
Ps 72:1, *225*
Ps 72:1–2, *188*
Ps 72:18–19, *216*
Ps 73, *18*, *45*, *130*,
    142, *223*
Ps 74, *18*, *219*
Ps 74:1–2, *71*
Ps 74:2, *125*
Ps 74:12, *179*
Ps 74:13–17, *63*
Ps 74:19, *222*
Ps 75, *18*, *140*, *223*
Ps 75:4–5, *223*
Ps 76, *18*, *102*, *103*
Ps 77, *18*, *219*
Ps 77:2, *18*
Ps 77:5, *126*
Ps 78, *18*, *219*, *223*
Ps 78:1–3, *155*
Ps 78:58, *223*
Ps 78:60–61, *166*
Ps 78:68–69, *160*
Ps 79, *18*
Ps 79:1, *126*
Ps 80, *18*, *219*
Ps 80:1, *224*
Ps 80:14–15, *71*
Ps 80:15, *126*
Ps 81, *18*, *45*, *71*, *219*,
    223
Ps 81:5–7, *156*
Ps 81:6 ff., *223*
Ps 82, *18*, *137*
Ps 82:1–5, *137*
Ps 83, *18*, *219*
Ps 84:6, *150*
Ps 84:7, *158*
Ps 84:10, *160*
Ps 84:9, *225*
Ps 85:1–2, *222*

Ps 85:8–9, *223*
Ps 86, *220*
Ps 86:9, *218*
Ps 86:13, *221*
Ps 86:24–25, *43*
Ps 87, *157*
Ps 87:4, *223*, *225*
Ps 87:7, *158*
Ps 88:3, *107*
Ps 88:5, *106*
Ps 88:10–12, *95*, *221*
Ps 88:11–12, *106*
Ps 88:12, *106*
Ps 88, *199*
Ps 88:2, *76*
Ps 89:3–4, 19–37, *225*
Ps 89:8–12, *63*
Ps 89:19–37, *191*, *225*
Ps 89:48, *221*
Ps 89:49, *126*
Ps 89:52, *216*
Ps 91, *152*
Ps 91:4, *165*
Ps 91:14 ff., *223*
Ps 92, *220*
Ps 92:5–6, *96*
Ps 93, *170*
Ps 93:1, *225*
Ps 93:2, *171*
Ps 93:3–4, *172*
Ps 94, *223*
Ps 94:19, *132*
Ps 95, *71*, *77*, *156*, *219*
Ps 95:3, *218*
Ps 95:6, *218*
Ps 95:6–7, *77*
Ps 95:7–8, *217*
Ps 95:7–10, *153*
Ps 95:8 ff., *223*
Ps 96–99, *170*
Ps 96:1, *29*
Ps 96:3, *61*
Ps 96:8, *42*
Ps 96:8–10, *173*
Ps 96:9, *218*
Ps 96:10, *225*
Ps 96:11–12, *224*
Ps 96:11–13, *173*, *225*
Ps 96:13, *62*
Ps 97:1, *170*, *225*

Ps 97:6–8, *173*
Ps 98:1, 9, *218*
Ps 98:2–3, *172*
Ps 98:3, *182*
Ps 98:5–6, *171*
Ps 98:8, *218*
Ps 99, *170*
Ps 99:1, *225*
Ps 99:3, 5, 9, *225*
Ps 99:3, *224*
Ps 99:6, *171*
Ps 100, *153*, *184*
Ps 100:4, *43*
Ps 101, *189*
Ps 102, *109*, *120*, *133*
Ps 102:10, *108*
Ps 102:24, *105*
Ps 103, *64*, *67*
Ps 103:3–5, *218*
Ps 103:19, *179*
Ps 103:19–20, *64*
Ps 104, *67*, *219*
Ps 104:14, *219*
Ps 104:27 ff., *219*
Ps 104:34, *64*
Ps 105, *219*, *220*
Ps 105:4, *58*
Ps 106, *219*
Ps 106:48, *216*
Ps 107, *85*, *91*, *220*
Ps 107:2–3, *85*
Ps 107:17, *109*
Ps 107:42–43, *220*
Ps 109, *220*
Ps 109:8, *119*
Ps 109:21–22, *132*
Ps 109:22–25, *221*
Ps 109:27, *97*
Ps 109: 30–31, *115*
Ps 110, *186*, *187*, *190*,
    196, *197*, *225*
Ps 110:3, *187*
Ps 110:4, *190*
Ps 111, *216*, *219*, *220*
Ps 111:1, *220*
Ps 111:4–5, *75*
Ps 112, *217*, *222*, *223*
Ps 113:5, *219*
Ps 114, *22*, *219*
Ps 114:5, *31*

Ps 115, 22, 223
Ps 115:4–6, 64
Ps 115:17, 221
Ps 116, 22, 101, 221
Ps 116:3, 99, 107
Ps 116:5–6, 84
Ps 116:7, 94
Ps 116:11, 220
Ps 116:14 ff., 94
Ps 118, 53, 86, 88, 220
Ps 118:1, 218
Ps 118:8, 30
Ps 118:18, 30
Ps 118:19, 43
Ps 118:22, 31
Ps 118:28, 93
Ps 119, 45, 139, 140, 217, 223
Ps 119:9, 29
Ps 119:13, 30
Ps 120:26, 146
Ps 121, 154
Ps 121:2, 219
Ps 121:4–8, 154
Ps 122:1, 149
Ps 122:5, 221
Ps 124, 102
Ps 124:8, 118
Ps 125, 139, 223
Ps 126:5, 130
Ps 127, 223, 139
Ps 127:1, 30

Ps 127:3–5, 115
Ps 128, 223
Ps 129, 102
Ps 131, 136
Ps 132, 167, 191
Ps 132, 199
Ps 132:6–8, 167
Ps 132:7, 165
Ps 132:10, 225
Ps 132:11–18, 223, 325
Ps 132:15, 222
Ps 133:1, 148
Ps 134, 146, 223
Ps 134, 157
Ps 134:2, 218
Ps 135, 219
Ps 135:3–4, 218
Ps 135:16, 29
Ps 135:19–20, 53
Ps 135:19–21, 218, 219
Ps 135:21–22, 31
Ps 136, 53, 218, 219, 220
Ps 136:4–7, 10, 13, 16, 17, 25, 61
Ps 136:23–24, 69
Ps 136:26, 218
Ps 137:5–6, 159
Ps 138, 220
Ps 138:2, 218
Ps 138:4, 83

Ps 138:4–6, 220
Ps 138:7, 130
Ps 139, 131
Ps 139:1–18, 221
Ps 139:23, 132
Ps 140:5, 221
Ps 141:2, 218
Ps 141:7, 107
Ps 142:2, 120
Ps 144, 184, 188
Ps 144:10, 225
Ps 145, 217, 219
Ps 145:1, 225
Ps 145:11–12, 220
Ps 145:13b–20, 219
Ps 146, 219
Ps 146:7 ff., 219
Ps 146:7–9, 62
Ps 147, 22, 219
Ps 147:1, 170
Ps 147:7–9, 75, 218
Ps 147:19–20, 161
Ps 147:20, 69
Ps 148:5–6, 219
Ps 148:2, 32
Ps 148:5–6, 121
Ps 149, 169
Ps 149:4, 222
Ps 149:5–9, 170
Ps 150, 59
Ps 150:3–5, 54

2. OTHER BIBLICAL QUOTATIONS
(See also appendix VIII)

Genesis
Gen 1, 75
Gen 2, 75
Gen 4:23, 39
Gen 4:23–24, 26
Gen 37:24, 25

Exodus
Ex 15, 40
Ex 15:1–18, 49
Ex 15:1–21, 69   [225
Ex 15:18, 177, 224,

Ex 15:21, 49
Ex 16:33, 224
Ex 17:16, 178
Ex 20:16, 113
Ex 20:19, 205
Ex 21:23–25, 221
Ex 23:6–8, 113
Ex 23:17, 146
Ex 25:22, 164
Ex 32:4, 52
Ex 34:23, 146
Ex 37:1–9, 224

Leviticus
Lev 10:11, 155
Lev 16:14, 224
Lev 17:11, 224
Lev 19:2 ff., 206

Numbers
Num 7:89, 164
Num 10:35, 39, 224
Num 11:11–15, 222
Num 17:10, 224
Num 21:17, 39

Num 23:21, *178*

Deuteronomy
Deut 4:32, *78*
Deut 5:3, *217*
Deut 6:20 ff., *217*
Deut 7:6–8, *70*
Deut 9:25–29, *125*
Deut 13:5, *219*
Deut 14, *220*
Deut 16:11, 14, *220*
Deut 16:16, *146*
Deut 17:8–12, *148*
Deut 19:18–20, *113*
Deut 26:5, 16–19, *217*
Deut 26:11, *220*
Deut 31:10–13, *149, 210*

Joshua
Josh 7:7–9, *222*
Josh 24, *42*

Judges
Judg 5:3, *50*
Judg 7:18, *178*
Judg 8:23, *178*

1 Samuel
1 Sam 1:3, *52*
1 Sam 1:11, *26*
1 Sam 2, *17*
1 Sam 2:1–10, *94*
1 Sam 2:6, *108*
1 Sam 3:3, *165*
1 Sam 4:3–10, *165*
1 Sam 4:4, *224*
1 Sam 5:1–3, *166*
1 Sam 6, *166*
1 Sam 6:20, *165*
1 Sam 7:6, *222*
1 Sam 7:16, *148*
1 Sam 8:1, *148*
1 Sam 8:5, *184, 193*
1 Sam 9:13, 23, 24, *220*
1 Sam 10:27, *174*
1 Sam 12:12, *178*

2 Samuel
2 Sam 5:3, *175*
2 Sam 6, *166, 167*
2 Sam 6:2, *165, 224*
2 Sam 7:1–2, *191*
2 Sam 7:11–16, *189, 194*
2 Sam 11:11, *166*
2 Sam 12, *112*
2 Sam 14:5, *26*
2 Sam 15:2, *114*
2 Sam 15:10, *174*

1 Kings
1 Kings 1:32 ff., *174*
1 Kings 1:37–47, *174*
1 Kings 1:39–40, *54*
1 Kings 8, *166*
1 Kings 8:33 ff., *222*
1 Kings 17:20, *222*
1 Kings 18:27, *121*
1 Kings 21, *112*

2 Kings
2 Kings 9:4, *184*
2 Kings 9:13, *174*
2 Kings 11:12, *174*
2 Kings 18–19, *102*
2 Kings 19:15, *224*
2 Kings 20:9, *222*

1 Chronicles
1 Chron 16:36, *55*
1 Chron 17:11–14, *189*
1 Chron 15:1–2, *18*
1 Chron 28:5, *184, 193*
1 Chron 29:20, *54*

2 Chronicles
2 Chron 5:13, *55*
2 Chron 6:12–7, 3, *56*
2 Chron 7:3, 6, *55*
2 Chron 7:10, *157*
2 Chron 7:17, *184*
2 Chron 20:6–12, *222*
2 Chron 20:19, *18*
2 Chron 20:21, *55*
2 Chron 23:11–13, *54*

2 Chron 23:19, *150*
2 Chron 29:28–29, *57*

Ezra
Ezra 3:11, *57*
Ezra 9:6–15, *222*

Nehemias
Neh 1:5–11, *222*
Neh 7–44, *18*
Neh 8, *210*
Neh 9:6–37, *222*
Neh 11:17–22, *18*

Tobit
Tob 13, *17*

Judith
Judith 4:8 ff., *222*
Judith 5, *70*
Judith 9:11, *40*
Judith 15:10, *55*
Judith 15:13, *51*
Judith 16:2–3, *51*

Proverbs
Prov 25:1, *20*

Isaiah
Is 1:11 ff., *223*
Is 1:12–14, *148*
Is 1:23, *112*
Is 2:2–3, *150*
Is 2:54, 60 and 62, *157*
Is 5:7, *112*
Is 5:23, *112*
Is 6:3, *50*
Is 8:19, *221*
Is 9:11 and 32, *195*
Is 11:1, *194*
Is 11:3–4, *112*
Is 14, *221*
Is 29:4, *221*
Is 29:13, *223*
Is 30:29, *150*
Is 38, *17*
Is 38:10, *220*
Is 38:10, 12, *105*
Is 38:10–20, *94*
Is 38:12, *109*

Is 38:14, *109*
Is 38:18, *221*
Is 38:18–19, *96*
Is 43:1, *78*
Is 43:6–7, *78*
Is 43:16 ff., *219*
Is 44:23, *17*
Is 45:8, *78*
Is 52:7, *175*, *225*
Is 54:5, *75*
Is 60 and *66*
Is 60:1 ff., *223*
Is 60:2–3, *180*
Is 65:17–19, *78*

Jeremiah
Jer 2:2, *70*
Jer 2:6, *219*
Jer 3:2, *223*
Jer 5:26, *221*
Jer 7, *223*
Jer 7:2, *223*
Jer 7:4–7, *160*
Jer 15:15–21, *17*
Jer 15:17–18, *222*
Jer 20:7, *222*
Jer 22:3, *221*
Jer 30:9, *226*
Jer 30:10, *223*
Jer 31:6, *149*
Jer 31:22, *78*
Jer 31:33, *162*
Jer 31:33 ff., *179*
Jer 31:31–34, *219*
Jer 31:35–37, *75*
Jer 33:10–11, *55*

Baruch
Bar 1:15–3:8, *222*

Ezekiel
Ezek 10:18 ff., *178*
Ezek 11:16, *161*
Ezek 34:23–24, *194*
Ezek 37:1–13, *161*
Ezek 37:24, *226*
Ezek 37:26, *179*
Ezek 40:6–37, *223*
Ezek 47, *161*
Ezek 47:1–12, *158*

Daniel
Dan 2:20, *17*
Dan 3:26, *17*
Dan 3:55 etc., *224*
Dan 3:57–88, *59*

Hosea
Hos 2:16–18, *219*
Hos 3:5, *226*
Hos 11:9, *207*
Hos 13:4–6, *70*
Hos 13:11, *193*

Joel
Joel 1:13 to 2:17, *124*
Joel 3:18, *158*
Joel 3:21, *161*
Joel 4, *161*

Amos
Amos 3:1, *219*
Amos 4:4, *149*
Amos 4:6–11, *130*
Amos 5:5, 21, *223*
Amos 5:12, *221*
Amos 5:23, *52*
Amos 7:10, *223*
Amos 8:10, 14, *223*
Amos 9:11, *194*

Jonah
Jon 2, *17*
Jon 2:2–9, *94*
Jon 2:4, *220*

Micah
Mic 4, *161*

Haggai
Hag 2:11, *155*

Zechariah
Zech 8 and 14, *161*
Zech 9:9, *196*
Zech 14, *161*
Zech 14:8, *158*
Zech 14:17–18, *150*

Malachi
Mal 2:7, *155*

1 Maccabees
1 Macc 3:47, *222*
1 Macc 3:50–52, *125*
1 Macc 4:37, *222*
1 Macc 4:54–56, *57*

2 Maccabees
2 Macc 2:4–6, *224*
2 Macc 2:13, *20*

Matthew
Mt 1:23, *162*
Mt 2:2, *226*
Mt 3:10–13, *181*
Mt 4:1–11, *72*
Mt 4:17, *181*
Mt 5:39, *145*
Mt 5:44, *145*
Mt 13:41, *226*
Mt 21:5, *196*
Mt 22:44–46, *196*
Mt 25:31–34, *226*
Mt 26:28, *212*

Mark
Mk 14:58, *162*
Mk 15:9 ff., *226*
Mk 15:16–20, *200*
Mk 15:26, *200*

Luke
Lk 2:34, *181*
Lk 4:18–19, *196*
Lk 9:31, *72*
Lk 18:2–5, *112*
Lk 24:44, *202*

John
Jn 1:3, *77*
Jn 1:14, *161*
Jn 2:2–9, *89*
Jn 2:21, *162*
Jn 3:14, *72*
Jn 5:24, *181*
Jn 6:15, *196*
Jn 6:48–52, *72*
Jn 7:38, *72*
Jn 9:2, *110*
Jn 11:55, *149*
Jn 13:1, *72*

Jn 15:19, *134*
Jn 17:16, *134*
Jn 18:36, *196*
Jn 19:3, 19, 21, 226
Jn 19:18–22, *220*
Jn 19:36, *72*

The Acts of the
   Apostles
Acts 2:36, *197*
Acts 4:10–12, *181*
Acts 14, *134*
Acts 17:7, *196*

Romans
Rom 1:8, *221*
Rom 3:24, *219*
Rom 3:25, *224*
Rom 8:2, *162*
Rom 8:17, 29, *134*
Rom 8:21–22, *79, 182*

1 Corinthians
1 Cor 3:16, *223*
1 Cor 5:7, *72*
1 Cor 6:19, *223*
1 Cor 10:4, *72*
1 Cor 11:26, *100, 101*
1 Cor 15:24, *182, 226*
1 Cor 15:24–28, *198*

1 Cor 15:25, *198*

2 Corinthians
2 Cor 5:17, *79*
2 Cor 6:16, *223*

Galatians
Gal 4:25, *162*

Ephesians
Eph 1:3–14, *73*
Eph 1:10, *78*
Eph 2:21–22, *223*
Eph 4:24, *79*
Eph 5:25–27, *197*

Philippians
Phil 2:2–11, *133*
Phil 3:10–11, *134*

Colossians
Col 1:12–14, *73*
Col 1:15–17, *77*
Col 1:15 to 18, *79*

1 Timothy
1 Tim 6:13, *98*

Titus
Tit 2:11, *210*

Tit 3:4, *210*

Hebrews
Heb 1:1, *162*
Heb 1:2, *210*
Heb 2:12, *221*
Heb 4:14 ff., *224*
Heb 4:14 ff., *224*
Heb 11:10, *162*
Heb 12:22, *162*

1 Peter
1 Pet 2:9–10, *219*

2 Peter
2 Pet 3:13, *79*

Revelation
Rev 1:5, *98*
Rev 3:12, *162*
Rev 3:14, *98*
Rev 5:9–10, *73*
Rev 7:14, *135*
Rev 11:19, *166*
Rev 15:3–4, *73*
Rev 19:16, *226*
Rev 21:1, 5, *79*
Rev 21:2, *163*
Rev 21:4, *135*

Also from Herder and Herder

WE DARE TO SAY OUR FATHER

LOUIS EVELY

Catholic piety, long suffering from its predominantly other-worldly character, has often created an unnecessary tension between one's religious and one's secular duties. And, as if to compensate for this lack of concrete roots in daily life, most spiritual writing has been marred by an emotionalism and sentimentality which only served to make it less palatable to the Christian engaged in the work of the world.

WE DARE TO SAY OUR FATHER is that rare book — already acknowledged in Europe as a classic — that speaks without the unctious clichés of the old "manuals of piety"; it contains no farfetched examples, no rapturous calls to an unattainable sanctity. Everything Father Evely writes is succinct, direct, and cogent. How many pious authors, for example, would say: "It matters little that prayer bores us; let us do it because it delights God"; or, "There is more communion in a railway car than at some of our Sunday masses"; or, again, "A set of egoisms coincide and we call it brotherly love"; or, finally, "We like to start to love, but it hurts to carry on"? Not since the sermons of Newman has there been so simple and penetrating an analysis of the Christian life, and so fine a union of biblical understanding and psychological insight.

Although Father Evely's reflections have been widely used at retreats and days of recollection, his book is intended to be meditated on not just during special periods of the year, but daily. It is this focus on day-to-day living which has made WE DARE TO SAY OUR FATHER one of the most widely read religious books of the past decade, and which led to its being applauded by the world-renowned theologian, Father Yves Congar, as a masterpiece of spirituality.

Also from Herder and Herder

MAN AND WIFE IN SCRIPTURE

PIERRE GRELOT

In recent years there has been a growing demand among all Christians for greater candor in the discussion of sexuality. Openness and frankness are among the dominant characteristics of the modern mentality, and therefore only a marital doctrine which strips away the constraints of a needless prudery will be acceptable to the man of the twentieth century. For that reason a return to the biblical sources of the Christian understanding of marriage is necessary not only because all moral life must be rooted in the scriptures, but also because the plain and forthright narrative of the bible speaks most convincingly to the man of our time.

MAN AND WIFE IN SCRIPTURE is a synthesis of what the bible teaches about the sexual bond. While not attempting to be a complete theology of marriage, it does provide in a concrete and graphic way the indispensable scriptural foundation for an understanding of marital relations which is not bound by scholastic or legalistic categories. Father Grelot traces the sacred character of sexuality in the ancient orient, differentiates clearly the Old Testament doctrine from various pagan practices, discusses such ideal couples as Abraham and Sarah, Isaac and Rebecca, and concludes with an analysis of the lyric dialogue of bride and groom in the Song of Songs. Throughout his examination of the Old Testament texts the author brings out the gradual revelation of the meaning of marriage as the counterpart of the union of Israel with God. This union culminates in the New Testament teaching in which Christ is the bridegroom and the human race is the bride whom he has redeemed. It is in this mystery that every other marriage finds its consecration and its significance.

The entire work creates, according to THEOLOGICAL STUDIES, the impression of the grand sweep of scripture moving progressively toward a theology of the human pair; and it is described by THE CATHOLIC BIBLICAL QUARTERLY as "a concise and fine synthesis".